WITHDRAWN

Realism and American Foreign Policy

Realism and American Foreign Policy

Wilsonians and the Kennan-Morgenthau Thesis

Steven J. Bucklin

Westport, Connecticut
London

Library of Congress Cataloging-in-Publication Data

Bucklin, Steven J., 1955–
   Realism and American foreign policy : Wilsonians and the Kennan-Morgenthau thesis /
Steven J. Bucklin.
      p.   cm.
   Includes bibliographical references (p.) and index.
   ISBN 0–275–96737–9 (alk. paper)
      1. United States—Foreign relations—20th century—Philosophy.   2. Morgenthau, Hans
Joachim, 1904–   3. Kennan, George Frost, 1904–   4. Wilson, Woodrow, 1856–1924.
   5. Internationalism.   I. Title.
   E744.B827   2001
   327.73'001—dc21   00–032370

British Library Cataloguing in Publication Data is available.

Library of Congress Catalog Card Number: 00–032370
ISBN: 0–275–96737–9

First published in 2001

Praeger Publishers, 88 Post Road West, Westport, CT 06881
An imprint of Greenwood Publishing Group, Inc.
www.praeger.com

Printed in the United States of America

The paper used in this book complies with the
Permanent Paper Standard issued by the National
Information Standards Organization (Z39.48–1984).

10 9 8 7 6 5 4 3 2 1

Copyright Acknowledgments

The author and publisher gratefully acknowledge permission to use the following material:

From Hans Morgenthau. *In Defense of the National Interest: A Critical Examination of American Foreign Policy*. New York: A. A. Knopf, 1951. Used by permission of Matthew and Susanna Morgenthau.

From George F. Kennan. *American Diplomacy*. Chicago: University of Chicago Press, 1984. © 1951, 1979 by The University of Chicago and © 1984 by George F. Kennan.

This book is dedicated to my mentors.

Contents

Acknowledgments

One of the opportunities the publication of this book affords is to thank the many people who have helped and supported me. It is a pleasant task to address them.

I am grateful to Heather Staines, the Board of Editors, Ellen Leiba, and the other personnel at Greenwood Press for accepting my proposal and publishing the book. They happily worked with and counseled me when I asked them what were likely very routine questions.

At the University of Iowa, Professor Lawrence E. Gelfand provided a patient, guiding force to focus my research and is the best of mentors. Professor Miriam Gelfand gave me guidance, food, and always welcomed my conversations. Professor Ellis Hawley influenced the way I organized the book. In addition, the Department of History supported me financially through awards and teaching assignments that enabled me to complete my work.

All of my colleagues at The University of South Dakota Department of History, past and present, played an invaluable role as mentors, too. In particular, Professors Stephen Ward, Gerald Wolfe, and Don Pryce encouraged me to study history. Professor Robert Hilderbrand pushed me to seek the Ph. D., helped me to think about the framework of the book, and has been a valued friend for years. Mary Nielsen and Jacque Manning gave me great secretarial support.

I am also deeply indebted to my family and friends. Clint and Shirlee Bucklin have supported me unconditionally for 45 years, as have my siblings, Stan and Sheri. My daughters, Clare and Grace, inspired me to work harder and give me tremendous moments of joy when I really need them. Kendall Staggs and Sylvano Wueschner each played an important role in the development of this book, not to mention providing me with great diversions. To my other friends and family members who have sustained me over the years, I extend my thanks as well.

Most importantly, I thank my wife, Stephanie. She has been an invaluable, loving, and patient resource for fifteen years. Without her, this book would not have been written.

Introduction: The "Realist" Critique of Wilsonian Internationalism

Critics have frequently attached Woodrow Wilson's policies and those of his disciples as being idealistic, asynchronous, somehow outside the interests of the United States. Isolated by their faith in international law and the cooperation of nations they were divorced, so the argument goes, from the realities of balance of power politics, of *machtpolitik*, and of the self-interested policies so necessary in a modern industrial democracy.

Henry Cabot Lodge and a small but influential group of Republicans and Democrats were among the earliest of these critics, but increasingly opponents came from the academy. Revisionist critics from Harry Elmer Barnes to Charles Tansill to William Appleman Williams argued that idealism did not serve the public good, either at home or abroad. Critics from the "realist" school, including Hans Morgenthau, George Kennan, Robert Osgood, and Louis Halle, criticized Wilsonianism's divorce from realism as the principal reason the U.S. had veered off course away from the true national interest.

Those critics employed a limited examination of Wilsonianism to arrive at their conclusions. After a more complete examination, the evidence is clear that Wilsonianism was as interest based as any "realist" approach to the problems of international organization and domestic reform. In fact, the terms "idealist" and "realist" serve students of history poorly. Woodrow Wilson's legacy is neither idealistic nor *realpolitik*. His legacy is the organization of the world's nations around a common body of law as the events of the last fifty years underscore.

The evidence reveals, too, that in the absence of such a system, Wilson carefully, though not without failures, maneuvered the craft of state through the course of power politics. That he was willing to use both force—in fact sometimes too willing—and diplomacy to accomplish national goals is additional evidence that he met the *sine qua non* of the realist school.

In a paper presented to the Mid-America Conference on History at Topeka, Kansas, historian Emily Hill observed that prominent interpretations of U.S. foreign policy commonly represent the focus on geopolitics during the Truman administration as a dramatic shift away from the "Wilsonian reveries" of the interwar period.[1]   She asserts, correctly, that the emergent "Morgenthau-Kennan" thesis of the late 1940s, early 1950s guided critics of idealism for the next fifty years.[2] Hill proposed a study of interwar scholarship, especially the works of Quincy Wright and Frederick Schuman, as a means to address the inadequacies of the realist assumption.[3]

Kennan expressed that thesis in his 1985 foreword to the expanded edition of his 1951 book *American Diplomacy.* Kennan lamented the "excessive legalism and moralism" of American foreign policy and asserted that during the first five decades of the twentieth-century, United States foreign policy lacked an "accepted, enduring doctrine for . . . achieving real, and desperately needed, results in our relations with others."[4] Morgenthau wrote in 1951 that Americans tended to "conceive of our actions in non-political, moral terms," thus preventing us from "seeing problems of international politics as they are" and subsequently developing an appropriate foreign policy.[5]

So entrenched had the Morgenthau-Kennan thesis become that few questioned its validity. It was so amorphous in its definition of national interest that proponents of the realist school could criticize anyone whose interpretation of the national interest differed from theirs on any given issue. Only recently have scholars begun to assail this principal assumption of the realist school. In a review essay in *Diplomatic History,* Regina Gramer observed that "not just realist but also revisionist scholars in diplomatic history and international relations uncritically mix factual and normative conceptions of national interest," obscuring the origins of those policies. Gramer calls for a critical analysis of that uncritical mix.[6] In an essay written for the journal *World Politics* the same year, David Baldwin asked why scholars have not examined the roots of modern international relations studies instead of accepting as an act of faith the realist interpretation.[7]

A study of the theories of Wright and Schuman, coupled with those of Denna F. Fleming, another prominent Wilsonian, reveals the roots of international relations studies and exposes several weaknesses in the realist critique of Wilsonianism and "idealism." These three political scientists carried on the work of Wilson for sixty years, and they did so through a more complex and often more rigorous ideological framework than that which the "realist" critique affords.

Why these three Wilsonians? They were in the vanguard of their discipline. They held the highest positions in their professional guilds. They advised Bernard Baruch, John Foster Dulles, J. William Fulbright, and many other influential statesmen and politicians. They were called to testify before United Nations committees, Congressional committees, and other prominent organizations. Each served on the influential Committee to Study the Organization of Peace. And each reached broad audiences through public appearances and widely read publications.

Of the three, Quincy Wright was a dean among twentieth-century internationalists. Wright was instrumental in establishing the study of international politics at the University of Chicago where he was Schuman's mentor. Wright was dedicated to what he called the Anglo-Saxon legal heritage of evolutionary change. His prescription declared that an enforceable international law was a self-correcting system.

Denna Fleming, professor of political science at Vanderbilt, was a well-known advocate of the League of Nations and collective security. He made a second reputation for himself after retirement as a champion of better relations with the Soviet Union during the Cold War. His was an early voice calling for the United States to deal with the Soviets "firmly," yet "require her to trust us as an equal."[8] Fleming's advice was based on his interpretation of the historical circumstances behind the Soviet drive to world power. He formalized his thoughts in his groundbreaking revisionist history *The Cold War and Its Origins* (1961), a two-volume work that remains influential.

His sympathy for the Soviet perspective of world affairs was expensive. The chancellor of Vanderbilt, where Fleming spent most of his career, branded him as a communist sympathizer and sent unsolicited messages to at least one prospective employer. That action cost Fleming a position at the University of South Florida.

Frederick Schuman was in many respects a more sophisticated Wilsonian than was Fleming. Schuman saw a Freudian side of human nature that included a more chaotic soul than the rational creature so many of his colleagues presupposed. Because of this, Schuman believed that it was equally necessary to appeal to the emotional side of humanity, to emphasize collective identity in creating the new world order.

Schuman provoked, aroused, and made people uncomfortable with the assumptions they held about the world around them. He also understood the role shibboleths, symbols, and myth play in power politics. This may explain his abiding understanding of power politics and the people who practiced them. He recognized Hitler for what he was in 1933. Schuman published a detailed and prescient account of what was happening in Germany and what was in store for the world in 1934 entitled *The Nazi Dictatorship: A Study in Social Pathology and the Politics of Fascism.*[9] As well, his textbook, *International Politics,* was in its seventh printing at the time of his death in the 1970s.[10]

Schuman also suffered for his identification with the Soviet Union. He was a vocal critic of U.S. policy toward the Kremlin throughout his career and advocated relaxed relations with the Soviet Union. As well, he courted causes and figures that many Americans labeled as "fronts" or "fellow travelers." Consequently, he was a target of state and national anticommunist campaigns during the '30s, '40s, '50s, and even in the '60s.

As Wilsonians, all three men believed in the need to organize the world around a common body of law. They recognized the efficacy of collective security, international organizations, and the rule of law as the best means for maintaining peace. But they did not hold these to be the only means, nor even the most desirable means under given sets of circumstances. As the evidence culled from their massive collective writings and equally impressive papers indicates, they not only understood balance of power, *machtpolitik,* and any other variable of the "realist" approach, they advocated such frameworks in the absence of meaningful international organization.

Fleming, Schuman, and Wright offered a dynamic Wilsonian analysis of world organization. For them, Frederick Jackson Turner's *requiem* had not announced the closing of the American frontier, but the shift of that frontier to a global landscape. World organization was a part of that new frontier. Ultimately, they meant to establish an institution like the League of Nations that bound its members to a code of law, but to reach that goal, they emphasized power, progress, and economics. Far from being idealistic utopians, these individuals, like Wilson before them, sought practical means to establish an effective structure of world organization.

Their mentor practiced balance of power politics diligently. A variety of evidence exists that demonstrates Wilson's affinity for power politics. Hans Morgenthau observed that Wilson and Alexander Hamilton were "one" when it came to their concern for maintaining the European balance of power.[11] Generally, Wilson believed that the fewer people involved in the creation and application of foreign policy, the more likely its success.[12] This was especially important in an international system of power politics. He was convinced that the president should be able to determine and execute foreign policy virtually unchecked. His disciples shared his vision of a strong executive, whether in the position of president of the United States or General Secretary of the League of Nations or the United Nations.

Wilson envisioned a presidency that would take the nation to new international heights. As chief executive, he expressed this dramatically in his 1916 speech to the League to Enforce Peace. On that stage, Wilson shared with the public his recognition that the United States now pursued global economic and political interests. In fact, they were universal interests. The nation's responsibilities would now include ensuring a stable world political and economic system friendly to U.S. interests. This declaration of universal interests was in effect the Wilson Doctrine. It was a doctrine that would shape the twentieth-century, for, despite Kennan's lamentations otherwise, here was a doctrine that other presidents vigorously pursued.

Wilson declared that the war then raging in Europe had "profoundly affected" U.S. interests. No longer could the citizens of the United States consider themselves above or beyond the concerns of other nations. "We are," he continued, "participants, whether we would or not, in the life of the world. The interests of all nations are our own also. We are partners with the rest. What affects mankind is inevitably our affair as well as the affair of the nations of the [world]."[13]

Gone was the confining tradition of the Monroe Doctrine. Gone too was the equally restrictive emphasis on the Pacific Rim. In an interdependent economic system, all nations, of course, some more than others, could affect U.S. interests. Perhaps those interests always had been global in scope, but Wilson articulated them in a new language. This universalism characterized not just Wilson's thought, but that of his followers.

Wilson clothed this universalism in the rhetoric of American moral mission as well as self-interest, but a willingness to engage in power politics was fundamental to the accomplishment of both. He maintained that the United States could succeed where other nations, less virtuous, had failed. Such a conviction was nothing less than Periclean. Similar beliefs had influenced Wilson's predecessors in office, as well as the foreign policy elite. Impassioned patriots, scholars, politicians, missionaries, and common folk had emphasized the unique nature, first of the "New World" and later of the United States and its global mission since the eighteenth-century. Wilson gave that impulse its first twentieth-century form.

At the same time, the general public believed strongly in a Caucasian-American dominated racial hierarchy. So too did their political leaders.[14] Even prominent leaders of ethnic and racial minorities, for instance Alexander Crummel and W.E.B. Du Bois, subscribed to the precepts of Social Darwinism. As will be seen, so did Morgenthau and Kennan.

Wilson acted on the international stage with the confidence of one who was convinced of not only his own righteousness, but that of his people, his race. The idea of racial pride and destiny was part of Wilson's religious and cultural heritage. Wilson's Southern upbringing, as well as his religious and political beliefs, contributed to his belief in the supremacy of the Anglo-Saxon race and its institutions.

It is a commonplace that Wilson's "New Freedom" domestic program was "for whites only." Wilson and his deputies, many of them Southerners, cut back the number and level of federal jobs open to black Americans. Segregation became official policy for federal employees.[15] In a letter to the influential publisher Oswald Garrison Villard, Wilson justified the policy as being in the best interest of African Americans who would otherwise experience discrimination in the office. Segregation, Wilson believed, eased the "friction, or rather the discontent and uneasiness, which had prevailed in many of the departments."[16]

His belief in racial/political superiority also influenced his foreign policies. The Mexican Revolution flew in the face of Wilson's belief in evolutionary social change and in the sacred nature of private property. In response to this revolution, Wilson established a *de jure* test to determine whether diplomatic recognition should be extended to a new government that replaced the *de facto* test the United States had employed since Jefferson's administration.

Willing to interfere in the political lives of peoples he considered inferior, Wilson made a comment about the Mexican people that haunts his legacy. In reference to Victoriano Huerta and his regime in Mexico, Wilson would not, he declared, recognize a murderer as head of state. Traditionally, this statement has been interpreted as an expression of Wilsonian idealism as well as hypocrisy, for the United States recognized many other heads of state, the tsar of Russia for one, who could easily be labeled murderers.

But the fact of the matter was that the Mexican Civil War threatened American investments, which were significant, and U.S. security. Although Wilson believed democracy would stabilize Mexico, when it became apparent in January and February of 1917 that war with Germany was imminent, Wilson sought a *modus vivendi*. He was quick to drop his insistence that the Mexicans be taught to "elect good men" and negotiated the withdrawal of the American

Expeditionary Force. What Wilson practiced in his relations with the Mexican Revolution was power politics under the guise of idealism.

There was, too, the fact that Wilson learned from his mistake in Mexico that there were limits to American military power. His reticence at committing U.S. troops to Russia during its Civil War was the result of his understanding of those limits. Realizing that military force was not always the answer to accomplishing the nation's interests, Wilson also refused to use force in China when the Japanese presented the 21 Demands and refused British overtures to commit U.S. forces to the Middle East in the period immediately following World War I. But when military power could be effectively used to protect American interests, two examples being the war against Germany and the intervention in Haiti in 1915, Wilson remained willing to use the military, and usually temperately.

His commitment of U.S. forces to the war against Germany was done in such a way as to ensure American goals would not be tied to Allied goals the United States did not share. The operation in Haiti was more problematic, especially given the legacy of American racism, but Wilson did succeed in protecting immediate American interests on the island and the strategic interest the nation stated in the Monroe Doctrine and the Roosevelt Corollary to it.

Wilson's idea of racial hierarchies also influenced his policies toward Asia and Asians. The president shared the conviction of many citizens that Asians were unassimilable in American society. Wilson stood for a "national policy of exclusion" as early as 1912. "We cannot make," he wrote, "a homogeneous population out of people who do not blend with the Caucasian race . . . . Oriental cooleism will give us another race problem to solve, and surely we have had our lessons."[17]

As well, Wilson rejected a statement of racial equality in the Covenant of the League of Nations that the Japanese government sought to redress racial biases. His refusal, though, was not solely racially based: he omitted such a declaration to ensure the membership of colonial powers like Britain and France in the League. Thus, his racism proved to be a source of realism in his approach to international relations, for he knew the League could not survive without the participation of the great powers.

Wilson's plans for the mandated territories provide more evidence of his faith in an Anglo-Saxon dominated racial hierarchy. The language of paternalism of Article XXI in the League Covenant is inescapable. The authors determined that many of the former colonies and territories of the defeated powers were "inhabited by peoples not yet able to stand by themselves under the strenuous conditions of the modern world." As a consequence, Wilson declared that those peoples should be placed under the tutelage of more "advanced nations" whose governments would accept such a role as a "sacred trust."

What is more, Wilson perceived different stages of development among the colonial peoples: he graded those stages of development, consciously or not, in descending order *according to the lightness of the skins* of the native populations. He held the former Turkish colonies, comprised mostly of light-skinned peoples, to be the most advanced. They would be "provisionally" recognized as independent states and allowed to exercise a great deal of self-government.

Central Africa, though, was judged to be at a stage of development so rudimentary that the Mandatory power would be responsible for civil administration and the maintenance of public order. The people of Southwest Africa and the South Pacific islands were deemed so aboriginal that they would best be served if their territories were incorporated directly as "integral portions" of the Mandatory.[18]

Despite the fact that one could interpret the above as a measure of Wilson's skepticism about democracy, he plainly valued it. But for him and his disciples, democracy was a system of merit, not of entitlement. Those who did not merit full participation would be denied it until they met certain standards. This, too, reflects Wilsonian realism.

Coupled with his belief in racial hierarchy, in fact derivative of it, was his insistence that an open playing field be the rule for the world market. Wilson believed, as did most U.S. citizens, that an "open door" to world trade was necessary to the well-being of the nation. Allowed to function unimpeded in that arena, they believed that the natural abilities and merits of Americans and their institutions would triumph over all competitors. These assumptions were crucial elements of Wilsonianism.

In his "Fourteen Points" speech, the third point called for the "removal, so far as possible, of all economic barriers and the establishment of an *equality of trade conditions* among all the nations consenting to peace and associating themselves for its maintenance."[19] That point was institutionalized in the League Covenant. The concept would remain one of the most enduring principles of Wilsonians and of U.S. foreign policy throughout the twentieth-century.

Wilson encountered massive obstacles in his quest to establish an international order based on the principles he had articulated in the short period between 1916 and 1919. Not least of these obstacles were partisan political opponents like Henry Cabot Lodge and foreign leaders who disliked him and what they considered American pretentiousness. Georges Clemenceau, who feared the loss of French prestige and influence, remarked that "God gave us the Ten Commandments, and we broke them. Wilson gives us the Fourteen Points. We shall see."[20]

To surmount these obstacles, Wilson set out to galvanize world opinion around his system. He insisted that an organized world opinion, presumably emanating from the League of Nations, would inevitably support his goals, an idea indelibly marked in the scholarship and rhetoric of his disciples.

Schuman especially, but Wright and Fleming as well, detected a spiritual void in the League. It held as one of its cardinal precepts the need to organize world opinion, yet the individual had no vested interest in League operations. Nowhere in the Covenant was there a provision for universal human rights. There was no call to "hold certain truths to be self-evident," no "Declaration of the Rights of Man and Citizen," and no provision for individual recourse to the institutions of the League. Such an organization would have difficulty rallying the masses to the barricades in time of distress. Fundamentally, this is a matter of power, and it was a problem each of these men attempted to solve.

To the most idealistic observer, the problem of organizing the world's diverse cultures and political systems around a set of common values would appear monumental. But the underlying assumptions these men held about organizing the world led them to believe that the task was not insurmountable. They were convinced that democracy equaled progress; that self-criticism allowed flawed policies to be amended or dropped. Wilson and his disciples advocated self-determination, constraints on national sovereignty, regionalism, and recognition of universal human rights as the best means to their end.

These scholars sought to regulate the abuses of power politics with modern management techniques. Where they perceived international chaos, they sought to impose order. They believed that *laissez-faire* sovereignty resulted in periodic wars. Alterations in the balance of power system acted as the "hidden hand," adjusting the relationships when necessary. Although one might accept the cost of unregulated economic markets—periodic depressions—war in the twentieth-century was no longer an acceptable debit. Accordingly, it was time for humans to regulate their affairs in the international arena to prevent war.

The means to do that would be collective security. In its most basic form, collective security would maintain the balance of power. Ideally, those nations that entered a system of collective security did so out of common need, respect for the law, and mutual opposition to aggression. But they also entered such a system with the knowledge that its ultimate effect would be maintenance of the balance.

Those powers that wished to alter the balance would have to seek means other than war or coercion to accomplish change. After all, peaceful change was the ultimate goal of international organization, not necessarily maintenance of the status quo. This was the great purpose of the League of Nations, and its appeal was simple and direct. But the complexities of tradition and the appeal power politics held for the Great Powers in their practice of international relations soon undermined the League.

These Wilsonians did not always agree with one another and they would sometimes pursue policies that might be interpreted as beyond the pale of Wilsonianism. But, like Wilson before them, they recognized that the goal of world peace was superior to any other and consonant with the national interest. To achieve peace, they sought to organize world opinion behind their policies. To prevent war, they endeavored to correct the anarchy of international relations. To bring all the world's peoples into the global political system, they encouraged policies of progress in the underdeveloped world. They shared an understanding that only an activist U.S. role in world affairs could obtain these goals.

When the fabric of international society dissolved once again in 1939, Wright, Fleming, and Schuman sought a new system to replace the one that had failed to keep the peace. The materials from which to craft a new world order were few. The failure of the League to stop the militarist states underscored the need to create a coercive power to enforce international law. Such a power would require physical as well as moral sanctions.

Of the reforms needed to create an effective world organization in place of the League, Fleming, Schuman, and Wright agreed that chief among them remained the diminution of sovereign power. By definition, a sovereign's power was ultimate, subject to no higher power. Consequently, the ultimate test between sovereign states was war. The costs of such a system had long been known: peace was maintained through the balance of power, and the balance required periodic readjustment, commonly accomplished through war. The most recent adjustment had wreaked devastation beyond the power of imagination; the adjustment to come defied comprehension.

And the fact remained that sovereign nations constituted Wilson's League. In fact, the League exalted the sovereign nation state. Despite claims to the contrary, Wilson's League placed no constraints on sovereignty. The flexible responses available to sovereigns in several of the League's articles assured this. Even Article X allowed for flexibility. In the case of aggression, "the Council shall *advise* upon the means by which [the member's] obligation shall be fulfilled." Articles XVI and XXI provided similar means to avoid military commitment.[21]

These three scholars, although unsympathetic to unchecked sovereignty, knew that, until a world organization could be created with sufficient coercive power to tame national sovereignty, international law would have to recognize the prerogatives of states. In addition, they recognized that regional interests of great powers, more commonly referred to as "spheres of influence," would play an important role in an effective world order. Such regional interests required a degree of autonomy within a world organization. Fleming, Schuman, and Wright recognized the need to accommodate great power interests in those regions in order to ensure the survival of a world organization.

Wilson's influence abounds in their collective works. Through them, Wilsonianism came to influence three generations of scholars, policy-makers, and politicians. Fleming, Schuman, and Wright shared several assumptions: that U.S. interests were universal; that the world's nations needed to be organized around a system of law; and that the "Open Door" was essential to a modern world economy. They were equally certain of their ideological, racial, and gender superiority. And they were willing to engage in power politics, in fact to champion the balance of power, to maintain peace until they could ensure the rule of law among nations. Theirs was as practical as any so-called "realist" approach to the problems of international relations.

The record of these men reveals a much different interpretation of Wilsonians than that which has been forwarded in the works of the realist school. The presumption that a lost realism had been reinvented at the onset of the Cold War is a false one if it is premised on the assumption that Wilsonians were idealists. The Wilson Doctrine that U.S. interests were universal has guided every administration from Franklin Roosevelt's to Bill Clinton's. From 1919 to 1945, three principal proponents of a realist/Wilsonian approach to U.S. foreign policy were Wright, Fleming, and Schuman. In the post-World War II environment, George Kennan's estimate of Soviet and U.S. behavior, Hans Morgenthau's *realpolitik,* and Henry Kissinger's *détente* were built upon the assumptions of Wilsonian internationalism. Wilsonian universalism, coupled with international law, has been the constant value in the equation of U.S. foreign policy for most of this century.

NOTES

1. Emily Hill, "The Myth of American Idealism?: Intellectuals and International Relations in the Interwar Years," paper presented to the Mid-America Conference on History, Topeka, Kansas, 1996, 1. The quote is from William Keylor, *The Twentieth Century World: An International History* (New York: Oxford, 1992), 263-264.

2. Hill, 2-3.

3. *Ibid.,* 7-8.

4. George F. Kennan, *American Diplomacy* (Chicago, IL: University of Chicago Press, 1984), vii.

5. Hans J. Morgenthau, *In Defense of the National Interest: A Critical Examination of American Foreign Policy* (New York: A.A. Knopf, 1951), 7.

6. Regina Gramer, "On Poststructuralisms, Revisionisms, and Cold Wars," *Diplomatic History* 19 (Summer 1995): 518.

7. David Baldwin, "Security Studies and the End of the Cold War," *World Politics* 48 (October 1995): 119.

8. Memo from Fleming to Bernard Baruch, 15 May 1946, 1, The Denna Fleming Collection, Vanderbilt University. Daniel Yergin notes that this memo was forwarded to President Harry S. Truman in *Shattered Peace: The Origins of the Cold War and the National Security State* (Boston, MA: Houghton Mifflin, 1977), 79.

9. Frederick L. Schuman, *The Nazi Dictatorship: A Study in Social Pathology and the Politics of Fascism* (New York: A.A. Knopf, 1935).

10. Frederick L. Schuman, *International Politics* (New York: McGraw-Hill, 1933).

11. Morgenthau, *In Defense of the National Interest,* 6. Morgenthau claims, though, that Wilson pursued the goal unconsciously.

12. See Woodrow Wilson, *Congressional Government in the United States* (New York, NY: Columbia University Press, 1908).

13. Woodrow Wilson, "Address to the League to Enforce Peace," Washington, DC, 27 May 1916, Public Papers, IV, 184-188, in E. David Cronon, *The Political Thought of Woodrow Wilson* (New York: Bobbs-Merrill, 1965), 419.

14. See Michael Hunt, *Ideology and U.S. Foreign Policy* (New Haven, CT: Yale University Press, 1987).

15. Cronon, 231.

16. *Ibid.*

17. *Ibid.,* 232.

18. "The Covenant of the League of Nations." In Cronon, 478-479.

19. "Address of President Wilson to the Congress of the United States, 8 January 1918." In Cronon, 442. Emphasis added.

20. Henry Blumenthal, *Illusion and Reality in Franco-American Relations, 1914-1945* (Baton Rouge, LA: Louisiana State University Press, 1986), 48.

21. "The Covenant of the League of Nations." In Cronon, 475-476, 47.

1

Wilson's Disciples

What had appeared in August 1914 to be a military conflict fought along traditional balance of power cleavages had rapidly escalated to a Social Darwinist winner-take-all, loser-receive-nothing contest where both sides claimed the other would stop at nothing short of world domination or total defeat. Hans Morgenthau observed that World War I represented the consummation of "the worldwide struggle for power."[1]

The concepts of balance of power, geopolitics, and *realpolitik* dominated discussions of international relations in the early twentieth century. Nations were believed to have a prerogative, if not a duty, to use their power for the aggrandizement of the nation-state. But the inability of traditional diplomacy to arrange a conclusion to the contest led many analysts to seek a new diplomacy, one that would provide a durable peace predicated on an effective arrangement of nations subject to international law. In short, they sought a new world order.

The Wilsonians developed a more sophisticated model of international relations than that of the realists. Like Peter Kropotkin, who perceived mutual aid as the corollary to struggle in the biological world, internationalists believed that law and mutual cooperation tempered the struggle between nations. In order to reduce the probability of war, it was definitely in the national interest to support international law and world organization.

It was not an easy task to convince the great body of public opinion that an international organization premised on the political equality of all states within the organization was necessary or even desirable, let alone essential for social progress. Internationalism was a word not yet widely used to describe a system of interaction among nations. As well, the concept of political equality among sovereign states was unfamiliar to many of the world's peoples. It was in this environment that Quincy Wright began his professional career.

Wright earned his Master of Arts in 1913 and Doctor of Philosophy in 1915 from the University of Illinois. He studied international relations under the direction of Professor James Garner, a leading internationalist and authority on international law. Following graduation, Wright held a research fellowship from 1915 to 1916 and accepted a series of one-year teaching appointments at Harvard from 1916 to 1919. In 1919 he joined the faculty of the Political Science Department at the University of Minnesota and in 1923 he accepted an offer from Charles Merriam, chairman of the Department of Political Science, to teach international law at the University of Chicago, where he remained until his retirement in 1956. After that, Wright accepted an *emeritus* appointment at the University of Virginia.[2]

Wright established his reputation as an analyst of international affairs and as an authority on international law early in his career. His dissertation was published in 1916 in the *University of Illinois Studies in the Social Sciences,* followed by several articles in the *American Journal of International Law.* His first book, *The Control of American Foreign Relations,* was released in 1921 and received the American Philosophical Society's Henry M. Phillips Crowned Essay Award, which brought with it a handsome sum of two-thousand dollars.[3] His growing academic stature led to his appointment as the Naval Intelligence Office "Special Assistant on International Law" during the Washington Conferences.[4] This was the beginning of several appointments to government that provided Wright the opportunity to affect policy directly and to reach a wider audience with his message of a new world order.

World War I generated wide discussion about international law, especially a law that would guarantee neutral rights. Wright wrote frequently about neutrality, especially during the period when the U.S. claimed to be a neutral party, and firmly embraced the historic rights of neutral nations as defined in international law. His reaction to German violations of neutral rights, though, was significantly harsher than his reaction to British violations.[5] His advocacy of neutral rights changed dramatically in the 1920s—in fact, he would anticipate the Kennan-Morgenthau interpretation by several decades—but during the war years Wright continued to argue for neutral rights.[6]

The war also encouraged demands in the United States and abroad for the creation of a "League to Enforce Peace," or a "Society of Nations" to maintain peace. In the United States, support for a league came from across the political spectrum and Henry Cabot Lodge and Woodrow Wilson were leading proponents. Quincy Wright, too, was among the early advocates of such an organization.

In a lengthy letter written to his father on Bastille Day, 1917, Wright declared that "world government" was needed to prevent future wars. To be effective, such a government would require power similar to the constitutional power of the U.S. Congress, especially the power to call the militia to enforce the law. A world federation would adjudicate international law through a single world court that would be the "*sine qua non* of a world organization." Equally important to him was the principle that the individual, not just the state, must have standing in the courts of international law.

This insistence on individual accountability in international affairs brought severe criticism from the foremost representative of the realist school in the post-World War II era. George Frost Kennan attacked what he labeled the legalistic-moralistic tradition of American foreign policy in a series of influential lectures given at the University of Chicago in 1950. Kennan condemned the belief that it was possible to apply the "Anglo-Saxon concept of individual law into the international field and to make it applicable to governments as it is to individuals."[7]

Yet Kennan also declared that "until peoples learn to spot the fanning of mass emotions and the sowing of bitterness, suspicion, and intolerance *as crimes in themselves*" war would continue to plague humanity.[8] In the face of historical experience that indicated peoples had little recourse to do anything about such activities within undemocratic states even if they were inclined to do so, Quincy Wright chose to offer change rather than stasis, hope rather than despair.

Wright's federation would have a central administration with a "Collegiate executive," and an international law that would be supreme over national laws in the manner that U.S. constitutional law was supreme over state law.[9] These areas of concern and his prescriptions or remedies remained, with few exceptions, substantively unchanged during his career.

Wilson's leadership and his plans for a just peace and a world order based on law appealed to Wright. His recognition of Wilson as a man of vision led Wright to become a Democrat in 1917. The President's Fourteen Points Speech of January 1918 and the debate over the League of Nations in 1919 cemented Wright's loyalty to Wilson, for he believed that the United States was obligated to lead the way to the new world order.

A few weeks before the election of 1918, Wright observed that the American people were united to win the war, but were uncertain what the fruits of victory should be. As a consequence, he believed U.S. voters would not vote for or against the war, but "for or against the ultimate political objects enunciated by the President." Wright thought loyal citizens, especially the Republicans, should rally 'round the President.[10]

Even though he was Wilson's disciple, Wright occasionally disagreed with the President. Wright criticized Wilson's unbending attitude about partisan disagreements as a serious liability. Wright opposed what he characterized as Wilson's rigid stand against reservations, no matter how moderate they might be. Compromise was the art of the possible, and Wright thought a compromise was necessary to the establishment of the new world order. Not only that, but he thought that such a compromise could be arranged.[11] Wright believed as well that for Wilson to make the League a political issue in the presidential campaign of 1920 would be "disastrous."[12]

Oddly enough, Hans Morgenthau later criticized Wilson for compromising his principles while negotiating in Paris. The advocate of realism from the University of Chicago declared that Wilson was "a compromised idealist, an empty-handed statesman, a discredited ally."[13] One can only wonder what Morgenthau's assessment would have been had Wilson succeeded.

Most opponents of U.S. entry in the League of Nations asserted that Article X of the League Covenant circumvented the constitutional authority of Congress to declare war and thus compromised national sovereignty.[14] This was an issue Wright examined in detail. He argued that courts had previously sustained the power of the executive to negotiate treaties that required certain types of military action and that the collective security aspects of the League did not result in a "delegation of power to declare war to the international commission."[15]

Wright cited a variety of evidence to support his position. The 1903 Treaty with Panama, approved and ratified, provided that the United States guarantee and maintain Panamanian independence, which could require a declaration of war in certain circumstances. As well, Congress had accepted limits on the war power when it approved the Treaty of Guadeloupe Hidalgo, the 1907 Hague Convention, and the Bryan Treaties, all of which prohibited war under specific conditions. Of course, the issue of delegation of powers had not been tested in these instances, and the Constitution specifically prohibits such delegation of powers between branches.

Perhaps his strongest argument was that the use of force under such a "concert of Powers" would not necessarily require a congressional declaration of war. He argued that Congress had long allowed the executive to determine when to use armed force and cited Lincoln's actions to suppress the Southern rebels to demonstrate that "force may be used to the greatest extent without a declaration of war by Congress."[16] This Wilsonian understanding of executive application of military force would indelibly shape the character of the twentieth century American presidency.

Wright concluded that if the subject matter of a treaty was appropriate for negotiation, if it did not conflict with the purposes of the Constitution nor any of its specific prohibitions, then once it was ratified it became a matter of what he referred to as a "constitutional understanding." Once such an understanding was reached, those departments of government whose approbation is necessary to ratification "are bound by their allegiance to the Constitution to perform the acts necessary to give it effect." He provided a *caveat* in that he thought it wise to consider the opinion of those branches of government whose consent was necessary for the ratification of treaties prior to signing such agreements, but this was not, he declared, a legal necessity.[17]

By January of 1920, determined congressional opposition to the League had prevented ratification of the Versailles Treaty. Wright renewed his call upon the president to accept certain reservations. Wright held the "remarkable" transformation of William Jennings Bryan, who had been "accused of radicalism and doctrinairism," but who was now an advocate of "reservations and opportunist compromise," as a model for Wilson.[18]

Wright endorsed the Democratic ticket of James M. Cox and Franklin D. Roosevelt in 1920. He declared in a letter to William Howard Taft that the question of U.S. membership in the League was the most important question the nation faced. Because American entry was practically certain with Cox and Roosevelt and doubtful with Harding, Wright would vote for the Democratic ticket.[19]

Taft countered that, in his opinion, Warren G. Harding was the surest way for the United States to join the League. But as Wright noted to a friend, Taft was wrong about Harding being the shortest route to the League, but perhaps right about his election being the shortest route for Taft to get to the Supreme Court.[20] Wright believed Republicans would destroy any chance the United States might have to join an effective League of Nations. Wright indicated, though, that despite Republican claims to the contrary, the Geneva meeting of the League Assembly, which Wright attended, was a great success.[21]

Although Woodrow Wilson's role in preventing U.S. entry into the League disappointed him, Wright ultimately held Henry Cabot Lodge and the Republicans responsible for the defeat of the treaty.[22] Wright likened Lodge to Pope Gregory VII in that the Senator delighted in "making his enemies come to Canossa." The Senator's vindictiveness destroyed the Versailles Treaty as the Republicans were determined to "accept nothing but unconditional surrender." This unbending policy wrought disaster in that it compelled Wilson to retreat from what Wright characterized as the President's conciliatory position announced in his January 26th letter to Senator Johnson.[23] Wright's loyalty to the League outweighed whatever reservations he may have felt about the methods Wilson employed to achieve Senate approval of the treaty.

This question of whether or not the Senate had the authority to contravene executive initiatives led Wright to produce *The Control of American Foreign Relations,* a work in which he defined his belief that the executive branch was solely vested with that authority. One of the constitutional "understandings" was that Congress would acquiesce to executive initiatives.[24] He believed that "the organs conducting foreign relations have their responsibilities defined by international law, while their powers are defined by constitutional law." In order to avoid confusion, a series of understandings developed (or must develop) in the experience of the U.S. government in order that it function effectively.[25]

Wright's analysis of the issue was historical. He provided various precedents that suggested the unique position of the executive branch in its relation to foreign policy. He was careful to include some of the arguments opponents had advanced and to address what he perceived to be their inadequacies.[26] He also documented several controversies that occupied international legal scholars, and he provided the reader with a cogent analysis.[27]

The feature of Wright's analysis that places him squarely as a Wilsonian was his belief in a strong executive, unbowed by Congress, and representative of the people's will. Such an executive would function best under a broad construction of the Constitution without a meddling Senate.[28] Wright identified closely with the recommendations Wilson articulated in his book *Congressional Government,* and concluded, as did Wilson, that "the result of over a century of experience under the Constitution illustrates certain necessities in an adequate control of foreign affairs."[29]

The foremost of those necessities in Wright's mind, and a *sine qua non* of the realist school, was unhampered executive initiative in foreign affairs. The development of constitutional understandings was critical to this goal. In "The Understandings of International Law," Wright asserted that the preamble to the Covenant of the League of Nations supported a flexible interpretation that allowed it to develop "understandings" like those that evolved under the English common law.[30] Wright envisioned similar understandings for the United States federal government.

He compared the condition of those understandings that had developed in the United States to those of the eighteenth century British constitution. He described the U.S. Constitution as a "jarring and jangling instrument" that created rocky conditions between the executive, its cabinet members, and the legislative branch. The institutions of the Constitution were good, he wrote, but the "constitutional manners which will make them work like a well-ordered dinner party" had not yet been developed.[31] The question, of course, was how to develop such understandings and it was here that Wright was less than effective, although certainly imaginative.

Like realists Henry Kissinger, who six decades later would call for "some more permanent conception of national interest," and George Kennan, who called for a "long-term approach" to foreign policy as a leavening agent to what they perceived to be the problems of American idealism, Wright recommended that Congress declare certain permanent general policies.[32] Those policies should guide, but not restrict, executive initiative. Wright sought to ensure that the principles of international law, a body of law that had enabled democratic institutions, especially American institutions, to thrive, would govern as much diplomatic activity as possible. A third requisite was that, with respect to potential interdepartmental rivalries over treaty negotiations, the government should cultivate tolerance, consideration, and respect toward "the exercise of powers which may collide with the powers of other departments."[33]

In retrospect, the inadequacies of these first three remedies are obvious. The declaration of any permanent policy outside the very general rhetoric of national interest would be restrictive, to say the least, and there are no guarantees that the Executive and Congress would be in concert even after the declaration of such policies. As for international law, little diplomacy actually occurred outside its recognized principles. The only means to ensure that as much "diplomacy as possible" did come under those principles would be to establish an effective world order with sufficient police power to coerce the objects of its law to obey it.

More importantly, to predicate interdepartmental relations on "toleration, consideration, and respect" betrayed Wright's naivete of governmental dynamics. He ignored the fact that the three branches often claimed prerogatives in the same areas and that the capacity or incapacity of political appointees varied between departments. As well, he assumed that there were officials to whom such "virtues" would appeal in the operation of government.

Wright's fourth and fifth recommendations were better suited to achieve his goal of an effective foreign policy. He described the maintenance of "close informal relations between the agencies of the government having to do with foreign affairs." To do so, Wright would have enlarged the cabinet to include representatives of the legislative branch in order to "form a Cabinet capable of reaching decisions on foreign affairs likely to secure cooperation from all departments of the government and yet not too large for business."[34]

Wright would also maintain, but always at the executive's initiative, direct relations with the Senate through more frequent addresses and explanations of executive policy to that body, and to congressional committees on foreign affairs.[35] Wright was anticipating the creation of the National Security Council in 1947. That group, although not comprised of the individuals Wright designated, served an identical purpose: to augment the strength of the executive to direct foreign affairs.

Ever mindful of those individuals and groups who feared a powerful executive, Wright emphasized the general nature of his prescriptions. Wright concluded that constitutional understandings would not limit the President's power in foreign relations, nor impair the need to act expeditiously. Instead, they would provide the executive a general direction and avoid or at least discourage congressional opposition to treaties and other presidential initiatives in foreign affairs.[36]

Wright's final prescription was to develop political traditions that threw "big men to the top." "The people and parties," Wright said, "must insist on men of experience and tried capacity as candidates."[37] George Kennan argued from a similar vantage for the creation of a foreign policy elite. "I firmly believe," wrote the former director of the Policy Planning Staff, "that we could make much more effective use of the principle of professionalism in the conduct of foreign policy."[38] Part of the remedy Wright suggested was to retain the expertise of former presidents and secretaries of state by establishing a tradition of electing them to the Senate after their executive service. He offered, though, no assessment of what to do in the event the men were deemed incompetent. Another part of the remedy was to establish an "understanding" of a hierarchical system of offices—governor to Senate to Vice-President to the Cabinet to the Presidency—as a means of preventing "dark horse" victories in presidential elections.

Again, he offered no counter to the inherent threat that this type of system posed in perpetuating an elite.[39] He alluded to the Senate of ancient Rome as a model, apparently unworried that even at its best the Roman Senate was an unresponsive, corrupt, and bloodthirsty body and that at its worst it was a tool of unresponsive, corrupt, and bloodthirsty emperors. Equally troublesome was whether many presidents would care to devote their next six years to the demands of the Senate after an exhausting one or two terms as chief executive.

Wright, like the realists who would follow him, used the vantage of expediency to argue for a strong executive. In "International Law in its Relation to Constitutional Law," Wright emphasized that legislative or public interference delayed and unnecessarily publicized treaties. Concentration of power in executive hands assured rapidity and secrecy, a fact at odds with Wilson's first point in the Fourteen Point Speech. Wright observed that constraints on the swift exercise of a power often made that power worthless.[40] His assumptions were based upon attributing an intrinsic value to speed and secrecy, something realists have long valued in foreign relations.

While the issue of executive control of foreign policy consumed much of his time, Wright continued to follow other developments that pertained to international law and organization. He was very interested in the issue of war crimes and the possible trials of war criminals. He saw great potential to bring international law to the forefront of world attention through these actions.

Equally important, Wright believed that to be truly effective, international law had to apply to individuals, not just states.[41] Wright believed that the trial and punishment of the Kaiser would be a precedent to deter future acts of aggression. It would also greatly enhance the power of the World Court. The trial never materialized, and Wright turned to other matters, but the subject continued to occupy his interest.

While Quincy Wright was fighting the battles of theory and policy, Denna Frank Fleming was learning the hard lessons of warfare on the battlefields of Flanders and France.[42] Fleming entered the "war to end all wars" as an enlisted soldier, trained as a machine gunner, and became an instructor in the operation of the "Lewis gun" at an aircraft machine gun school in France for six months.[43] He was an early victim of the world flu epidemic shortly after becoming a gunnery sergeant. Upon his recovery he was detailed to ordnance duty where, among other responsibilities, he and his squad dug graves.

This journey, both intellectual and physical, greatly affected the young man who was, he wrote, "born in the bosom of isolationism in the heart of the Mississippi Valley" at Belle Ridge, Illinois on 25 March 1893. Fleming had remained an isolationist Republican until 1917. During that year, he came to believe that President Woodrow Wilson had done all he could to keep the United States out of the European conflict and that his country was no longer able to remain neutral in World War I.[44]

The war's senseless squander and the possibility that it could happen again left Fleming a determined Wilsonian. Fleming sought to relocate power in a new global community at the expense of independent national sovereignty. Among the many problems he faced, though, was the unknown quality of the new world organization. He would fight against the centralization of power in the legislative branch of the U.S. government that he believed was unresponsive to the people, yet he would rely upon the power of a new organization that held the potential to become the greatest of all institutions of centralized power.

Fleming left the army with a diploma from Eastern Illinois Normal School earned in 1912, and a B. A. in Political Science earned in 1916 from the University of Illinois. There was little demand for machine gun instructors in civilian life, but there was employment for teachers. Fleming had been a high school teacher and principal from 1912 to 1917 and he resumed these careers upon his return from the war.

He found time as well to pursue a master's degree from the University of Illinois, which he received in 1920. In 1922 he graduated from teaching high school students to educating college students at Monmouth College where he served as an assistant professor of social science, an associate professor, and eventually as chair of the department from 1924 to 1927.

In 1927 Fleming was granted an extended leave of absence in order to pursue a Ph.D. at the University of Illinois. While there, Fleming, like Quincy Wright, studied under the supervision of Professor James W. Garner. Garner was an influential educator and an advocate of Wilsonian internationalism. Garner's impact on both men was profound and helped to shape their world outlook: it was his devotion to law as the agent for world organization that shone through in his two most famous students' work.

As part of his doctoral program, Fleming enrolled at Columbia University in New York City in order to audit the lectures of James T. Shotwell, Arthur W. McMahon, and Joseph P. Chamberlain.[45] These men were important peace activists and they, especially Shotwell, came to influence Fleming's future.

Fleming was particularly interested in the Senate's defeat of the League of Nations, and he took partial manuscripts of two books, his dissertation, *The Treaty Veto of the American Senate,* and *The United States and the League of Nations, 1918-1920,* to Shotwell for review in 1927. Shotwell, who along with Salmon Levinson was a principal architect of the Kellogg-Briand Pact, found Fleming's works so promising that he forwarded them to the Woodrow Wilson Foundation. The manuscripts were greeted enthusiastically—so much so that Norman Davis, one of the foundation's board members, suggested to the Chancellor of Vanderbilt University, James H. Kirkland, that Fleming would make an admirable addition to the Vanderbilt History and Political Science faculty.[46]

Fleming earned his Ph.D. in 1928, but his dissertation defense was difficult. Several of his committee members criticized what they characterized to be the polemical quality of his work, a charge that would revisit him in later years regarding other works.[47] Ultimately, though, Fleming's defense was successful. Putnam published his dissertation in 1930 and found it necessary to run a second printing the same year.[48] Fleming then applied to Vanderbilt University for a position in the Department of History and Political Science. In due course, he was appointed in 1928 and began a relationship that lasted thirty-three years until McCarthyism drove him from Vanderbilt.

Fleming focused his early career on what he considered the Senate's obstructionist role in defeating the Versailles Treaty.[49] In addition to his dissertation, he published two other books early in his career that became influential: *The United States and the League of Nations, 1918-1920* and *The United States and World Organization, 1920-1933*.[50] In these books Fleming reiterated the belief, popular among Wilsonians, that the Senate alone was responsible for the botched effort at world organization following World War I and that Henry Cabot Lodge and his followers had sabotaged the League for personal and partisan reasons.[51]

The battle between Wilson and the Senate over the League set Fleming's political agenda for the remainder of his career. Fleming's included both institutional and individual conflicts in his early analysis and sought to synthesize the interpretations of the rift between the Senate and the Executive branches of government.

He defined the problem of Senate interference in the making of treaties through historical analysis, carefully documenting the precedents for Senate influence, including the role of individual senators and presidents. In later efforts to quantify the injustices of the Senate in regard to executive treaty making, though, his data allowed for a conclusion at odds with his agenda. "Four-fifths of all the treaties submitted to the Senate," he wrote, "have been approved by it without any change whatsoever . . . Likewise, the failure of 62 treaties to be approved by the Senate in any form has had serious consequences in not more than a fifth of the situations resulting." Another conclusion would be that the Senate was, for the most part, a reasonable body that found few occasions to object to the unhampered power the executive branch wielded in making treaties.[52]

Fleming did not propose radical alternative models for American government, nor did he offer a comparative analysis of the U.S. system with other systems. Instead, he proposed minor modifications to the U.S. system, but they were modifications that would drastically reduce the Senate's influence and greatly expand the power of the presidency. In this, he was at once a Wilsonian and a realist.

What is revealed in his book *The Treaty Veto of the American Senate* is not so much Fleming's disappointment with the system as his disappointment with certain Senate decisions, decisions at odds with his agenda, his antagonism toward Henry Cabot Lodge, and his idolization of Woodrow Wilson. Fleming, like Wilson, believed that a parliamentary system would rectify this type of problem much quicker than did governments "where the theory rules that independent branches of the Government must watch and check or block each other."[53] Power should be concentrated in the hands of the executive.

As fervid an Anglophile as Wilson, Hans Morgenthau shared this assessment. He declared that the parliamentary form of government created in the cabinet a "mechanism that enables a majority of the elected representatives of the people to control the foreign policies of the government [and] compels the government to speak in foreign affairs with one voice."[54] Such a system, if adopted in the United States, would reduce the possibility of foreign powers misinterpreting American foreign policy.

Kennan, too, called for the U.S. to adopt a parliamentary system. Noting that many called for such a constitutional reform, Kennan wrote that "if I had any doubts before as to whether it is this that our country requires, those doubts have been pretty well resolved in my mind by the events of the past weeks and months."[55] Nonetheless, he was so pessimistic regarding the chance of such a reform being approved that he cautioned the reader to "dismiss the possibility as one that might have any particular relevance to our present problems."[56]

As for his disappointment with the Senate's actions, Fleming did not approve the result of the opposition's manipulation of public opinion, but he knew its value. He believed that these opponents had "resisted the demand that we should take our high place in the League, gradually wore it down and had finally overcome it by arousing counter feelings of infinite number and variety." As a Wilsonian he believed that organized public opinion was essential to the cause of internationalism.[57]

Fleming described the Senate's role as "both irritating and unfair" and he accepted the editorial analysis of the *Nation* when it attacked the "growing tendency to make the management of our international relations subservient to the purposes of party politics—which is another way of saying, of growing indifference to national reputation."[58] Fleming believed that the Senate had undermined the intent of the Founding Fathers and that it was now arrogating power in a day of increasingly important foreign affairs.[59]

Nothing demonstrated this, in Fleming's mind, more amply than what he considered to be Henry Cabot Lodge's role in scuttling the League of Nations. After all, Lodge had originally defended the idea of a League. Recognizing the difficulties encountered when a politician advocated anything resembling an alliance, Lodge still believed that Washington's Farewell admonition should not be construed to prevent the United States from accepting responsibility, along with other "civilized" nations, of maintaining peace if the appropriate means for coordinating their actions were found.[60] But after the war, Lodge became, in Fleming's view, a crass partisan who disregarded his earlier convictions regarding U.S. commitments to global responsibilities.

Fleming accepted the substance and the rhetoric of President Wilson's war address to Congress.[61] Americans, Wilson declared, would fight for the things they held dear: a democratic government responsive to its people, equality among nations, and the "universal dominion of right by such a concert of free peoples as shall bring peace and safety to all nations and make the world itself at last free." And, said Wilson, Americans would consider it their privilege to sacrifice both blood and treasure for these principles, principles that shaped the creation of the nation and assured its peace and happiness. "God helping her," he urged, "she can do no other."[62]

Whether or not the United States really had some other recourse than intervention in 1917 continues to be debated. Fleming believed that German unrestricted submarine warfare, coupled with the intrinsic threat Prussian militarism posed to free and democratic societies, so jeopardized the national interest that it made neutrality untenable. He concluded that the United States and Wilson could indeed "do no other"—especially when the British provided compensation for the goods they seized.[63]

Like Fleming, "realists" declared that the only mistake the United States made was its delay in entering the war. Kennan argued that American leaders, especially Wilson, were slow to appreciate the impact an Allied defeat would have on U.S. national interest. Citing a passage from Wilson's speech to the League to Enforce Peace in May 1916, Kennan argued that Wilson's declaration that Americans were "not concerned" with the causes of the war was a betrayal of his failure as a statesman.[64] Once we entered the war, though, Kennan observed that "we had no difficulty in discovering—and lost no time in doing so—that the issues involved in it were of the greatest significance to us."[65]

But Kennan failed to provide the context of the speech. In the same passage, it is clear that Wilson was correct: as a nation, it was too late to be concerned with the origins of the war. What Wilson said was that "the interests of all nations are our own also. What affects mankind is inevitably our affair as well as the affair of the nations of Europe and Asia."[66] Clearly, Wilson recognized the importance of a stable balance of power in Europe to the national interest of the United States.

Morgenthau was equally critical of Wilson. According to Morgenthau, Wilson's failure to recognize that the European balance of power was the "traditional guarantor of American security" led him to temporize in his response to World War I. Even when the United States entered the war, Morgenthau decried the fact that it was for the wrong reason. Wilson sought not to "restore a new, viable balance of power, but to put an end to the balance of power once and forever."[67]

What Wilson actually said was that the United States was not interested in a "new attempt" to maintain the peace through "nothing" but the balance of power. Wilson knew that balance of power alone could not maintain peace. Balance of power politics inevitably led to war because some nation always challenges the balance. Furthermore, the United States would not join a combination of exclusively European powers. The United States was interested in more than just the peace of Europe; the United States sought world peace.

As for suggestions that Wilson should have accepted a compromise with the League's opponents, Fleming argued that to do so would have been a rejection of principle.[68] This was less than effective given Wilson's willingness to compromise the principle of self-determination in the service of world peace and Fleming's own conversion from neutrality to intervention during the war. Fleming observed that in his Fourteen Points Speech to Congress, the President specified that there must be a general association of nations. Specific covenants would govern it so that "mutual guarantees of political independence and territorial integrity" could be effected for great and small states alike," a most important aspect of post-war international organization.[69]   Any compromise would likely result in a truncated league.

What Fleming would not admit was that people who opposed Wilson's League might do so because they believed that it did not represent the interests of the nation. In the long struggle to define the Constitution, both the Executive and the Legislative branches traditionally avoided entangling alliances, sought to check the other's attempts to aggrandize their authority and power, and tried to rein in the masses to keep the country safe from the "dangers" of democracy. The Senate's charge to provide advice and to consent to, or dissent from, treaties was designed to protect the country from rash decisions *and* to protect elite interests against radical developments. It is possible many Senators accepted that charge seriously, for they believed the Executive Branch had strayed dangerously from established precedent.

It is problematic whether Wilson's exclusion of ranking Republicans from the Peace Commission resulted in the Round Robin of 4 March 1919. It is entirely possible that nothing could have tempered that group's resolve to oppose the Treaty. Certainly, this is the interpretation Fleming forwarded. The caucus of Senate Republicans declared that without revision the Senate would not consent to the President's idea of the League. Wilson envisioned a League whose covenant bound its members to protect peace, free trade, and the territorial integrity of every member nation: contracting parties would conceivably act multilaterally against aggressor nations in order to protect one another's rights.

This was what the Senate opposition feared most, for they thought this League obligation would circumvent congressional power to declare war and thus augment executive power. But there were significant problems in this belief, for there was no coercive device to force the contracting parties to action. The League would have no independent military force to add power to its authority, most League decisions would require a unanimous vote, and the member states reserved to themselves the right to take independent action in the event that they considered it "necessary for the maintenance of right and justice."[70]

Although these factors made the Reservationist arguments against the League moot, they also appeared to make the League a body without substance. The League's sole authority rested in the moral suasion it exerted on international public opinion—again, there was no binding, coercive agent to enforce its rules and regulations, and the Reservationists, at least the discerning ones, knew this to be the case. But appearances were deceptive. A concert of great powers, many now dependent on the economic goodwill of the United States, could, if united, force their policies on the world.

Fleming's description of the above events paid homage to the story of President Washington's first experience with the Senate and its role of giving advice and consent over a proposed treaty in order to demonstrate "the friction inherent in the attempt to give two independent bodies power over treaties."[71] The Constitutional Convention wanted a limited role for the Senate, Fleming explained, and the Senate had immediately gone beyond that role: disputatious Senators like William Maclay in the eighteenth century or Henry Cabot Lodge

in the twentieth should not constrain the President.[72]   "There are," wrote
Fleming, "always likely to be lawyers in the Senate who can think of something
that ought to be changed.   There are always some who are of the opinion that
the executive must be watched, or it will betray us."[73]

"Realists" would later share that distaste for legalism.   In addition, they in-
veighed against undue congressional interference with Executive initiative.
Kennan made no effort to conceal his contempt for the Senate in his *Memoirs*
when discussing the Vandenberg Resolution.   He described the Senators of the
Foreign Relations Committee and their questions during testimony as "typical
of that mixture of arid legalism and semantic pretentiousness that so often
passes, in the halls of our domestic political life, for statesmanship."[74]   Morgenthau wrote that the fear of congressional investigation hung "constantly over the
heads of all members of the executive department" and decried the time State
Department officials had to spend defending their policy or their loyalty.[75]

Fleming believed that the "scrutiny of treaties" ought to be turned over to
the House of Representatives, a body of individuals who relied more "upon
good sense and less upon rigid legislative methods" than did the Senate in order
to counter the overly "legalistic" tendency of the Senate.[76]   This seems anoma-
lous for a man who so highly valued "the reign of law."[77]   Perhaps part of the
explanation for this incongruity is the strong sense of populism his interpretation conveys.   Internationalism in the twentieth century was presented as a
"peoples" movement whose message was empowerment of the world's people in
their affairs.

Whatever their origin, his views on this issue place him squarely in the realist school.   George Frost Kennan and Hans Morgenthau based much of their
critique of U.S. foreign policy on the overly legalistic and moralistic elements
of its conduct.   On more than one occasion, Denna Fleming and Quincy Wright
developed the critique long before it became associated with the realists.

At this time, Fleming identified "the people" with the House of Representatives.   His basis for this identification was his belief that there were fewer lawyers in the House, therefore its membership was less inclined to litigious inter-
pretive battles over constitutional law and more inclined to exercise common
sense. He thought the limits of what he identified as a senatorial mindset were
serious.   In an unintended self-parody of his own profession, he concluded
"Words mean everything to many of them."[78]   It was, of course, a naive belief
to think that the members of the House were any less corruptible, any less partisan, or any closer to the people than the members of the Senate.   Nonetheless,
Fleming held that a broadening of congressional responsibility for treaties
would at least on the surface better serve the cause of democracy.

Equally contemptuous of the Senate, Morgenthau wrote that obsessive executive fears of Congress were based on the false assumption that it was representative of public opinion.   "That the temper of Congress and especially of the
Senate is not of necessity truly representative of public opinion," he wrote, "is
evident from a consideration of the factors that limit the representative function
of Congress."[79]

Fleming transposed the populists' community ideology to what was now,
in his view, the global community.   His villains were the same as the populists'—lawyers, the wealthy interest groups, the robber barons—all those who

would deny "progress" and expression of the public will. Fleming indicted multimillionaires like Henry Clay Frick and Andrew W. Mellon for having contributed millions to defeat the League.[80] And Fleming singled-out financiers Thomas W. Lamont and H. P. Davidson, along with Elihu Root, for having provided Lodge with a copy of the Versailles Treaty prior to official publication. Fleming charged jurists John Bassett Moore and Charles Evans Hughes with dereliction of duty.[81] But most of all the Senate, that isolated group of lawyers and wealthy businessmen who clung to a superannuated sense of national sovereignty and to a reactionary foreign policy, received Fleming's ire.

Ironically, Fleming noted that the Founding Fathers themselves sought to prevent the popular will from exerting undue influence on the measured considerations necessary to conduct foreign policy, and to provide a check on a powerful executive branch. Because of this, and after much deliberation, the Constitution was designed to give the Senate (or a small minority thereof), a body of indirectly elected, influential officials, the power to stay the implementation of treaties.[82]

This, of course, was the result of the "infamous" two-thirds rule, a rule that doubled the value of every vote against a treaty, and a rule Fleming believed should be abolished.[83] But even though the intent clearly had been to protect an ill-informed, sometimes rash public from unfortunate decisions and not merely to perpetuate the interests of the ruling class, such had also been the intent behind the indirect election of Senators, something that the public had seen fit to change.

Fleming described the role of the Senate in foreign policy and treaty ratification as the "irreparable" mistake of the Constitution.[84] After all, Fleming argued, the President was responsible to all the people and as such should be able to negotiate treaties without undue Senate interference.[85] This was a characteristic Wilsonian interpretation of the need for a strong executive. The Senate could not always be trusted to see the utility of a treaty outside the context of regional or party interests, and, in the event that it did not, Fleming concluded that the country should recognize that instead of a new treaty it needed a new Senate.[86] An elite group of partisan senators, separated from the true interests of their constituents, often refused to pass measures that were for the good of the collectivity.

Instead, the Senators claimed that they checked the "authoritarian," "unrepresentative," and even "monarchical," occupants of the executive office and declared further that they, the Senators, were duty bound to protect the republic from mobocracy. According to Fleming, the Senate would oppose any transfer of power to the House, because the Senate sought to protect its institutional prerogative and retain its members' position of oligarchy in the creation of foreign policy despite its members' protests that the system served the interests of democracy.[87]

Fleming provided as well the example of the Roman Republic, which, according to his interpretation, fell "when the Senate [which had been entrusted with the power to make treaties] gathered executive, administrative, and legislative powers in its hands and ruled the state. The Empire followed."[88] The warning is not lost on even the least discerning reader, although Fleming's reading of Roman history is subject to a very different conclusion.[89]

Fleming also appealed to the reader's sense of progress and modernity in order to augment his argument. Organizational technique and technology, he declared, were rapidly shrinking the world.[90] He noted that the temporizing of the Senate while it awaited assurances of "complete safety and perfect equality" in treaties caused the United States to lose ground in a world that continued to move ahead rapidly. It was a world in which an international organization was developing means to settle disputes peacefully, and the United States was without significant input in the process.[91] A country that was too rigidly tied to the past was in jeopardy of being left behind, of missing the new organizational structure of international society.

Fleming thought this rigid traditionalism was one of the great tragedies of the old system. Why, he asked, must a nation of air travel and radio be bound by the assumptions of men who lived in the days of sail and oxcart? In a day when the pace and scope of international events had increased greatly, why should a small group of anachronistic Senators be allowed to block progress?[92]

Fleming realized that the Senate was not going to divest itself willingly of the right to influence foreign policymaking. He believed the Senators would prevent a constitutional amendment in the foreseeable future, but he noted that it had once been thought that the Senate would be immobile in its opposition to the popular election of its members. Taking small hope in this, though, he wrote that "The Senate resisted that reform until a long campaign compelled its submission. It will take even longer no doubt to lead the Senate to modify its power over treaties."[93]

What, then, short of revolution, should the future course be for those who wished to change the system? The pressure of "organized public opinion" was a basic Wilsonian tenet, and Fleming turned to it to force the Senate into action. Citing the numerous constitutional developments that World War I and the peace had wrought, he suggested that the people opposed to change could be made to see the way of the future. He called attention to the governments of the newly constituted countries of Europe as examples: Germany, Austria, Poland, Czechoslovakia, Estonia, Finland, and Yugoslavia had all rejected the U.S. structure for upper house involvement in the governance of foreign policy and treaty making.[94] These governments had chosen the lower house to check foreign policy making, which reaffirmed representative government and helped prevent elite control of the government.[95]

As for Senate opposition to such a loss of power, Fleming preempted it with rhetoric from the Senate. Senators from all parties had at one time or another proclaimed that nothing was less suited to the purposes of democracy than a small group of men, isolated from the people, who exercised power in their name. Especially vehement had been the protests of the opponents to the League about the impact of a few men in Geneva or The Hague sitting in judgment of U.S. policy. It would be difficult for Senators who had thwarted the treaty process to object to such a broadening of popular control as Fleming advocated. How could they, he wondered, "insist upon the right of a small group of Senators, varying in number from a dozen to thirty-three, to rule the foreign affairs of the American nation?"[96]

Surely, he argued, the Senate, like our allies and enemies, could be persuaded that a system where a simple majority vote of *both* houses was required for consent to treaties was a progressive step and should be adopted. Fleming thought it would be very difficult for any reasonable person to oppose such a system.[97] Of course, the Senate did not (and still does not) employ reason as its sole criterion for decision-making. Even if it did, given the perspective of some of its more influential members like Hiram Johnson and William Borah, the Senate could "reasonably" assume that the precedents Fleming cited were meaningless or they could arrive at the conclusion opposite of Fleming's.

By the presidential campaign of 1920, Wright and Fleming had defined their core beliefs regarding Wilsonianism. While Wright had arrived at his ideas solely through scholarship, Fleming had come to his through action in World War I. The two men shared many beliefs, among them the need for an international organization with teeth and the need for an executive branch of government capable of delivering effective foreign policy in a new era. They would spend much of the next decade seeking both.

In large part, these men recognized the limits of American power. No nation alone could accomplish what was necessary to assure peace and stability. Their advocacy of the League of Nations and international law was explicit recognition of the "greater humility in our national outlook" that George Kennan declared essential to a realistic approach to international affairs.[98] The flexibility of response afforded in the League Covenant was exactly what the United States needed to exercise "greater restraint than we have shown . . . in involving ourselves in complex situations far from our shores."[99]

NOTES

1. Hans Morgenthau, *In Defense of the National Interest: A Critical Examination of American Foreign Policy* (New York: A.A. Knopf, 1951), 42.

2. Louise Wright, *A Bibliography of Quincy Wright: 1890-1970* (Pittsburgh, PA: The Clifford E. Barbour Library, 1974), 5; Charles Merriam to Quincy Wright, 17 April 1923, Box 4, addenda 2, folder 10, The Quincy Wright Collection, University of Chicago.

3. Quincy Wright, *The Control of American Foreign Relations* (New York: Macmillan Co., 1922).

4. Navy Department to Quincy Wright, 28 June 1918, Box 1, addenda 2.

5. The fact that Great Britain compensated for lost neutral property influenced Wright's position regarding the Germans. See Quincy Wright, "The Destruction of Neutral Property on Enemy Vessels," *American Journal of International Law* 11 (January 1917): 358-379.

6. For his changed position on neutrality, see Quincy Wright, "The Future of Neutrality," *International Conciliation* 242 (September 1928): 1-98. Wright writes "neutrality in the sense used by the law during the past century is incompatible with a society of nations organized to prevent violence," 17.

7. George F. Kennan, *American Diplomacy* (Chicago, IL: University of Chicago Press, 1984), 94.

8. *Ibid.,* 62.

9. Wright to Father, 14 July 1917; for additional material on supremacy of international law over municipal law, see Wright "Conflicts of International Law with National Laws and Ordinances," *American Journal of International Law* 11 (January 1917): 1-21; as for the need of an international law superior to national laws, see his dissertation "The Enforcement of International through Municipal Law," *University of Illinois Studies in the Social Sciences* (Urbana, IL: University of Illinois Press,

1916): 1-264. Wright used the municipal model throughout his career as the basis for a federal world order.

10. Wright document, "Issues of the Campaign," 28 October 1918, Box 18, folder 7.

11. Wright to Mother, 16 December 1919, Box 2, addenda 2, folder 3. Wright's use of ratification here is somewhat fuzzy as he later indicates that the executive ratifies, the Senate provides only its advice and consent. See, too, Wright to Rex, 19 December 1919, Box 2, addenda 2, folder 1, for further criticism of Wilson's position.

12. Wright to Rex, 19 December 1919, Box 2, addenda 2, folder 1. For more of Wright's criticisms of Wilson see Wright to Father, 18 January 1920, Box 2, addenda 2, folder 3; Wright to Prof. Wilson, 16 February 1920, Box 2, addenda 2, folder 2; and Wright to Father, 28 February 1920, Box 2, addenda 2, folder 3.

13. Morgenthau, *In Defense of the National Interest,* 27.

14. See H. C. Lodge to Wright, 25 February 1919, Box 18, folder 8, for a discussion of the opposition's general fears.

15. Quincy Wright, "Treaties and Constitutional Separation of Powers in the United States," *American Journal of International Law* 12 (January 1918): 72-76.

16. *Ibid.,* 76-77.

17. *Ibid.,* 93-95.

18. Wright to Father, 18 January 1920, Box 2, addenda 2, folder 3.

19. Wright to W. H. Taft, 28 September 1920, Box 3, addenda 2, folder 1; Wright to "Pit," 31 October 1920, Box 2, addenda 2, folder 8.

20. William H. Taft to Wright, 10 September 1920; Wright to Rex, 30 May 1921, Box 2, addenda 2, folder 4.

21. *Ibid.*

22. See Wright to Mother, 16 December 1919, Box 2, addenda 2, folder 3; Wright to Rex, 19 December 1919, Box 2, addenda 2, folder 1; Wright to Father, 18 January 1920, Box 2, addenda 2, folder 3; and Wright to Denys Myers, Box 1, addenda 2, folder 5 for Wright's comments on Wilson's responsibility.

23. Wright to Myers, 24 March 1920, Box 1, addenda 2, folder 5.

24. Wright, *The Control of American Foreign Relations,* 42.

25. *Ibid.,* ix, 7-9.

26. *Ibid.,* 6. Wright notes John Jay's argument against those who opposed treaties as the "supreme" law of the land. See also 361-365.

27. *Ibid.*

28. *Ibid.,* 25.

29. *Ibid.,* 366-68. Wright refers to Woodrow Wilson, *Congressional Government: A Study in American Politics* (New York: Meridian, 1956), 266; 273-274. Wright also cites "Corwin" following the quotation provided here but clearly the implication of the preceding text is that Wilson shared this conclusion. Arthur Link refers to *Constitutional Government in the United States* (New York: Columbia University Press, 1908), 77-78 to demonstrate that "Wilson believed that the president was a virtual sovereign, responsible only to public opinion and not to Congress, in the conduct of external affairs." As cited in Arthur Link, *Wilson The Diplomatist* (Chicago, IL: Quadrangle Books, 1957), 132.

30. Quincy Wright, "The Understandings of International Law," *American Journal of International Law* 14 (October 1920): 379, fn 45.

31. *Ibid.,* 369.

32. Walter Isaacson, "Kissinger's Realism Without Morality," in Thomas Paterson, *Major Problems in American Foreign Relations, Volume II: Since 1914* (Lexington, MA: Heath, 1995): 631; Kennan, *American Diplomacy,* 94.

33. Wright, "The Understandings of International Law," 370-371.

34. *Ibid.,* 371.

35. *Ibid.,* 371-372.

36. *Ibid.,* 372.

37. *Ibid.,* 373.

38. Kennan, *American Diplomacy,* 93.

39. *Ibid.*

40. Quincy Wright, "International Law in its Relation to Constitutional Law," *American Journal of International Law* 17 (April 1923): 234-244.

41. Quincy Wright, "The Legal Liability of the Kaiser," *American Political Science Review* 13 (February 1919): 123, 128.

42. Fred Rennik to Denna F. Fleming, 11 October 1943, Box 3, The Denna F. Fleming Collection, Vanderbilt University.

43. Fleming noted that the Lewis gun "sometimes shot backward instead of forward." Notes from Doris A. Fleming to Steven J. Bucklin, 23 January 1989, 4.

44. Denna Fleming to Mr. Schreiner, 11 February 1957, 1; Fleming, *The United States and World Organization, 1920-1933* (New York: Columbia University Press, 1938), 16. Doris A. Fleming revealed that Denna had been a Republican to me in a telephone conversation on 12 February 1989.

45. Doris A. Fleming to Steven J. Bucklin, 23 January 1989, 5.

46. *Ibid.*

47. Doris Fleming wrote that Denna's defense "was a hard battle." In a conversation with me on 12 February 1989 she used the term "polemical," although on page five of her notes of 23 January 1989, she writes that the committee criticized the dissertation as being "not academic enough, would not sell, etc., etc." As for later criticisms, see Paul Conkin's *Gone with the Ivy: A Biography of Vanderbilt University,* (Knoxville, TN: University of Tennessee Press, 1985), or several of the reviews of Fleming's *The Cold War and Its Origins, 1917-1960* (Garden City, NY: Doubleday, 1961). Fleming's dependence on newspapers, especially the *New York Times* and the *Nashville Tennessean* made his scholarship suspect in the eyes of his critics.

48. Notes from Doris Fleming to Steven J. Bucklin, 6.

49. Fleming to Sen. Elbert D. Thomas, 1 February 1935.

50. Denna Fleming, *The United States and the League of Nations, 1918-1920* (New York: Putnam, 1932) and Fleming, *The United States and World Organization, 1920-1933.*

51. Fleming, *The United States and World Organization,* 17-22.

52. Denna Fleming, "The Role of the Senate in Treaty-Making: A Survey of Four Decades," *American Political Science Review* 28 (August 1934): 583.

53. Denna Fleming, *The Treaty Veto of the American Senate* (New York: G. P. Putnam's Sons, 1930), 313.

54. Morgenthau, *In Defense of the National Interest,* 225.

55. Kennan, *American Diplomacy,* 94-95.

56. *Ibid.,* 95.

57. Fleming, *The Treaty Veto of the American Senate,* 172.

58. *Ibid.,* 43; 62. This is just one example of Fleming's use of the liberal press to corroborate his opinion. What is noticeably lacking is reference to the other perspectives surrounding the issue of the Senate's role in policy making.

59. *Ibid.,* 272.

60. Frederick L. Schuman, *International Politics: An Introduction to the Western State System* (New York: McGraw-Hill, 1933, 1937), 252.

61. Presidential Address to Congress, 2 April 1917, Public Papers, V, 6-16, as found in E. David Cronon, *The Political Thought of Woodrow Wilson* (New York: Bobbs-Merrill Co., 1965), 337-348.

62. *Ibid.,* 348.

63. Fleming, *The United States and World Organization,* 8; 10.

64. Kennan, *American Diplomacy,* 63-64.

65. *Ibid.,* 65.

66. Cronon, *The Political Thought of Woodrow Wilson,* 419.

67. Morgenthau, *In Defense of the National Interest,* 26.

68. Fleming, *The United States and the League of Nations,* 487-500; *The United States and World Organization,* 30.

69. Address to Congress, 8 Jan 1918, Public Papers, V, 155-162, as cited in Cronon, 444.

70. "League of Nations Covenant," as cited in Cronon, 468-481. There are no provisions for a League military force in the Covenant and it is implied that any joint military action would be a cooperative effort presumably under a command structure like that of the Allies and Associated Powers during World War I; Article V; Article XV.

71. Fleming, *The Treaty Veto of the American Senate,* 21.

72. *Ibid.,* 5-15.

73. *Ibid.,* 76. Fleming was not fond of lawyers. See Fleming, "The Role of the Senate in Treaty-Making: A Survey of Four Decades," *American Political Science Review,* 28 (August 1934): 596-597, or "Planning For The Post War World," 4 *Current History* (March 1943): 9.

74. George F. Kennan, *Memoirs, 1925-1950* (New York: Pantheon, 1967), 409.

75. Morgenthau, *In Defense of the National Interest,* 227.

76. Fleming, *The Treaty Veto of the American Senate,* 291-292.

77. Fleming dedicated *The United States and World Organization* to "Those in every nation who have sought, and to those who in the future will seek, 'The reign of law based on the consent of the governed and sustained by the organized opinion of mankind.'"

78. Fleming, *The Treaty Veto of the American Senate,* 292.

79. Morgenthau, *In Defense of the National Interest,* 231-232.

80. Wright shared this view of Harvey. See Wright to Rex, 30 May 1921, Box 2, addenda 2, folder 4.

81. Fleming, *The United States and the League of Nations,* 209-211. Fleming cites George Harvey, *Henry Clay Frick the Man* (New York: Charles Scribner's Sons, 1928), 220-221; 324-326. On Hughes and Moore and their role in scuttling the League see *The United States and World Organization,* 75-78; 248-249. Fleming refers to Elihu Root as the "chief attorney" for the Republican party, certainly a pejorative use of the term, *The United States and World Organization,* 27.

82. Fleming, *The Treaty Veto of the American Senate,* 11-14.

83. *Ibid.,* 111; 286-287; Fleming to Senator Elbert D. Thomas, Utah, 1 February 1935, 1.

84. Fleming, *The Treaty Veto of the American Senate,* 292-293. Fleming attributed the phrase to Secretary of State John Hay.

85. *Ibid.,* 45. This, of course, does not take into consideration the role of the Electoral College or the intent behind its creation.

86. *Ibid.,* 80; 83; 98; *The Boston Herald,* as quoted in Fleming, 99. Fleming was prone to cite the news media as evidence that the Senate was not "in tune" with the public interest. See pages 99-100 of *The Treaty Veto of the American Senate.*

87. *Ibid.,* 290. The non-representative theme occurs frequently in Fleming's book. See 98, 270, 272, 282, 283, 286, 288, 292, 293, 305, and 311.

88. *Ibid.,* 311.

89. One could argue that it was the dispersal of power to the Tribal Assembly and the Tribunes of the People that led to the calamity of the social war, the civil war, and then the establishment of empire and dictatorship.

90. Fleming, *The Treaty Veto of the American Senate*, 289.
91. *Ibid.*, 276.
92. *Ibid.*, 282-283.
93. *Ibid.*, 283.
94. *Ibid.*, 295-297.
95. *Ibid.*, 298.
96. *Ibid.*
97. *Ibid.*, 300-301.
98. Kennan, *American Diplomacy,* 178.
99. *Ibid.*

2

Wilsonianism and the New Era

The opening of the New Era brought a commitment from the Harding Admini-stration of noncommitment in the sphere of international affairs. The United States would not join the League of Nations, nor would it bind itself to alliances. Instead, as scholar Joan Hoff Wilson has noted, the United States began a course of independent internationalism.[1]

The realists had little to say about the New Era and its foreign policy. Ken-nan wrote that Charles Evans Hughes and Henry Stimson were men of integrity. Irreproachably loyal, modest, and kind and generous "to all who were weaker and more dependent" Kennan declared them "our finest contribution to the vari-ety of human species in this world [who come] closest to embodying our na-tional ideal and genius."[2] Nonetheless, Kennan concluded that there had been "a significant gap between challenge and response in our conduct of foreign pol-icy" under their stewardship.[3]

Hans Morgenthau condemned the policy of isolationism that he believed dominated New Era foreign policy and was equally hostile to internationalism. Both were, he claimed, "strangers not only to the first, realistic phase of Ameri-can foreign policy, but to its whole tradition."[4] Both, he noted with contempt, were blind to political reality.

For Quincy Wright and Denna Fleming, Republican victory in 1920 meant a setback for U.S. entry into the League and for a stronger U.S. commitment to internationalism. "Normalcy," the mantra of the Republican presidential candi-date Warren G. Harding, was to Fleming a conservative conspiracy, a reaction to the visionary progressive leadership of Woodrow Wilson and the Democrats. "Normalcy" was a policy designed to offset what Fleming called Wilson's "amazing program of [domestic] action." The old ruling classes and powerful economic groups found that Wilson's domestic program conflicted with their interests, and when they returned to power in 1921 they were determined to reverse Wilsonian reforms.[5] By inference, if one defeated the Republicans, there was great potential to bring about U.S. membership in the League.

As for foreign policy, Fleming believed Wilson's rhetoric about a move toward open diplomacy, a move he equated with denying power to the old elites, or at least forcing them to share it. And Fleming believed this policy was popular. Writing about the 1920 presidential election, Fleming asserted that Wilson's foreign policy was then so popular that Harding could not afford to campaign without making appeals to the overwhelming public support for a League of Nations.

Harding and his campaign managers, Fleming wrote, misled the public by alternately condemning the League of Nations and promising to sponsor a new association of nations, or to rehabilitate the one in Geneva. The condemnations were necessary to appease Republican senators who wanted to keep the United States out of the League but, according to Fleming, all indications within the Republican party led one to conclude that pro-League Republicans controlled party leadership. And this leadership urged the public to support Harding "as the way into the League."[6] It was, therefore, another Republican betrayal of public trust that led to Harding's victory, according to Fleming, for the irreconcilable opponents to U.S. membership in the League had no intention of letting their candidate tie the United States to that organization.[7]

Consequently, Wright and Fleming called on the government to cooperate with the League. They wrote prolifically in defense of the League and in explanation of its impact on international law, but if it was presidential minds they sought to sow with the seeds of internationalism, the field was indeed a difficult one to plow.

The New Era presidency was very much the antithesis of the strong executive the Wilsonians and the realists envisioned. Harding—affable, fond of women, drink, and gambling—delegated authority to some able and some not-so-able subordinates. Among the more able was his Secretary of State, Charles Evans Hughes. Hughes would set the stage for cooperation with the League of Nations when it became politically opportune to do so in 1922.

Calvin Coolidge was remarkably unremarkable. "Silent Cal" entrusted his foreign policy, and maybe powers of speech, to first Hughes and later to Frank Kellogg. Kellogg was chiefly memorable for the effort he and Aristide Briand made to make war an illegal act.

And, of course, there was Herbert Hoover. Certainly, Hoover was more of a Wilsonian than many people imagined, at least insofar as he wielded the presidency in foreign affairs. He was a forceful foreign policy president. His influence over Henry Stimson in response to the Japanese invasion of Manchuria is but one example where the stolid Iowan's mark could be found on American foreign policy.

What these three presidents held in common, though, was their continued need to placate isolationist senators like William Borah and pockets of isolationist public opinion. In order to get anything done, they had to make sure their treaties would be met with two-thirds senatorial approval. The political lesson of Woodrow Wilson and the Democrats in 1919 and 1920 was not lost on these presidents, nor was it lost on the realists and their idealist counterparts.

In 1921, Wright was given an opportunity to influence policy when the Navy Department retained him as a special expert on international law at the Washington Conference.[8] Through interpretation and counsel he exercised a degree of influence over certain proceedings and policies. Wright's personal correspondence contains little reference to his experience at the conference, but he did produce a commentary, "The Washington Conference," about the treaty systems that the delegates produced.

Wright compared the Four Power Treaty with Article X of the League Covenant and found their obligations to be similar. Given that there were no measures to enforce the obligations under any of the Washington Conference treaties, this demonstrates again that Wright believed in the principle of flexible commitment, a principle that the League Covenant allowed in the event of collective action. But despite his praise of the conferences, he emphasized that the Washington Conference system was no substitute for the League of Nations.[9]

Still, Wright proclaimed the Washington Conference a success. Hans Morgenthau concurred. He wrote in the 1954 second edition of his textbook, *Politics Among Nations,* that the Washington Naval Treaty, or Five Power Treaty, was "[t]he only outstanding success of its kind."[10]

Another issue with which Wright grappled was the creation of machinery for peaceful change. This may well have been the most important contribution of his scholarship. If the League were to be successful, something more than a perpetuator of the *status quo,* it had to develop means for peaceful change. As Elihu Root noted in a critique of the League, if Article X were perpetually enforced "it would be mischievous. Change and growth are the law of life" and Article X would "attempt to preserve for all time unchanged the [present] distribution of power."[11]

George Kennan shared Root's concern. Kennan believed that the effort to impose a legal system on the nation-states of the world "ignores the law of change."[12] He emphasized the fact that a system of international relations must function to ease transitions, not to impose a "a legal straight-jacket" on change.[13]

Yet much of both Kennan's and Morgenthau's scholarship could easily be interpreted as neo-isolationist. Never vague in their proclamations that the national interest should move American foreign policy, both were ever vague in defining what constitutes the national interest except in retroactive terms. As close as Morgenthau would come to a definition was that the national interest is "conceived as power among other powers."[14]

As for their paeans to change, both men offered only more of the same: traditional diplomacy, maintenance of the balance of power, and power politics. Morgenthau in particular was critical of Wilson for declaring that it was "a very perilous thing to determine the foreign policy of a nation in the terms of material interest."[15] Tied to the idea that the enduring national interest of the United States was the maintenance of the balance of power in Europe, Morgenthau and Kennan resisted change.[16]

In a time when much was made of agreements to maintain the status quo, whether in the form of the Washington Treaties or the Locarno Pact, Wright's vision led him to realize that the need to provide peaceful vehicles for change was essential to progress. Rather than rely on traditional diplomacy, which was the only solution Kennan and Morgenthau offered, Wright was willing to experiment. He was willing to consider changing the system.

An area that required experimentation was the colonial world. Wright feared that if the growing nationalist movements in colonial and mandated areas were not given proper vent, they would fuel yet another war. For Wright, the mandate system provided for peaceful transitions of power and for the fulfillment of obligations that industrially and culturally advanced nations held for less advanced ones.

"Backward" was the term he used most frequently in reference to the people who lived in the mandates, which reflected his perception about races and racial hierarchy.[17] In 1925, Wright received a Guggenheim Fellowship to study the mandatory system under the League of Nations.[18] The resulting book, published in 1930, is a glowing tribute to the League system and to the advances dependent peoples had made under mandatory tutelage.

Wright saw the mandate system as a means to enable the dependencies to prepare for independence. His research confirmed the right of Mandatory powers to be compensated for administrative costs and noted with approval the continued progress people, usually people of color, made under the benevolent rule of Western nations.[19]

The professor was particularly sympathetic to the virtues of the British model for governing mandates, especially when compared to the French in Syria.[20] Wright concluded that with British guidance, there had been material progress in the mandate of Iraq since 1921. Although taxation was heavy, revenues "appeared" to have been spent wisely, and he doubted that "unreasonable profits" had gone to foreign governments or merchants. Iraqi art, literature, and science, Wright continued, could not compare to Belgium's, Czechoslovakia's, or Norway's, so that Iraq's great hope was in continued British paternalism. Iraq, whose people Wright characterized as "adolescent," illustrated what was best about the League of Nations system of mandates.[21]

His assessment is shockingly one-dimensional when one considers the British massacre at Amritsar, India only seven years before his assessment. As for profits and plunder, it was commonplace that the British were engaged in plotting the systematic plunder of the Middle East's and Iraq's one resource, oil, which was not renewable. And the fact remains that Iraq's cultural heritage was absolutely stellar when held to that of the countries to which Wright compared it. Many contemporary residents of Ireland, India, or any other imperial possession or mandate of Great Britain's would likely have provided a very different assessment from Wright's.

Wright's belief in the mandate system demonstrated his willingness to sacrifice the needs of smaller powers to the great ones. It is not surprising that Wright and Fleming had little to say about American interventions in Latin America during the Progressive and New Eras. Just as Henry Kissinger would refer to Vietnam as a "footnote in history" when compared to the greater idea of détente, Wright and Fleming believed the needs of world peace and of international organization were superior to the needs of the underdeveloped world.

Kennan offered a similarly racist interpretation of the U.S. acquisition of the Philippines, but he had no suggestion for a different approach to "backward" peoples. "It was also fairly clear," he wrote, "that the inhabitants [of the Philippines] were hardly fit for self-rule, even if there had been a chance of their being left alone by other powers, which there was not."[22] Despite the fact that Emiliano Aguinaldo and his supporters had written a constitution and kept the superior armed forces of the United States at bay for four years in a war for independence, Kennan declared the Filipinos inferior to the demands of self-government.

As well, Kennan argued that U.S. national interest in the area was "nil." As a realist, he declared that the reason the United States invested its prestige, its fortune, and its citizens' lives to take the Philippines was that if we did not, someone else would.[23] Such logic had the potential to involve the United States in numerous engagements that were beyond the pale of what Kennan declared to be the national interest.

Morgenthau was equally racist. He declared the westward expansion of the original thirteen colonies to be "an act of civilizing rather than of conquering."[24] As for the global power of Europe, Morgenthau insisted that it derived from "its predominance over the colored races. It was the cultural, technological, and political differential between the white man of Europe and the colored man of Africa and Asia which allowed Europe to acquire and keep its dominion over the world."[25] The faults in such assertions require no explanation here. Morgenthau's Eurocentrism led him to a variety of false conclusions.

Such beliefs, so common among the realists, would serve as breeding grounds for discontent and for the violent nationalist movements that characterized the second half of the twentieth century. Despite the fact that his prescription was less than desirable, at least Wright recognized the problem. And Wright's idea of mentoring democratic institutions and eventual independence through non-invasive means was far more realistic and in-tune with the national interest than was the attitude of the fathers of the realist interpretation.

Another essential element of Wright's effort to devise means for peaceful change was his conversion to the belief that neutrality was an anachronism in the modern world. Wright believed that to extend neutral rights on the assumption that they would assure peace was an egregious error.[26] Neutrality was antithetical to the basic assumption of collective security and Wright noted that the legal concept of neutrality was not compatible with an organization of nations dedicated to non-violent solutions of international disputes.[27]

When Senator Theodore Burton offered a resolution on 15 December 1927 that would prohibit the exportation of armaments or other sinews of war to any nation engaged in war with another nation or nations, Wright offered a counterpoint. If the United States adopted such a policy, it would be prevented from supplying arms to victims of aggression.[28]

Wright's call for flexibility in the ability of the United States to provide war materials to the victims of aggression places him squarely within the model of realism that Hans Morgenthau enunciated. And while ideologues like John Foster Dulles shared Wright's condemnation of neutrality in the 1950s, Wright's interpretation was based on principle and a reading of international law, not on emotion.

Wright, like Wilson, also believed that U.S. economic interests made neutrality impossible. In a world rapidly integrating on political, economic, and moral levels there would be a consonant "decrease in the rights and increase in the obligations of neutrals" which would make the policy of neutrality more and more untenable.[29] States, he wrote, must recognize "a new status between war and neutrality [called] 'partiality.'"[30] In 1941 he declared that during the last twenty-five years the policies of isolation, neutrality and impartiality had failed to prevent war or to keep war from escalating. Such a record demanded a departure from those failed policies.[31]

One such departure would be to hold individuals and nations accountable for crimes against international law. Unlike so many of its critics, Wright passionately believed that the Paris Peace Pact of 1928 would lead to great accomplishments in the international system. He thought the Pact would light a path to the elimination of the historic definition of neutrality. He shared with Secretary of State Frank Kellogg the hope that the United States would abandon strict neutrality and that the Pact would help it do so.

His first analysis of the Pact was "The Interpretation of Multilateral Treaties." Here he wrote that "[t]he significance of the peace pact is in the field of politics and public opinion rather than in that of law . . . If the [Pact is] effective, it will be because it presents a standard about which public opinion can organize, and the standard will in practice be the simple formula of the text, not the complex discussions of the notes."[32] He included as well an explanatory model based on municipal law in which he asserted that multilateral treaties were equivalent to statutes while bilateral treaties were equivalent to contracts. Statutes, he suggested, were less subject to interpretation because greater care was practiced in their legal phrasing.[33]

Denna Fleming was less enthusiastic about the promise of the Paris Pact. Fleming found nothing positive in the fact that the Senate had rapidly approved the Kellogg-Briand Pact. Although some analysts believed that the Senate had seen the error of its ways in the League debate, for it was now willing to attach reservations in committee reports rather than directly to a treaty, Fleming was not among them.[34] The Kellogg-Briand Pact did not portend any great changes in Fleming's estimation.

He warned that there were no provisions to enforce the pact, no sanctions to be implemented against aggressors. It was only because the treaty required no commitment on the part of the United States that the Senate had approved it. Had it required the United States to act, Fleming assured the reader that "the amendments and reservations offered by the preservers of 'the traditional policies of the United States' and by the defenders of the Senate's power over treaties would doubtless have been many and varied."[35]

Of course, the realists panned the Pact. Kennan held it up as an example of the failure of the "legalistic-moralistic approach to international problems."[36] Morgenthau said that the Pact was impossible to define, thereby begging the question of what constituted a violation of its proscription.[37]

The legal significance of the Peace Pact came to hold greater importance for Wright. In 1933 he claimed that "[t]he legal character of the Pact seems to have stood the test of practice . . . and it is acquiring certain sanctions, although these sanctions may not be entirely adequate."[38] He should have remembered his admonition of 1925 that "Laws which are flaunted do more harm than good for they break down respect for the law." Until 1933, the only severe test of the Pact had been the Japanese invasion of Manchuria, and that test left few people convinced that the Pact would ever serve the greater good.[39] Wright concluded that war and armed violence in international affairs was completely devoid of legal foundation, but the problem of making the international society mirror the proscriptions of law remained.[40]

To make society adhere to the standards of international law would require manipulation of public opinion. Wright co-authored with James T. Russell an article entitled "National Attitudes on the Far Eastern Controversy" that sought to establish a predictive model of national behavior through the measurement of public opinion.[41]

In this study the authors identified the methods and goals of international relations and declared that state attitudes could and should be empirically measured. What followed was a very uncritical attempt to measure state attitude, but in the early 1930s the state of opinion sampling was at a primitive stage, inadequately developed. Nonetheless, the authors believed that they were presenting "a method of measuring the attitude of one state toward another through newspaper sampling and judging."

If newspapers existed within a state, the authors maintained that at least one of them would likely represent the attitude of those who controlled the interests of the state.[42] Wright and Russell thought agencies could be developed along the lines of those that forecast business trends. These agencies would provide analyses based on the material culled from huge quantities of newspapers that would graph the changing attitudes of states. The authors believed these graphs would prove to be worthy regulating devices if distributed to statesmen throughout the world. Danger spots would be not only readily identifiable as "matters of opinion," they asserted, "but as measurable quantities." In order to succeed in preventing war, the League must mobilize public opinion before an act of war. These scholars reasoned that these analyses might provide the data necessary to effectively organize world opinion.[43]

Serious difficulties attend this model—the existence of representative newspapers, biased judging, biased editing, the ability of the state to influence the content of any newspaper, regardless of its perspective, through false leaks or black propaganda, misquotes, typos, and a variety of other possibilities. Wright would later admit that his conclusions were "not based upon an adequate sampling of the press."[44] What was important, though, was his continued effort to organize world opinion through its manipulation. Political scientists would persevere in their efforts to map and otherwise measure public opinion over the next three decades. Wright was a pioneer in this important dimension of the study of international relations.

The realists also recognized the need to influence public opinion. But Morgenthau, who was taken with the concept of individual will in leaders, declared that success in foreign policy often required that a leader take an unpopular position. The "peculiar qualities of the statesman's mind," he wrote, "are not always likely to find a favorable response in the popular mind."[45] Like Machiavelli's prince, the statesman "must be able to temporize, to compromise, to bide his time."[46] One of the unfortunate, and according to Morgenthau, never changing, characteristics of democratic foreign policy was that those who conduct it "must either sacrifice what they consider good policy upon the alter of public opinion, or by devious means gain popular support for policies whose true nature they conceal from the public."[47]

Fleming, like Wright, tried to influence public opinion to accept an international role for the United States. Among the issues that occupied Fleming before World War II, besides the Senate's role in treaty-making, were attempts to gain U.S. entry into the World Court, the evolution of the League of Nations, and what he perceived to be the isolationist trend in American foreign policy.[48]

Fleming continued to pursue his studies of the League after he settled in Nashville, and he sought further assistance in the form of a Penfield Traveling Scholarship from the University of Philadelphia. He received one in 1932 and another in 1938.[49] The first scholarship enabled Fleming to live in Geneva and study the League of Nations in action. During his six months in Geneva he witnessed the "last phases of the Disarmament Conference and the [debates over] the Lytton report on the Manchurian war."[50]

His research resulted in a third book, *The United States and World Organization, 1920-1933*. In this book, Fleming developed his theme that the major failure in American diplomacy since the defeat of the League had been the pursuit of isolationism and neutrality. The work in many ways typifies the "progressive" interpretation of the 1920s.[51]

Fleming asked his readers to identify the leaders and policies that had destroyed what he called the "greatest promise ever held out to man"—the League of Nations. What leaders and policies had allowed destructive forces greater than any previously known to be unleashed? What were the consequences for the nation now that it entrusted its security and well-being to the policies of neutrality and isolation?[52] Fleming held that the Republican leadership and their decade-long policy of "normalcy" were responsible for the precarious state of U.S. security.[53]

His solution? There was, he wrote, "no substitute for the League of Nations strong enough to keep the peace, and . . . none can be invented."[54] Order was as essential to the international system as it was to the local community, Fleming wrote, and he quoted Cordell Hull to support his beliefs. "The all-embracing preoccupation of all of us," Hull said, "may be summed up in one word—order. Order in international relations is just as vital as it is in the relations within a nation."[55]

Fleming noted that the most crucial obstacle that world order faced was the relationship that the United States would have with the League. Presumably, the prospect of some *Pax Americana* left him unmoved. As long as the relationship between the League and the United States remained unsettled, he believed the international situation would continue to deteriorate.[56]

With this in mind, Fleming expressed his disappointment to President Franklin D. Roosevelt at the Senate's defeat of U.S. entry into the World Court, asking him to throw his full power into a future effort to gain U.S. participation. He counseled the president that both his prestige and the welfare of many nations depended on this outcome. Fleming thought it "intolerable" that William Randolph Hearst, "allied with an importunate radio priest and a half dozen other violent individuals, should defeat the will of the nation, your leadership, and dominate our foreign policy."[57] Fleming entreated the president not to accept future congressional reservations to U. S. entry in the World Court. Fleming understood any opponents of such entry to be obstructionists dedicated to the maintenance of their privileged position in the world order.

It was in the milieu of the waning New Era that another voice would join Fleming's and Wright's. A decade after Wright and Fleming had become committed Wilsonians, Frederick Lewis Schuman began his career as a member of the second generation of Wilsonian internationalists. Schuman devoted his career, which spanned fifty years of the twentieth century, to the analysis of power politics, international relations and world organization. His contributions as author, scholar, and pedagogue influenced a generation of citizens, students, academics, and politicians, especially through the writing of a widely adopted text, *International Politics,* and those contributions continue to offer insight to those who read international theory.[58]

He was Quincy Wright's student at the University of Chicago. From an early date, Schuman's interests gravitated toward U.S.-Soviet relations and he would contribute extensively to that historiography. He believed that a more fundamental appeal than reason would be necessary to grab the public imagination and compel it to accept the new world order. Wilsonian internationalism influenced his beliefs, but the model Schuman advocated for international order was a different version from the one Wilson had earlier envisioned.

Schuman accepted much of the Wilsonian model in that he called for leaders and publics who understood the interdependence of political societies, who saw beyond narrow chauvinistic sovereignty and class distinctions. He ardently believed that an educated world public, one instilled with new myths, aware of agents of international cohesion, a public concerned with more than domesticity, was a prerequisite to world order.

Schuman devoted most of his scholarship and a considerable portion of his personal life to this "mission of education." He desired not the "global village" of Marshall McLuhan, but a "global cosmopolis." But if that world failed to materialize, Schuman had an alternative model that was far less liberal and decidedly less democratic than that of traditional Wilsonianism. It was a model based on power politics.

Schuman was born in Chicago on 22 February 1904. In 1920 he enrolled at the University of Chicago where he studied as an undergraduate, graduate scholar and fellow, and where he received a Ph.B. in 1924 and a Ph.D. three years later. By the 1920s, the University of Chicago was among the foremost institutions of learning in the country, "the intellectual center of American academic life, especially in the rapidly growing social sciences" and "the most influential center of the new political science."[59]

While a student at Chicago, Schuman studied with several very influential political scientists including Charles E. Merriam, Harold Lasswell, Leonard White, and Quincy Wright. The relationship he developed with Quincy and Louise Wright became the most important. The Wrights were his mentors, confidants, and colleagues during his years at Chicago. They were social activists whose agenda included domestic and international issues. As we have seen, Quincy Wright enjoyed a prominent reputation as a leading expert in international relations, and he exerted considerable influence on Schuman.

To Schuman, U.S. foreign policy was painfully unsophisticated, a quality evident in the refusal to join the League and in the non-recognition policy applied to revolutionary regimes.[60] Although they might not cite the same two examples, the realists certainly shared his characterization of American foreign policy.

For Schuman, the Bolshevik government was a Manichaean presence in the Western psyche that generated both hope and fear. Sympathizers saw in Bolshevik industrial planning a model for the United States and the world. Even Henry Ford found something to admire in the Soviet model.[61] And many political scientists believed that the ability to plan and apply policy effectively on a state or international level was one of the principle benefits of their new discipline.

But in other people there reposed nothing but hostility and a visceral hatred for this Russian social experiment. From 1917 onward, many U.S. citizens harbored fears and misgivings about the Russian revolution and its champions. Government and privately sponsored propaganda, especially the near hysteria generated during the Bolshevik phase of the revolution and the Allied intervention that followed, created much of this attitude. But perhaps because the revolution was so iconoclastic, because it so represented modernism and the disruption of traditional beliefs, it appeared to threaten the West in real terms as well.

Public perceptions about the Bolsheviks and Russia notwithstanding, Schuman developed a lifelong affinity for the country and for its Marxist experiment. It was an almost romantic attachment that led him to write his dissertation. In that dissertation he challenged the then current historical interpretations and anticipated later revisionist and New Left studies, especially William Appleman Williams' *American Russian Relations, 1781-1947.*[62]

Schuman's first trip to the Soviet Union in 1928 included "a most interesting half hour with Litvinov."[63] Schuman first saw a hard-bound copy of his dissertation, published by International Publishers, on the foreign minister's desk during his interview. Litvinov praised it as a "valuable contribution."[64]

Schuman's world vision reflected certain contemporary intellectual currents. One of these was an apprehension that the United States was sending mixed signals to the rest of the world. He feared that cultural confusion in the United States was being juxtaposed to an international political level.[65] The world's newly unbound Prometheus, it seemed to him, was losing the initiative and had excluded itself from vital processes within the international community.

The realists often noted such a failure on the part of U.S. officials to communicate foreign policy intentions. Although speaking specifically of the Open Door policy, Kennan sounded a criticism that he would apply to United States foreign policy during nearly the entire twentieth century. The failure of the U.S. to adopt a realistic approach to its foreign policy cultivated "bewilderment, suspicion and concern . . . in the foreign mind."[66] Morgenthau noted simply that American foreign policy and its makers needed to "relearn the great principles of statecraft which guided the republic in the first decade" of its existence.[67]

For Schuman, who sought to reshape the international community, the 1920s had an urgent quality about them. He felt keenly the need to spread his message, for he believed in the necessity of an informed, persuaded public. He accepted an instructorship at the University of Chicago in 1926, a position he held until 1936 when he accepted an assistant professorship in political science at Williams College in Williamstown, Massachusetts.

During the summer of 1929, Schuman traveled to England and France on a grant to conduct research for Quincy Wright's *The Causes of War and the Conditions of Peace*.[68] Schuman's research turned not only to the work for Wright, but for what would be Schuman's second book, *War and Diplomacy in the French Republic*.[69]

Schuman followed the book on the French Republic with *International Politics: An Introduction to the Western State System*.[70] The text became a standard in many universities and colleges in the United States and by 1968 was in its seventh edition. He employed an historical approach to international politics, and this text established both his penchant for making predictions and his advocacy of a new world order.

That order was predicated on an institution for international organization that Schuman hoped would differ structurally and theoretically from the League of Nations. He presented these views in the first edition of *International Politics* (1933), in which he criticized the League and its inability to enforce collective security. He also criticized Woodrow Wilson, who Schuman perceived in terms of the former President's "facility at phrase-making," and whose ideas of a "league of honor, a partnership of opinion" as an agent to enforce peace Schuman had come to deem naive.[71] Here was an internationalist pre-empting the later realist critique of the League of Nations.

His next book, *The Nazi Dictatorship: A Study in Social Pathology and the Politics of Fascism*, established both his national and international reputation.[72] He conducted much of the research in what he referred to as "the madhouse of Hitler's Berlin" where Schuman watched the Nazis seize and consolidate power.

But although he called it a madhouse, and although Hitler's methods were mostly opprobrious to Schuman, he saw value in the use of propaganda, in the cultivation of new myths, and in the *volkgemeinschaft* policy. The book was published at a time when it was not altogether commonplace in certain Western circles to bash National Socialism, and also very unpopular in the United States to advocate, as Schuman did, collective intervention to prevent the spread of fascism.[73] Like their response to the alarm others sounded, Western politicians, pressmen, and publics whose fear of Communism often nourished admiration for Fascism ignored his warnings—with predictably disastrous consequences.[74]

Schuman's evaluation of the Nazis was prescient. Even before *Nazi Dictatorship,* he wrote in *Current History* that Hitler's agenda sought to incorporate Austria, most of Czechoslovakia, the Baltic states, and any other regions that could be appropriated to the advantage of the Pan-Germanic nation.[75] As early as 29 October 1933, Schuman offered a cogent assessment of Hitler's future policy.[76] Schuman accepted Hitler's stated intentions and demonstrated in the same article the *Führer's* consistency in public policy speeches that began as early as 1920.

Schuman recognized the threat Nazi Germany posed to U.S. national interests almost immediately. For George Kennan, it was difficult even in 1951 to say that the United States should have acted in defense of its national interest and against Hitler earlier than it did. Part of the reason for this may lie in Kennan's belief that nations cannot judge each other's "domestic institutions and requirements, and we have no need to be apologetic to anyone, unless it be ourselves, for the things we do and the arrangements we enforce within our own country."[77]

For Kennan, the West might have stepped into German domestic affairs in 1933, 1935, or 1938, but to what effect? He claimed that no one knew who or what would have replaced Hitler. And, indeed, that is true: the Nazi movement may have survived without Hitler or the army may have taken control. But to declare that the real problem was "the weakness of German society which made possible his triumph" and in the next paragraph state that we "did nothing to harm Weimar Germany" is to divorce a realist from the responsibility to recognize what is in the national interest.[78] Despite the fact that Kennan continued by way of saying that the United States should not have left Weimar to its own devices, he offers nothing by way of explanation as to what U.S. policy should have been. In fact, he seems persuaded that isolationism in the case of U.S. relations with a great power can be a good thing.[79]

For Schuman and the other internationalists, realism had failed just as miserably as any substitute for it during the 1920s. In many respects, Schuman viewed the Versailles system as an instrument to maintain, if not the old order, then its close replica, for those who sought to use it still operated on the assumptions of the old diplomacy. It was in the United States, Schuman said, that traditional attitudes were most deeply entrenched. He believed that the United States had the greatest interest in a world society because a continuation of international anarchy stood to prevent the order and stability U.S. leaders saw as essential to the spread of free enterprise and democracy.

Yet despite its paramount interest, the United States remained reluctant to play the role necessary to create an effective world organization. More than any other great nation, the U.S. remained "committed to the ancient ways which offer so little hope for the salvaging of a sick acquisitive civilization composed of self-seeking communities."[80]

The next year Schuman declared that the United States must reassess the "attitudes, values, ideologies, symbolisms, and mythologies of the ruling classes of the nation-states" and commit to a policy of "transformation . . . transvaluation . . . [and] revolution." It was imperative that the United States, as the only one of the "bourgeois Great Powers" not in the League, lead the way.[81]

Schuman had reservations about the League and international organization, but he believed that if the world's peoples and nations failed to reorganize in accordance with his prescribed model, then the League could still serve as an alternative to ethnic nationalism. In this, he shared Wright's concern about nationalist movements as a source of future warfare. The League's institutions, he thought, could become the new traditions, the new shibboleths, the new symbols of a world consciousness. The problem with this, though, was that he saw the world situation in immediate terms, yet the transformations he advocated took time, more time than he believed the Western state system had before catastrophe struck. What was lacking was the power, coercive power, to enforce unity upon "the recalcitrant States of the world society."[82]

Yet Schuman had no ready solution for this problem. He noted that Machiavelli recognized the same dilemma in his *Discourse on Livy*. The Florentine wrote that "we cannot change our opinions and sentiments so frequently as the times vary: first, because we cannot easily oppose ourselves to what we have been accustomed to desire; secondly, that, having repeatedly been prosperous in one way, we cannot easily persuade ourselves that we shall be equally so in another."[83] The public and its leaders, especially the upper classes, would be unwilling to accept a new system when the old system provided tangible benefits.

Maintenance, or controlled change, of power plagued international security and peace as well. Balance of power was the key ingredient to world peace under the League system, but there did not yet exist a peaceful method to alter the balance that was universally accepted. Most nations had found it necessary to fulfill their security needs through national armaments and military alliances; international security guarantees were meaningless given a nonexistent binding force, moral or physical, to which all parties could appeal. Schuman wrote that the problem with guaranteeing international security was that there existed no "collectively organized, coercive authority in the existing structure of international government to restrain lawbreakers and preserve order."[84]

This is the basis of all arguments against international legal systems: that unlike national law, there is no instrument to coerce the objects of international laws to conform to the norms those laws prescribe. The debate was between those who demanded a League with super-state powers, especially a strong military institution, and those who believed that the collective nations could and would act rationally without extraordinary force.

Schuman regarded this debate and the form it took over the League of Nations in the context of the application of sanctions. He believed that the sanctions system of the Covenant was untenable. Self-interest motivated states, and the further a conflict is from the borders of a state, the less likely the people and leaders of that state are to perceive the resolution of that conflict as vital to their interests. Like Woodrow Wilson, Schuman accepted the premise that all conflicts are of interest to everyone on some level. But Schuman knew as well that few states would be willing to sacrifice either the blood or money necessary to make sanctions effective against aggressor states that had not attacked them.[85]

Schuman concluded that no nation was willing to allow an international body to compromise its sovereignty, yet the system he advocated revolved around just such a circumstance. No meaningful security could be established without the means for adjusting the *status quo* peacefully and the only way that Schuman could envision this to occur without world dictatorship involved dominant states conceding sovereignty, concessions he indicated they would not willingly make.

Not only that, but his system provided the states no formula to ensure that such a concession would be in their interests.[86] Assuming there existed no supranational force to guarantee that sanctions would be applied universally in the event that they were necessary to stop an aggressor, there was little reason to believe that any sanctions a League of Nations could provide had the slightest chance of success.

As of 1933 Schuman had not offered a viable solution, but he did offer a clear analysis. He believed that the problem central to the twentieth century was uncontrolled acquisitive capitalism combined with power politics, profits, and prestige: any solution, then, rested on a satisfactory conclusion of class antagonisms.[87]

Schuman believed that the two major sources of friction and conflict that confronted modern society were "the divergent and seemingly irreconcilable interests of those who own wealth, manage industry, and reap the profits of business, and of those who own nothing but labor power and who work for wages." Society knew only one method to unite the classes and that was to appeal to a common identification with the state. Love of and loyalty to nation superseded that of class bonds. Nationalism was the great unifying agent of the twentieth-century. Policies of aggrandizement appealed to elements of all classes, and although they benefited the ruling classes far more than the working classes, they were perceived as benefiting the nation.[88] Schuman believed that such policies, when successfully pursued, alleviated social unrest within a domestic context, but that such policies in an international context led to war.

This thesis laid the blame for wars directly on those who profited from them: on the capitalists, the financiers, the munitions-makers, and by inference, even on the working class. Schuman's theory depended upon a cycle in which war disrupted the world economy, which in turn generated labor unrest, which then brought about conditions favorable to fascism, which then further exacerbated world tensions. The cycle had to be broken, he thought, for it led to "irremediable disaster for the whole social and political structure of the world society."[89] But how to break the cycle?

In 1933 Schuman offered only vague nostrums that required the "organized application of social intelligence on a world-wide scale for the purpose of easing tensions, preventing conflict, and integrating divergent class and national interests into a new synthesis of values adequate for the political reformation of the world society."[90] Ironically, his solution was to transfer those values that created nationalism in sovereign states to a universal level; not unlike the Bolsheviks, who despised bureaucracy but found it absolutely essential to maintain their revolution, Schuman found nationalistic myths and conformity essential for his world order.

Despite his insistence upon the need for symbols that appealed to the emotions, he also called for economic planning and international organization as "the requisite roads to salvation." Both required "the organization of technical knowledge and socially directed intelligence for the rational solution of the [world's] problems." Both required that reason be substituted for "emotion, superstition, and blind faith in outworn formulas."[91]

But Schuman recognized certain cultural limitations to the promise of reason. After all, reason operated in an environment that current "superstitions and mythologies" limited. Nations had to acknowledge common interests on an international scale that would "prevail over selfish class loyalties and ancient tribal allegiances" or reason would be ineffective. He reiterated his belief that the institutions of capitalism prevented, or at the least made very difficult, the establishment of a genuine consensus of interests between the classes.

On an international scale, Schuman believed that the institutions of the Great Powers served an analogous function to those of capitalism. They were, he wrote, "formidable obstacles [to] a true world community." Without the "social and psychological bases of cooperation and coordination," world organization was likely to flounder. Schuman remained skeptical as to whether or not "consciously directed effort" could manufacture such bases of cooperation and coordination, but he warned that "the crisis of the world society is rapidly reaching high tide and that solutions must be devised soon, or they will be useless."[92]

As Franklin Roosevelt and the New Dealers reinterpreted and reinvented New Era policies, Fred Schuman, Denna Fleming, and Quincy Wright were devoted to developing a system that would rely on a common police force to maintain the peace. In addition, they sought a greatly empowered international organization to settle an increasingly unsettled world. But in the absence of such an international police force or strong international organization, they advocated a strong executive who could use American power without the fetters of Congressional interference. They were as much realists as any other analysts of the planning and implementation of American foreign policy.

NOTES

1. Joan Hoff Wilson, *American Business and Foreign Policy, 1920-1933* (Boston, MA: Beacon Press, 1973), x.

2. George F. Kennan, *American Diplomacy* (Chicago, IL: University of Chicago Press, 1984), 92.

3. *Ibid.,* 93.

4. Hans Morgenthau, *In Defense of the National Interest: A Critical Examination of American Foreign Policy* (New York: A.A. Knopf, 1951), 29.

5. *Ibid.,* 24; 46.

6. Denna Fleming, *The United States and World Organization, 1920-1933* (New York: Columbia University Press, 1938), 35.

7. *Ibid.,* 37-41.

8. Navy Department to Quincy Wright, 27 August 1921, Box 3, addenda 2, folder 12, The Quincy Wright Collection, University of Chicago. Wright's pay was $13.33 *per diem,* $1200 for three months, Navy to Wright, 31 August 1921, Box 3, addenda 2, folder 12.

9. Quincy Wright, "The Washington Conference," *American Political Science Review* 16 (May 1922): 290-297.

10. Hans Morgenthau, *Politics Among Nations: The Struggle for Power and Peace,* second edition (New York: A.A. Knopf, 1954), 169.

11. Philip C. Jessup, *Elihu Root,* 2 volumes (New York, 1938), volume 2, 392-393, as cited in Arthur Link, *Wilson the Diplomatist* (Chicago, IL: Quadrangle Books, 1957), 136.

12. Kennan, *American Diplomacy,* 98.

13. *Ibid.*

14. Morgenthau, *In Defense of the National Interest,* 223.

15. *Ibid.,* 23. The Wilson quote comes from his 27 October 1913 speech at Mobile, Alabama.

16. Morgenthau, *In Defense of the National Interest,* 25-26; Kennan, *American Diplomacy,* 5.

17. Quincy Wright, "Sovereignty of the Mandates," *American Journal of International Law* 17 (1923): 691-703; see also Wright to Pitt, 30 May 1921, Box 2, addenda 2, folder 8, where Wright uses racist language and stereotypes; Quincy Wright, *Mandates Under The League Of Nations* (Chicago, IL: University of Chicago Press, 1930), 5, fn 3a. Wright uses "race" in reference to ethnic groups, i.e., Switzerland has "three races," "The Palestinian Problem" *Political Science Quarterly* 41 (1926): 412. Wright went to great lengths to justify his use of "backward" in characterizing certain peoples, though: see *Mandates Under The League of Nations,* 582-584.

18. Wright correspondence, 29 May 1925, Box 6, addenda 2, folder 5.

19. Wright defined "three important types of backward areas--the Moslem, the Negro, and the Oceanic," each of which is noticeably non-Anglo. Wright, *Mandates Under The League of Nations,* 586.

20. Quincy Wright, "The Government of Iraq," *American Political Science Review* 20 (1926): 747-751.

21. *Ibid.,* 768-769.

22. Kennan, *American Diplomacy,* 16-17.

23. *Ibid.,* 13.

24. Morgenthau, *In Defense of the National Interest,* 8.

25. *Ibid.,* 45.

26. Quincy Wright, "The Project of the American Institute of International Law on Maritime Neutrality," *American Journal of International Law* 21 (1927): 127-136.

27. Quincy Wright, "The Future of Neutrality," *International Conciliation* 242 (September 1928): 17.

28. *Ibid.,* 13.

29. *Ibid.,* 17; 23.

30. *Ibid.,* 25.

31. Quincy Wright, "The Lend-Lease Bill and International Law," *American Journal of International Law* 35 (April 1941): 313.

32. Quincy Wright, "The Interpretation of Multilateral Treaties," *American Journal of International Law* 23 (1929): 101-103.

33. *Ibid.* Wright also noted problems of "authorial intent," especially in reference to notes.

34. Among those who placed great hope in the Paris Pact was Quincy Wright.

35. Denna Fleming, *The Treaty Veto of the American Senate* (New York: NY: G.P. Putnam's Sons), 268.

36. Kennan, *American Diplomacy,* 94.

37. Morgenthau, *Politics Among Nations,* 259-60.

38. Quincy Wright, "Meaning of the Pact of Paris," *American Journal of International Law* 27 (1933): 50.

39. Quincy Wright, "The Outlawry of War," *American Journal of International Law* 29 (January 1925): 96.

40. *Ibid.,* 61.

41. Quincy Wright and James Russell, "National Attitudes on the Far Eastern Controversy," *American Political Science Review* 27 (1933): 555-576.

42. *Ibid.,* 557.

43. *Ibid.,* 560.

44. Quincy Wright, *The Causes of War and Conditions of Peace* (London: Longmans, Green & Co, 1935), 112.

45. Morgenthau, *In Defense of the National Interest,* 223.

46. *Ibid.*

47. *Ibid.,* 224.

48. See Fleming's articles of the thirties, entitled "The Role of the Senate In Treaty-Making: A Survey Of Four Decades," *American Political Science Review* 28 (August 1934); "The Advice of the Senate in Treaty-Making," *Current History* 32 (April-September 1930); a response to the neutrality argument in "Neutrality Controversy," *Congressional Digest* 15 (January 1936); "America's Stake in the Far East," *The China Weekly Review* 88 (20 May 1939), and those of the early forties including "War Without Shooting," 1 *Current History* (September 1941); "Roosevelt and Churchill Confer," *Current History* 1 (October 1941); "The Coming World Order, Closed Or Free," *The Journal of Politics* 4 (1942); "Planning For The Post War World," 4 *Current History* (March 1943); "America and the World Crisis," *Vital Speeches* 10 (15 October 1943); and "Is Isolation Dead?" *Vital Speeches* 11 (1 December 1944), for his continued critique of neutrality and isolationism. He was also interested in the child labor laws and supported federal authority to address that problem. Fleming to J. Pardue, (editor of *The Evening Tennessean*) 25 February 1937, The Denna Fleming Collection, Vanderbilt University.

49. Fleming document entitled "Data Concerning D. F. Fleming," undated (but prepared sometime post 1966), Fleming Collection; Fleming, *The United States and World Organization,* viii; notes from Doris Fleming to the author, 6.

50. Fleming, *The United States and World Organization,* viii.

51. See for example Arthur Schlesinger, Sr.'s interpretations, or John D. Hick's *Republican Ascendancy, 1921-1933* (New York: Harper and Row, 1960).

52. Fleming, *The United States and World Organization,* viii.

53. *Ibid.,* 34.

54. *Ibid.,* 529.

55. *New York Times,* 23 October 1937, as found in Fleming, *The United States and World Organization,* 546.

56. *Ibid.*

57. Fleming to Franklin D. Roosevelt, 1 February 1935.

58. Frederick L. Schuman, *International Politics: An Introduction to the Western State System* (New York: McGraw-Hill, 1933).

59. Edward A. Purcell, Jr., *The Crisis of Democratic Theory: Scientific Naturalism and the Problem of Value* (Louisville, KY: University of Kentucky Press, 1973), 3; 17. Purcell cites a survey from Albert Somit and Joseph Tanenhaus (New York, 1964), 66, that asked political scientists who had had "the greatest impact on the profession before 1945, [and] the top three places went to Charles E. Merriam, Harold D. Lasswell, and Leonard White--all at [the University of] Chicago." Purcell, 17.

60. Schuman wrote that "A successful and far-sighted foreign policy is impossible for the United States so long as the persistence of isolationism and provincialism paralyzes . . . the president and the State Department." "American Foreign Policy," *American Journal of Sociology* 37 (May 1932): 887; as for U.S. recognition policy, see the above article, 84, and with specific reference to the Soviet Union, see Schuman "Benighted Diplomacy," *The Nation* 134 (18 May 1932): 563-564, in which Schuman wrote that the "Hoover Administration, in Russian matters as in others, is more Bourbon than the Bourbons."

61. Milton Cantor, *The Divided Left: American Radicalism, 1900-1975* (New York: Hill and Wang, 1978), 73.

62. William Appleman Williams, *American Russian Relations, 1781-1947* (New York: Rinehart, 1971). Schuman requested an introduction for his book from Senator William Borah, who supported normalized relations with the Soviet Union. Borah declined because of time constraints. The Frederick L. Schuman Collection, American Heritage Center, University of Wyoming, Laramie, Wyoming, Number 7824, Box 12, William E. Borah to Schuman, 21 March 1928.

63. Schuman to Quincy Wright, 21 August 1928, Wright Collection, Box 23, addenda 1.

64. Schuman to Scott Nearing, 8 February 1972, 1.

65. Schuman, "American Foreign Policy," 888.

66. Kennan, *American Diplomacy,* 46.

67. Morgenthau, *In Defense of the National Interest,* 3.

68. Wright, *The Causes of War and the Conditions of Peace.*

69. Frederick L. Schuman, *War and Diplomacy in the French Republic* (New York: AMS, 1931).

70. Frederick L. Schuman, *International Politics: An Introduction to the Western State System* (New York: McGraw-Hill, 1933).

71. *Ibid.,* 254-257.

72. Frederick L. Schuman, *The Nazi Dictatorship: A Study in Social Pathology and the Politics of Fascism* (New York: A.A. Knopf, 1934,1935).

73. Schuman's book raised the ire of the "Association of German Veterans of the World War" whose members protested it to the University of Chicago Board of Trustees, 14 December 1935, Box 12, The Frederick L. Schuman Collection, University of Wyoming.

74. *Ibid.*

75. Frederick L. Schuman, "Nazi Dreams of World Power," *Current History* 39 (February 1934): 537. Schuman displayed an uncanny appreciation of the consequences, current and future, of the Nazi seizure of power in "Germany Prepares Fear," *The Nation* 77 (7 February 1934): 353-355, "The Political Theory of German Fascism," *American Political Science Review* 28 (April 1934): 210-232, and "The Third Reich's Road to

War," *Annals of the American Academy of Political and Social Science* 175 (September 1934): 33-43.

76. Schuman to Wright, 29 October 1933, Wright Collection, Box 2, addenda 1.
77. Kennan, *American Diplomacy,* 53.
78. *Ibid.,* 80-81.
79. *Ibid.,* 81.
80. Schuman, "American Foreign Policy," 888.
81. Schuman, *International Politics,* 802, 821.
82. *Ibid.,* 842.
83. *Ibid.,* 845.
84. *Ibid.,* 717.
85. *Ibid.,* 720-721.
86. *Ibid.,* 853.
87. *Ibid.,* 849.
88. *Ibid.,* 847.
89. *Ibid.*
90. *Ibid.,* 847-848.
91. *Ibid.,* 848.
92. *Ibid.*

3

Wilsonians, Neutrality, and the Fascist Threat

The end of the New Era brought trying times both for the League of Nations and for Wilsonians. The Japanese invasion of Manchuria severely tested the world organization's ability to enforce collective security or to implement meaningful sanctions. Earlier problems between Italy and Albania and China and the Soviet Union underscored the League's need for military might in the face of attacks against the peace. By 1933, both Japan and Germany had left the League.

What was equally disturbing to Wright, Fleming, and Schuman was the unwillingness of the United States to accept the mantle and responsibility of power. Neutrality, a policy foisted on the United States by conservatives who claimed to better understand the realities of national interest than did the Wilsonian internationalists, threatened to allow the fascist states to expand at the expense of democracy and a liberal world order. Each time Congress passed a Neutrality Act in the 1930s—in 1935, 1936, 1937, and 1939—nations with leaders opposed to peace took advantage of the opportunities these inflexible policies offered them.

Wright was convinced that technology continued to shrink the world to such an extent that the theoretical basis for neutrality was no longer plausible.[1] This was a theme common to these three internationalists. He also observed that neutral behavior served frequently to perpetuate aggression, or even reward it; at other times it seemed to serve no purpose at all.[2] With the consequences of World War I lingering in his mind, Wright turned to the works of Hugo Grotius (who abhorred neutrality) and Thomas Aquinas (who had refined Augustine's concept of "just war") in an effort to demonstrate the futility of neutrality.

In 1935, as fascist forces began their plunder of Ethiopia, Wright wrote a Public Policy Pamphlet entitled *The United States and Neutrality,* in which he emphasized that both the Paris Peace Pact and the Budapest Articles of Interpretation were means of war prevention, not the avoidance of war, a paradox if ever there was one. He criticized the traditional concept of neutrality and provided a four-point policy that he believed would help maintain international stability at all times, not just in times of crisis.[3] The pamphlet was part of a series produced under the editorship of Harry Gideonse designed to bridge the chasm between the concentration of scholarly journals on issues that the public deemed peripheral and the superficial commentary of popular magazines.[4]

Wright's critics, including George Sokolsky, noted specialist on the Far East, were less optimistic about the Paris Peace Pact. In an earlier letter to Wright, Sokolsky criticized Wright's interpretation of the Pact, saying that Wright wanted peace "only if it is legal" and that Wright would "condemn the whole human race to constant warfare" so long as the law was upheld.[5]

This seemed in part a valid criticism, especially when Wright had written earlier, in "When Does War Exist?," that a legal definition was necessary to prove violation of Article XII of the Covenant and necessary for the sanctions that Article XVI imposed and to prove violation of Article I of the Paris Peace Pact.[6] It appeared that Wright believed war could be legislated away without any coercive power to bind the objects of such legislation.

But Wright had also written in the same article that "Article II of the Pact may be violated even though legal war does not exist."[7] As a man who believed that law was the essential ingredient to world order, Wright maintained the importance of the Pact as a precedent for sanctions against future aggressive acts. Wright suffered no illusion that the Pact would eliminate war, but it would allow for the prosecution of, or application of sanctions against, the aggressor in future situations. This conviction led him to claim that Japanese violations of their obligations under the Paris Peace Pact, the Nine Power Treaty, and the Hague Convention of 1907, provided the president justification to impose "negative reprisals" such as discriminatory measures against Japanese goods.[8]

He invoked the Pact as well to justify Franklin Roosevelt's Executive Agreement in 1940 to supply Great Britain with destroyers in exchange for bases. He noted that most of the international community recognized that Germany had "initiated hostilities in violation of its international obligations under the Pact of Paris and other instruments." Because Germany was an initiator of aggressive war, it was not a lawful belligerent, and parties to international agreements with Germany were no longer obligated under international law to observe neutral obligations toward Germany and her allies as they had broken the dictum *pacta sunt servanda.*[9]

Again, reference to the Pact may seem unnecessary when considering action against Japan and Germany, but in a world organized around law it was essential. The need to establish the law as definitive may explain why Wright insisted that what existed in Europe after September 1939 was not legally a state of war under the Pact of Paris. He insisted that "violence by certain governments in violation of international obligations was being opposed by other governments acting in defense, or acting to give assistance to those defending themselves, or acting as a police force . . . as a universal *posse comitatus.*"[10] Perhaps only lawyer could arrive at such a distinction. Certainly, such semantics fed the Kennan-Morgenthau criticism that some Americans were overly legalistic in their approach to foreign policy.

Neither Kennan nor Morgenthau directly addressed the issue of neutrality, but their opposition to it as a static policy can be inferred from their comments on U.S. policy during the years 1914-1917 and 1933-1941. Of the pre-World War I era, Kennan wrote that it "seems hard to understand" why the United States clung so tenaciously to neutral rights. "New modalities of warfare," he insisted, had rendered most neutral rights obsolete.[11] As for the pre-World War II period, Kennan blamed the desperate character of the Allied position in late 1941 on earlier "mistakes" that had created both military weakness and the need to ally with the totalitarian Soviet state.[12] Morgenthau, who believed "the question central to the national interest of the United States [was] the balance of power in Europe and Asia" argued that the isolationism of the periods before both world wars, of which neutrality was a key component, obviously failed to meet the national interest.[13]

Wright's assessment of appeasement, including the agreements reached at the Munich Conference of 1938, was another area of agreement between him and the "realists." Writing in the *American Journal of International Law* in 1939, Wright examined the strategy of appeasement as a means of peaceful change. He cited precedents for Munich-type agreements and declared that even Wilson held the peace of the world "superior in importance to every question of political jurisdictional boundary."[14] Yet because extra-legal threats of war forced the issues at Godesburg the Munich agreements, Wright wrote, were not likely to yield justice. Munich was not an example of effective peaceful change to him because it was a *diktat*, a view he now held of the Versailles Treaty.[15] So although Wright did not accept the procedural aspect of this appeasement, he held little against it in principle.

This was consistent with Hans Morgenthau's approach to diplomacy. He wrote that the term appeasement "has exercised a nefarious influence upon the policies of the West by being used to discredit all attempts at establishing peace through negotiations."[16] Citing Churchill's dictum that "Appeasement from strength is magnanimous and noble and might be the surest and perhaps the only path to world peace," Morgenthau declared that a negotiated settlement was "the sole rational alternative to war."[17]

Kennan was somewhat ambiguous about Munich and appeasement. He blamed the rise of Hitler not on the West, but on the "weakness of German society which made possible his triumph."[18] But when writing about the collapse of Japanese-American relations, Kennan declared that in his opinion, "a policy carefully and realistically aimed at the avoidance of a war with Japan and less encumbered with other motives would certainly have produced . . . different results."[19] Given that Neville Chamberlain, Eduoard Daladier, and even Mussolini were trying to accomplish just that at Munich—avoidance of a war—it is safe to conclude that Kennan, too, harbored no ill-will toward the concept of appeasement.

The so-called "isolationists" in the United States claimed that continued refinement of neutrality legislation would best serve U.S. security interests. For Fred Schuman, though, events in Europe during the 1930s required a more complex response. He wrote in the preface to the second edition of *The Nazi Dicta-*

torship that Hitler had won the first engagements of the next war "without firing a shot."[20] The Fuhrer ended not only the mirage of French hegemony, but crushed the French defensive bloc. As well, Schuman believed that the League system of collective security had "probably been dealt a fatal blow" when the British cabinet refused to honor Britain's Locarno Pact obligations and apply sanctions against Germany.

To Schuman, fascist imperialism was the only beneficiary of isolationism and neutrality. What was needed to reverse that trend was a renewed sense of Wilsonian universalism, but that was a dead issue with the U.S. public. "The forces of liberalism and peace," wrote Schuman, "have again abdicated before the Nazi menace."[21] Schuman called for the use of force. He believed that German revisionism was the greatest immediate threat to world security and that all the powers, great and less great, should oppose it. Hitler's mission, according to Schuman, was to achieve equality with the victors of World War I, and that in order to realize that goal the Germans must recover all their lost provinces, unite all German speaking peoples, restore their overseas colonies, and gain adequate *lebensraum*. And, Schuman wrote, Hitler knew and depended on the fact that these goals could not be achieved through peaceful means.[22] Collective security was the only hope for the West and the Soviets to prevent Hitler from fulfilling his goals.

There were many reasons why a prophet of war drew little positive response from the public or U.S. policy makers in 1935. Less than twenty years before, the United States had entered a European conflict, the "war to end all wars," the war to "make the world safe for democracy." Yet when that war was concluded the United States repudiated the world order that its president and other peace-makers envisioned. A growing number of policy makers and average citizens alike rejected the commitments necessary to Wilsonian internationalism.

As well, public doubt about the reasons for U.S. entry in World War I had grown exponentially since 1917. By 1935 many people found the 1934 Nye Committee report on the arms industry's role in bringing the United States into the "Great War" deeply disturbing. A growing body of voters also listened to the anti-internationalist rhetoric that came from Father Charles Coughlin, William Randolph Hearst, and even Will Rogers.[23] And, of course, a national hero, Charles Lindbergh, praised Hitler's new order unconditionally and called on the public to support it. In a speech given on 13 October 1939, "Lindy" declared that "It is the European race we must preserve; political progress will follow. Racial strength is vital; politics is a luxury. If the white race is ever seriously threatened, it may be time for us to take our part in its protection, to fight side by side with the English, French, and Germans, but not with one against the other for our mutual destruction."[24]

There was, too, the Senate defeat in 1935 of U.S. entry into the World Court, which reiterated that Wilsonian internationalism of any sort was still anathema to that elite body. There were so many opponents to international commitment that it appeared on the surface that there existed a consensus behind an isolationist foreign policy. To characterize the foreign policy of the thirties as isolationist, though, is to deny the reality of policy, both domestic and foreign, but isolationism did influence the public.

Warnings from Schuman went unheeded. Immediate reaction to his predictions notwithstanding, they did create interest in him as an international political and foreign affairs analyst, especially for German affairs. Besides the book *The Nazi Dictatorship*, Schuman had written several articles during the thirties on the Nazi threat, including "Nazi Dreams of World Power" in *Current History*, "Germany Prepares Fear" in *the New Republic*, "The Political Theory of German Fascism" in the *American Political Science Review*, and "The Third Reich's Road to War" and "The Conduct of German Foreign Affairs" in the *Annals of the American Academy of Political and Social Science*.[25]

Denna Fleming considered the need for U.S. cooperation in the new international organization so important that he could not afford to confine his message to books and articles addressed to a scholarly audience. He had seen how effective the obstructionists' methods had been in "organizing the opinion of mankind," and he was convinced that "a large number of people" throughout the country were interested in his views.[26] He began new projects in the 1930s designed to broaden his audience and to aid his effort to organize public opinion.

Edith Osburn of the League of Nations Association asked him to write columns for a commercial syndicate.[27] Fleming replied that he was very interested and had been seeking a wider audience for some time. He had written a total of two hundred, twice-weekly front page columns for the *Nashville Tennessean* during the last year-and-a-half, and public interest in them had continued to grow.[28] Although this particular opportunity for syndication did not materialize, he wrote another fifty articles for the local paper before he would be embroiled in what he called the "conservative-liberal tussle" going on inside the *Nashville Tennessean* that led to his resignation in 1937.[29]

Soon after he left the paper, Fleming began a ten year association with radio station WSM in Nashville, during which time he broadcast 750 programs that were heard in 30 states and Canada.[30] He valued radio's ability to reach wide audiences and was concerned that the public receive opinions that countered those of "the new radio kings," an obvious reference to Father Coughlin and to Huey Long's successors.[31] Fleming provided his audience a range of fare, including pleas to accept the exchange of destroyers for naval bases, a dramatization of the takeover of Czechoslovakia, and a discussion of the charge that the motion picture industry pandered to warmongers.

His beliefs in liberal democracy, in Wilsonian world organization, and in the need for the United States to use its power to the benefit of peace infused his broadcasts. Fleming repeatedly reminded his audience that the nation's leaders had made the gravest mistake in modern history when they rejected U.S. membership in the League of Nations. He referred to Woodrow Wilson as the first world statesman that the United States had produced, and lamented the fact that the people had betrayed Wilson's vision, a betrayal whose cost Fleming believed the United States continued to pay.[32] Fleming also made clear that it was his desire to support the democracies as the first outposts of the nation's interest. Even George Kennan asserted that "the cause of the British and the French could really be called the cause of freedom and democracy" during the period before the German attack on the Soviet Union.[33]

It was not unusual for internationalists to be the focus of radical criticism during the 1930s. Schuman developed a certain mystique during the decade that appealed to a large political minority and he capably exploited this popularity. Maybe because of this he was in demand on the lecture circuit, where he commanded a substantial fee. Regardless of the reason, he had a constant forum from which to popularize his ideas.[34]

His mystique resulted from his identification with leftist causes and his acceptance of the "party line" explanation of the "Great Purge Trials" in the Soviet Union that the guilty had been found guilty through due process and that the accused had, almost to a person, admitted their guilt. This position opened him to accusations that he was a Stalinist, and he dealt poorly with his critics. Regardless of his protests to the contrary, he was, according to contemporaries and later analysts, at the very least a fellow traveler.[35]

Schuman confronted reactionary and ultrapatriot charges in the Illinois Senate as a result of the "Dilling Accusations" in 1934. Mrs. Albert W. Dilling, the author of The Red Network, was a rabid anticommunist and Schuman's experience with her charges offers certain insights into his later conduct toward people he believed were oblivious to the reactionary dangers in the United States.[36] In her book, Mrs. Dilling placed Schuman, Eleanor Roosevelt, Newton Baker, Harold Ickes, Rexford Tugwell, Louis Brandeis, William C. Bullitt, William Borah, Gerald Nye, Burton Wheeler, Quincy Wright, and many, many others, on a list that purported to include "the most dangerous radicals and revolutionaries in the United States."[37] The list, though, was incomplete, for Mrs. Dilling should have included herself among the "dangerous radicals" in the United States.

On 17 July 1922, Mrs. Dilling and her mother, Mrs. Elizabeth Kirkpatrick, conducted an armed raid on the home of Mrs. J. D. Clark, who, according to Mrs. Dilling, was competing for Mr. Dilling's affection. Brandishing guns and smashing windows, the two women burst into the Clark home and confronted Mrs. Clark with her alleged improprieties: Mrs. Clark called the police. When Chicago's finest arrived they arrested the "Dilling Gang" on charges of concealed weapons and disorderly conduct.

But Mrs. Dilling's apparent zeal did not stop at private vendettas—she pursued her political opponents with equal fervor. Schuman noted that when he was scheduled to deliver a lecture in Kenilworth, Illinois on 26 March 1935, Mrs. Dilling canvassed the homes of prominent Kenilworth citizens. Upon being received into their homes, she distributed copies of a pamphlet linked to Schuman entitled "Culture and Crisis," denounced Schuman as a Communist, and demanded that he be refused permission to lecture in the city. On this occasion her goal eluded her.[38]

In an effort to combat her tactics, Quincy Wright suggested that perhaps Schuman should collect information about Mrs. Dilling that would discredit her in the public mind. But he also warned him that "an effort to organize a general campaign on this question might do more harm than good [as] it is usually undesirable to enter into competition with a skunk with a skunk's weapons."[39]

The Dilling accusations and Schuman's other political activities came to the attention of the University of Chicago's administration. Schuman alleged that on 14 November 1934 the Hearst owned *Chicago Herald-Examiner* had misquoted him, and when Schuman pursued a correction, the paper's executives launched a vicious attack on him. By 16 March 1935 Hearst and his paper called for Schuman's dismissal, alleging that Schuman had mounted "a direct challenge to American institutions in the name of communism."[40] Schuman in turn charged that Hearst employed tactics that Göring, Goebbels, Rosenberg, and Hitler would admire.[41] It was not unusual for Hearst to attack academics, and some members of the university community may have deemed this a rite of passage, even a mark of having been in the thick of battle. On the surface it appears that this was the case with the university administration.

But it also seems that the pamphlet "Crisis and Culture," which Mrs. Dilling claimed implicated Schuman in subversive activities, may have caused a minor sensation in the president's office. Schuman felt compelled to explain in detail his association with the pamphlet. He wrote to Robert M. Hutchins, the president of the university, that he had "foolishly" given permission for the publishers of the pamphlet to use his name as an endorsement without having first read the pamphlet. He claimed that only after its publication did he become aware that it was done so under the lead of "League of Professionals for Foster and Ford," and that there were fifty-one other names included, none of whom, he claimed, were avowed Communists or Communist party members. How he knew the latter to be true is curious indeed.[42]

Schuman claimed that he had never belonged to the Communist or Socialist parties, "nor to any organizations even remotely affiliated with them."[43] He also explained that professional interest in "political attitudes and behavior among Chicago negroes" motivated his attendance at the dinner banquet for James Ford, an African American and candidate for the vice-presidency in 1932. In his memorandum to the investigating committee, Schuman revealed that he had voted for Roosevelt and Garner, an obvious effort to acquit himself of the reckless accusations of an individual whose emotional stability was questionable.[44]

Mrs. Dilling's ardor would be redeemed in the near future. Unfortunately for Schuman, the accusations, coupled with his previously suspect activities, took on an independent life and became the basis for further burdens, including U.S. House Un-American Activities Committee investigations in 1943 and still more accusations during the McCarthy years.

Given the political environment and the continuing "Red Scare" in the United States, Schuman's problems, even if the evidence for his involvement was little more than fanciful or circumstantial, were nevertheless substantial.[45] After all, his dissertation, *American Policy Toward Russia Since 1917*, challenged U.S. policy toward Russia and defended Marxist-Leninist revolutionary goals and methods.[46] And he had culled from it articles that provided the evidence his critics used to portray him as a "Communist sympathizer."

Schuman believed in the "Popular Front" as a defense against pan-fascism, a belief that served as further proof to some that his "travelling" companions were suspect. By 1935, the year after the Soviet Union joined it, he had come to believe that the League of Nations was "a grand alliance of liberalism and communism for mutual defense against fascism." Sanctions were an effective reality, all because of the unity that the common enemy of fascism provided the disparate nations represented at Geneva. He believed that if the League stopped Mussolini, fascism would be dealt a "stunning" blow.[47] This was, of course, not far removed from the official party line in Moscow.

The young professor invested much faith in the "Popular Front," and when the United States failed to participate in it, he feared fascist victory.[48] Having observed the failure of League sanctions to hamper Mussolini's attack on Abyssinia, Hitler's juggernaut of diplomatic victories, and Japan's domination of China and the Far East, Schuman may have lost his professional objectivity. After all, he saw the struggle as a final one, with the victor to determine the future. For him, it was not the time to act with decorous attention to logic, but to join in common cause. Liberalism and communism, he maintained, were reconcilable.[49]

In an article published in the *Southern Review* in 1936 entitled "Liberalism and Communism Reconsidered," Schuman declared the two ideologies fundamentally compatible. "Democracy," he observed, "as a mass faith . . . is not at all ideologically incompatible with communism." Marxism, after all, was a product of liberalism, and both systems trusted "in Reason and the Common Man."[50] He argued that the Bolsheviks were forced "reluctantly" to adopt "nondemocratic forms of political power in order to remove economic and social inequalities and injustices" and that the leaders "hoped" one day to restore political democracy. Both liberals and communists were "dedicated to freedom, to tolerance, to the pragmatic discovery of truth through experimentation and free discussion in the market place . . . and . . . to the application of reason to human affairs." [51] Noticeably absent, though, was any direct evidence for this opinion.[52]

Schuman reached several uncritical conclusions regarding the Soviet State.[53] The arguments with those conclusions are obvious, but his conclusions regarding the differences between the two ideologies require further analysis. Schuman wrote that liberals were inclined to believe that reason, if properly applied, could solve all human problems while the communists had realized that "emotions, mysticism, and mythology" were as important as reason and economic self-interest in motivating human masses. They, like fascists, recognized that "non-logical symbols of warmly felt collective experience" could be used to manipulate humans to a desired action.[54] The Communists had proven that "consciously directed effort" could manufacture "the social and psychological bases of cooperation and coordination."[55] Schuman saw value in the Soviet success at manipulating public opinion.

"No great mass movement," he wrote, "no profound revolution, no transvaluation of values is possible without the psychological equivalents of religious supernaturalism."[56] And liberalism, he declared, had lost its vital myths. Schuman realized that where old shibboleths were lacking, the public must be induced to value new ones; that those people in control must be willing to wield unrestricted power to reshape society. He had as evidence to buttress this belief the success of *gleichschaltung* in Germany and the First Five Year Plan in the Soviet Union. They demonstrated that determined governing elites, through planning and "organized social intelligence," could manipulate public myths with state power.

World War II led Schuman to advocate the use of power in unencumbered terms. In a letter to the editor of *The Nation,* he considered a "new" form for future government: "Caesarism." Schuman defined it as "a world order in a world imperium in which government will cease to govern nation-states and local land plots and begin to govern the world as an economic and social unity." He was careful to explain that he did not attribute to this new form of government the despotism usually associated with the term "Caesarism." Instead, Schuman constructed the term to mean "the supremacy of politics" over anything else. In this new social structure would be leaders who were willing to lead, governments that truly governed, and a society that believed in and supported mass values. A new social militancy—"'totalitarian' in scope and efficacy if not in purpose"—must consume the public.[57]

Schuman had learned these lessons from the fascists and Bolsheviks. "All these forms of power," he wrote, "and tools of action are common to fascism and to any effective socialism. . . . These are the prerequisites of survival in the twentieth century. . . . If the ends of democracy are to be served, democrats must learn at once to do what must be done."[58] He believed that any new political organization would have to be focused on "a new economy ruled by a self-conscious, respected, and purposeful political élite wielding authority in areas far wider than the nations or even the 'great powers' of today."[59]

This was a strong remedy, one that might kill the patient, yet it was Schuman's prescription. How he believed such a prescription would serve the "ends of democracy" is difficult to ascertain. It is certain, though, that passages like the one above served to demonstrate the charges of his critics that he valued power above all else.

His idea that a world government could take form was not something that Hans Morgenthau found idealistic. Morgenthau observed thirteen years later, in 1954, that for the first time in history, "conquest of the world" was possible. The confluence of modern technological developments in transportation, communication, and warfare under the control of one superpower not only made world conquest possible, it made it possible for the conqueror to "keep it conquered."[60]

Quincy Wright grappled with the same issues in his book *The Causes of War and Conditions of Peace,* a compilation of lectures delivered at the Graduate Institute of Higher International Studies at Geneva, Switzerland, in October and November of 1934. *The Causes of War* represented an innovation for Wright. He changed his approach to the examination of the issue of war and its control from "why war" to "how is peace organized?" "War," he wrote, "can less and less be treated from the historical, deterministic and predictive point of view. More and more we must consider it from the engineering, constructive and control point of view. We can less profitably be interested in the *causes of war,* more profitably in the *conditions of peace.*"[61]

Social control was the key element of Wright's prescription. He sought to identify "elements of the total situation during peace which we can effectively manipulate and which, if properly manipulated, will preserve the peace."[62] He believed that to cultivate the conditions of peace, everyone must renounce "*intransigent* opposition to existing [conditions]" by which he meant "the renunciation of opposition to these [conditions] . . . not subject to restraint in the adaptation of means to ends."

In anticipation that not everyone would renounce intransigence, Wright called for "an organization of the world community adequate to restrain conflicts . . . so that violence will not accompany them." The basis for such a world organization to intervene in conflicts would be "the realization in international relations of a system of law intolerant of violence except as a legally controlled instrument of execution." In addition, he recognized the need for "continuous application of peaceful techniques for preventing extreme departures from equilibrium among the material forces in the state system."[63]

More simply put, he wanted to prevent abrupt alterations of the balance of power. Wright demanded only the "most gradual changes in the relative position of states with respect to armaments, status, influence and policy" because only the gradual change of social conditions could ensure peace.[64] Yet, there is something very Orwellian that pervades his concept, especially when he began to advocate not just control of conflict, but controlled conflict.[65]

Wright believed that qualitative, quantitative, and moral disarmament were the most promising ingredients for maintaining equilibrium among the states.[66] That equilibrium, he wrote, was the prerequisite to the development of effective international law and an empowered League of Nations.[67] Wright also seemed to foreshadow future U.S. nuclear deterrent policy in his remarks that concerned the impact of mutually assured destruction on the possibility of peace.[68]

Wright offered a possible solution to the criticism that balance of power politics perpetuated the *status quo* and inevitably invited war: that through more "accurate measures of the changing situation [in] armament and industrial statistics, it is possible that disturbances could be observed before they had become serious. A council mainly of the great powers might with such data bring pressure by debate to rectify the balance."[69] This faith, of course, was a direct result of his research with Richard Russell. Wright realized as well that the collection of accurate data required peacetime international inspections and verification.[70]

Wright also addressed in *The Causes of War* some of the criticisms leveled against the theories of world organization. Foremost, he came to advocate a loose confederation rather than a strong federal union of nations. Several reasons compelled him to abandon the U.S. federal model. He believed that the U.S. government had become too centralized and was now more than likely a unitary state rather than a federation.[71] His world organization would be loosely modeled after the confederations of the past and dependent on regional organizations within the greater body. This would, of course, be the model the United

Nations chose with the adoption of Article 52 and the concept of regional security organizations.

Wright moved as well toward a stricter interpretation of the constitution of a world organization, for he believed that the purview of central government would have to be reduced and that guarantees of the autonomy of the members would have to be stipulated.[72] But he noted that none of his prescriptions would be completely effective unless the world organization was truly universal in its membership. And for that he was willing to pay a price.

Wright cited League failures during the Manchurian Crisis in 1933 and during the Chaco War between Bolivia and Paraguay in 1938 as proof that a world organization could not deal effectively with major crises unless all the powers, great and small, were members. This was especially true of those nations who were immediate neighbors of litigants or belligerents. Wright believed that the League must become universal, even at the expense of amendments to the Covenant that eliminated formal obligations respecting sanctions but that incorporated the Pact of Paris.[73]

There remained for Wright the problem of developing both state and individual loyalty to the League and its institutions. In this area, he shared Schuman's concern about the need to develop myths and common beliefs. Wright thought it wise for the League to assume the World War I debts of member nations and to develop the mandates as League territories, and he cited the U.S. annexation of the Northwest Territory in 1783 and assumption of state debts in 1791 as proof of the method's viability. He called, too, for the League to adopt symbols around which individual loyalty could be rallied through vigorous education and propaganda. To facilitate this, the League must become, in Wright's opinion, the forum for "real, dramatic and obvious" conflict in order to maintain the people's interest, for "people," he wrote, "are interested in conflict."[74]

If armed conflict or aggression occurred, a regional force should respond to the transgression. Wright believed it would be years, perhaps decades, before the League could field an armed force capable of policing the world; therefore, physical sanctions should be regional and Articles X and XVI of the Covenant should be amended to reflect such organizations. This, of course, would be a key element in the United Nations Charter. As well, Wright came to believe that to implement effective military operations, any world organization would have to exercise a monopoly over military air power.[75] This assumption would become a principal feature of future collective actions under UN auspices.

Wright, too, assessed the problem of applying sanctions to states. He observed that to punish an entire state for the actions of its government would likely bear the moral stigma of punishing the innocent as well as the guilty. This is a charge that critics continue to level against the application of sanctions. Application of sanctions might, too, resemble the act or acts of war. And, of course, there was the lack of sufficient coercive power to enforce League sanctions without universal membership.

For Wright, the solution was the universal application of moral sanctions. Sanctions could only work if all the powers were behind their immediate application. "If that moral solidarity exists," Wright insisted, "adequate methods can be devised [for the application of physical sanctions] even if not provided beforehand."[76] Wright was a gradualist, and he approached the concept of world organization from that perspective. Such organization was in an almost embryonic stage, so that to give such a world organization immediate and all-inclusive powers might be to doom it from inception.

It was at this juncture that the issue of sovereignty plagued Wright. In a system that allowed a court of appeal to negate state laws contrary to the laws of the international organization, states might perceive a "dangerous encroachment upon [their] existing sovereignty" that could be used to provide justification for secession.[77] Consequently, Wright set his sights to limit national sovereignty. Opponents of U.S. membership in the League used the issue of infringement of sovereign rights as a shibboleth to encourage nationalist-based fears among the public. Sovereignty was synonymous with national prestige, or so it was argued, and any limitation upon national sovereignty resulted in a concomitant loss of prestige.

As with any other confederation, certain powers would be left to the member states and certain powers to the central government. Although this solution, presented in a dispassionate way, may have been acceptable to many citizens, others feared that a world government might defy the wishes of the United States. That fear plagued the efforts of people like Wright. Some limitation of national sovereignty was essential to the establishment of machinery for peaceful change.

The League did not have adequate machinery to provide for peaceful change. The reason for that situation was the lack of a world legislative authority, an authority that would require far greater sacrifices of national sovereignty than an organization designed exclusively for the prevention of aggression. Peaceful change, said Wright, required effective legislation, especially if the changes contemplated were territorial boundaries or economic policies, two areas traditionally associated with the prerogative of sovereign nations.[78]

Policy matters such as these had always produced sharp exchanges between revisionist and status quo states, with status quo states having little reason to accept a voluntary system of change. In order to effect meaningful change during peacetime, there would have to be an international legislative authority powerful enough to compel status quo states to accept change under appropriate circumstances and to compel them to sacrifice certain advantages they thought they possessed under a traditional interpretation of national sovereignty.[79]

Fleming, too, continued to argue for a more effective international organization. After the passage of the First Neutrality Act in 1935, Fleming hoped that the sentiment for neutrality in the United States had peaked and that the United States would accept its responsibility to help maintain world order.[80] His hope unfulfilled, he renewed his efforts on behalf of collective security toward the end of the decade.

Fleming attacked neutrality both as a concept and as legislation. He was especially concerned that the Neutrality Acts would hinder members of the League of Nations in the event they were compelled to use force to restrain an aggressor. As well, he observed that the Neutrality Acts unnecessarily limited the ability of the president to respond forcefully and effectively to world problems.[81]

He now attacked what he referred to as "the new explanation" of historical revisionists for U.S. entry into World War I. The revisionist critique, which according to Fleming was "unduly at variance with the facts," had been used to buttress the neutrality legislation of the 1930s.

In his application to the Rockefeller Foundation for a research grant, he wrote that the debate over the question of U.S. neutrality had replaced the debate over U.S. entry into the League of Nations as the dominant controversy in foreign affairs. He noted that a "new, revised version" that purported to explain U.S. entrance into the "great war" now dominated U.S. foreign policy, but assured the Foundation that many people held the revisionist interpretation to be at odds with the facts. Because of this, he believed that a study was warranted to allow for greater understanding of the historical bases for the course of U.S. neutrality.[82] The Rockefeller Foundation rejected his request on grounds that his historical approach did not meet the criteria of those studies ordinarily included in their international relations program.

Fleming did receive a second Penfield Traveling Scholarship in 1938 and, although it interrupted his radio career, it enabled him to pursue his new project. Vanderbilt not only matched the funds from the University of Pennsylvania, but provided expenses as well.[83] His third book, *The United States and World Organization, 1920-1933,* had just been published, the result of his first Penfield, and he set out to conduct research for the next.

He spent the last months of 1938 in New York City and the first ones of 1939 in Great Britain, where he listened to news from Geneva of the League of Nations' continued decline. Caught in the heady atmosphere of pending European disaster, his project was delayed, to say the least: it was not until 1968 that Doubleday published his book *The Origins and Legacy of World War I.*[84]

Fleming returned to Nashville with a sense of urgency, as he believed that Britain and Western Europe constituted the first line of defense of the United States and for civilization.[85] This was not the opinion of an idealist who sought to accomplish with words what must be accomplished with force. Fleming's assessment of American interests in Europe demonstrates again the inability of labels like "idealist" to explain anything about the individuals to whom they are applied.

Until the United States entered the war, much of the substance for Fleming's addresses over WSM was devoted to condemnations of America Firsters, of Senators Robert LaFollette and Burton K. Wheeler, and especially of Charles Lindbergh. Fleming praised the policies of Churchill, Roosevelt, and the Atlantic Community. But his views were not completely Eurocentric: he was also aware of the stake the United States held in the Pacific. Fleming had condemned the actions of the Japanese in China since their seizure of Manchuria in 1931-1932, as did most Wilsonians, but by 1939 his tactic was to awaken in the public a sense of China's importance to the future of U.S. interests.

Fleming was not deluded about the immediate potential that a Chinese consumer market held for the United States, but he held visions of a gigantic future export market for U.S. goods in Asia. He wrote in an article for the *China Weekly Review* that "a vast demand for American goods has never developed [in China], and can never develop, until China is modernized under a stable, enlightened government."[86] He declared further that it was easy to conclude superficially that "our present trade with China, or with the Far East, is not worth a war." Still, Fleming warned, "the Pacific is the region of the future [and] the United States . . . is compelled to be a Pacific power."[87] Here was both an accurate prediction and an acute observation.

His views about China, though, were those of a nationalist, not an internationalist. He denied the existence of a *de facto* Japanese sphere of influence in the Far East, both military and economic. Statistics Fleming cited demonstrated clearly that U.S. investment in China was, at $242,000,000, only one-fifth of Japan's investment of $1,137,000,000 as of 1931. They revealed, too, that U.S. trade with Japan was far more important than with China, as the Japanese imported twice the value in U.S. goods that the Chinese did, and that 43 percent of all U.S. trade in the Far East in 1935 was with Japan.[88] It was possible to conclude that better relations with Japan should have been the focus of U.S. foreign policy, not the defense of China. He also failed to mention the equally brutal, if less effective, methods of government of the Nationalist Chinese and their gross corruption. If Fleming believed Chiang Kai-shek's regime capable of establishing a "stable, enlightened" Chinese government, then the professor's optimism belied the available evidence.

What Fleming wanted was to preserve the Open Door. He observed that it was "not for nothing" that the world's greatest nation had "invented" the means to span the globe in search of "the things we desire and require. Every continent and every clime needs the products of our industry, as we need theirs," so it was absolutely essential that Asia and the world remain freely accessible to American "inventiveness, initiative and ability."[89] Like Wilson, Fleming realized that American economic interests were universal.

Second, he wanted to defend China in order to have a stable neighbor to the West. The only way for that to happen, in his opinion, was for the United States to ensure that China won its "courageous fight for liberty," a strange liberty indeed, given the nature of the Nationalist regime.[90] What Fleming meant, though, was Chinese victory in the struggle for independence from Japan. In an effort to ensure Chinese victory, Fleming called for the United States to raise tariffs on Japanese goods 25 percent, even in disregard of the Geneva Accords against punitive tariffs that the United States had signed and had not abrogated. An aggressive policy toward Japan was not what the State Department or the U.S. Navy then favored. Although Fleming most likely took heart when an embargo policy was adopted in 1941, that policy put the Japanese military into preparations for direct confrontation with the United States and made war between the two powers a foregone conclusion.[91]

Quincy Wright continued to address the theme of the Open Door through his assessment of the League mandate system. In 1939, he wrote that the mandate system amplified the twentieth century trend against imperialism and that the mandate system complimented the current theory of international organization and self-determination. "Native rights," he concluded, "and the open door have been protected in the mandated territories."[92]

What is revealed as well are Wright's priorities for the mandates in his insistence upon maintenance of the Open Door. This doctrine was an integral part of his prescription not just for mandates, but for the entire world.[93] Although the only variety of mandate to be specifically subject to Open Door guarantees was the type B mandate, Wright insisted that it be extended to all mandates.[94]

In fact, mandatories like Great Britain, whose leaders wished to maintain privileged trade relations within the Commonwealth and later "sterling areas," pressured the League to apply the Open Door selectively rather than universally to all mandates. The only countries to push hard for universal adoption of the Open Door were Japan and the United States, and the impact their capital development had on "backward" areas was even by this time legendary among their inhabitants.[95] Despite the probable intentions of the British, theirs was the best policy.

Throughout this discourse, Wright devoted little attention to assessing the problems the Open Door caused in China and seemed oblivious to the detrimental impact that a strong capitalist society and its extension of trade might have on a more traditional society. This was especially true in mandated areas that had but one or two valuable resources. And although Wright was correct in his assessment that commercial discriminations in "backward areas often led to conflict in the past," so too did application of the Open Door.[96]

Too often traditional societies found their labor devoted entirely to the production of the resource with export value and as a consequence became dependent on other countries for fundamental needs—food stuffs and clothing, among other items. When the resource was depleted, the "backward" area was left just about as "backward" as it was when the Open Door had been applied. And, if a mandate were to be accepted with "scrupulous good faith," then part of that good faith might include the establishment of protective tariffs or export taxes with the revenues earmarked for infrastructure development, especially if one accepted the parent-child analogy so apparent in Wright's analysis.[97]

Clearly, Wright's recognition of the value of third party adjudication for changing mandate status was his signal contribution to the argument for perpetuation of the system. He was aware of the inertia implicit in a dependency system, for on the occasion in the past that a people demonstrated competency for independence, the imperial power seldom realized or acknowledged the condition until faced with revolt. The mandate system, noted Wright, addressed this problem through the introduction of a "disinterested body . . . to examine the situation . . . from the native and world points of view, appraising particularly the evolution of a capacity for self-government."[98] Of course, as with so many other areas of Wright's plans, no mention is made of specific criteria to be applied to the determination of "a capacity for self-government," and the Eurocentrism of the goals for the entire mandate system he accepted without demur.

The realists were mixed regarding Fleming's and Wright's assessment of the Open Door and its function on behalf of the national interest. Morgenthau saw the Open Door as a mechanism through which to maintain the balance of power in Asia, a goal consonant with his estimate of the national interest. "However unsure the United States has been in its Asiatic policy," he noted approvingly that "it has always assumed that the domination of China by another nation would lead to so great an accumulation of power as to threaten the security of the United States."[99]

Kennan did not share that assessment. He believed that "no two-word formula or symbol" could adequately reflect the complex circumstances surrounding foreign trade activity in China.[100] Equally inadequate of definition was the idea that the United States would defend the "territorial and administrative integrity of China." Kennan believed that the "trouble with the Open Door Doctrine and the integrity of China as political principles was simply that these terms were not clear and precise ones which could usefully be made the basis of a foreign policy."[101]

As the likelihood of direct U.S. participation in World War II became apparent, Fleming used his forums as vehicles to arouse public opinion in support of the Allies. Now almost fifty, he had seen world order collapse twice in his lifetime, along with countless bloody local and regional conflicts: he was now less concerned with the formalities of scholarship than with the need to arouse the public to its responsibilities for the future world order. Of course, the themes he pursued varied little from those on which he had conducted extensive research during the course of publishing his books, perhaps in that sense justifying his rhetoric.[102]

After twenty years, Fleming still seethed at the isolationist forces he held responsible for the duration of the First World War and for the inability of the United States to use its great power, both moral and economic, to prevent the Second World War. In an article for *Current History* entitled "War Without Shooting," Fleming attacked isolationists in the U.S. Senate, who he would later call the last vestiges of aristocracy in the United States, as well as Herbert Hoover, who opposed aid to the Soviet Union, the Nazis, the Japanese militarists, and the Italian fascists.[103] This was standard fare, a characteristic polemic, of a supporter of the Atlantic Alliance.

Two elements, though, stand above the other exhortations. First, he appealed to the people of the United States to accept their manifest international responsibilities. Second, his early sympathy for the Soviets offered an important insight to Fleming's later interpretation of the origins of the Cold War. They were themes he repeated, not just the following month in another article for *Current History* entitled "Roosevelt and Churchill Confer," but throughout the war and for the rest of his career.

Fleming feared that the U.S. public was unwilling to make the sacrifices necessary to win the war against the triple headed monster of fascism, National Socialism, and militarism. He feared that Americans were unwilling to give up their "Sunday gasoline," that the nation would return to the "orgies of Normalcy."[104] Congressional failure to extend periods of service for "selectees, national guardsmen, and reserve officers" for the duration of the emergency compounded his fears that the public was either unaware of or unwilling to accept the sacrifices necessary to win the war.[105]

Fleming goaded his readers with the words of Philander C. Knox. Secretary of State for William Howard Taft, Knox warned that "If the time ever comes when we Americans are unwilling to fight to preserve the freedom we have inherited, those freedoms will be destroyed and taken from us by a stronger breed of men who retain the courage to fight for what they have and for what they want." Strength was thus equated with a willingness to fight. Fleming believed, too, that many Americans viewed themselves as a "privileged people, exempt from the pains of actual fighting for liberty." Duty, he wrote, was incumbent upon Americans, for it was the "functioning of American democracy that [was] decisive for the fate of all free nations including our own--and always will be so long as we allow international anarchy to rule the world."[106]

As for the Soviet Union, Fleming referred to Hitler's aggression eastward as a mixed blessing. He wrote of Stalin's "wisdom" in exercising control over the area that stretched from the Karelian Isthmus to Bessarabia after 1939. This was a surprising appraisal from an internationalist, one who professed a respect for international law and the right of self-determination, but Fleming explained his appraisal in the language of *realpolitik*. Stalin's brutal policies from the 1930s onward could now be better appreciated, "for here was absorbed, well in front of the main Soviet defense, the first shock of the sudden and treacherous German attack."[107]

So much for Finland, Poland, Estonia, Latvia, Lithuania, and the Rumanian provinces of Bessarabia and northern Bukovina. It seemed that Fleming was willing to sacrifice principle to expediency, to allow the end to justify the means. This was as realist a denial of idealism as a realist could hope for! There was, too, a flair for brinkmanship in Fleming, indicated by his remark in October 1941 that the President should "[keep] pace with whatever degree of shooting the Nazis and their allies wished to incur."[108] But with the Soviet Union and its actions, here was an instance of a theorist who thought he had seen the future. Those countries and territories whose sovereignty had been so flippantly ignored were simply the first to succumb to the vanguard of the world state. Still, in an arena where international law lacked the coercive element necessary to enforce it, those who stood on principle were likely doomed to fall to the outlaw aggressor states.

As the world stood on the brink of World War II, Frederick Schuman's rising reputation as a prolific author, prominent academic, and well-known public figure, brought him an offer from historian Tyler Dennett of Williams College. Dennett, formerly of the State Department, had aided Schuman with a portion of his dissertation research and had received a glowing recommendation from Quincy Wright in support of Schuman.[109] Williams is located in Williamstown, Massachusetts in the central Berkshires. The town was a small Yankee community and the college, which admitted only men, had a reputation as a liberal institution. Schuman, who observed that Williams was not equal to Chicago in status or in intellectual diversity, moved anyway in the fall of 1936 and spent the next thirty-two years there as a professor. He was named Woodrow Wilson Professor of Government in 1938 and he quickly became a public figure on campus and in the community.[110]

As the Schumans moved to Williamstown, developments in Europe continued to provoke internationalists and "isolationists" alike. The continent had experienced a diplomatic revolution when Hitler exposed the French security system for the fraud that it was. Polish, Belgian, Czechoslovakian, Yugoslavian, and Romanian policy makers reevaluated their countries' alignments with France, and other countries seemed to have little choice but to follow suit. In Spain, the Civil War demonstrated that U.S. neutrality legislation was ineffective. And all the while the League of Nations continued to flounder on the shoals of collective security, unequal to its charge to keep world peace. The Soviet Union, alone among the powerful nations, vigorously supported collective security at the time, but without success. Given Schuman's belief in collective security, it is not surprising that he defended the Soviet government.

By 1941, Schuman refined in *Design For Power* [111] a theme that appeared earlier in *The Nazi Dictatorship* and one that became popular in later revisionist works: he declared that the West had pursued a policy calculated to encourage the *Drang nach Osten*.[112] Schuman charged that Chamberlain, Daladier, Halifax, and Weygand had conspired to use Hitler's war machine to destroy the Bolshevik government in Moscow.[113] As early as 1935, Schuman had warned that neither Britain nor the United States could remain neutral if Russia were attacked after a French defeat. Further, he predicted that Japan would enter such a war with the dual aims of occupying Siberia and forcing the United States from the Western Pacific.[114] His message was not well received.

Wright's pre-war analysis revealed two crucial elements in his estimate of how to organize the world for peace. First, he addressed the issue that Elihu Root had so forcefully noted years before—that the nature of the League served first the interests of the status quo. Second, he clearly indicated the need for some form of coercive power that would supersede the sovereignty of independent nations in specific situations, most importantly war, in order to "compel [them] to sacrifice certain advantages."[115]

These two ideas represented the consistency and the evolution of his approach to the problem of organizing the world for peace. Wright had maintained from the beginning of his career that some limitations on national sovereignty were essential to organize the world for peace. To do so, he had emphasized, at least since the 1930s, the need for an effective international police force to be at the disposal of the League of Nations or its successor. To Wright, the League as it was embodied in 1919 was simply "the first step toward organizing the force of the whole to be used against a recalcitrant part."[116] The next step was to give the central body of world government requisite authority and power to maintain peace. The most viable means available for the establishment of the peaceful settlement of disputes was, according to Wright, a strong world political organization.[117]

The Wilsonians sought every opportunity to demonstrate to the public that fascism, militarism, and nazism threatened the national interest. Like their realist critics, they called for action to defend American interests in Europe and in Asia. Fleming, Schuman, and Wright consistently argued that in the face of an ineffective world organization, the United States must take measures to protect the balance of power from *revanchist* states like Germany and expansionist states like Japan in the Far East. Implicit in both was the recognition that American national interests required that the balance of power be maintained.

NOTES

1. Quincy Wright, "Lansing and Neutrality," *Southern Review* 2 (1936-37): 419-420.

2. See Quincy Wright, "Amending or Developing the U.N. Charter," *Common Cause* 2 (June 1949): 410, where he writes that an "isolationist neutrality policy . . . encouraged aggression." Although this quote is ten years from the time above, it reflects his sentiments during the thirties as well.

3. Quincy Wright, *The United States and Neutrality*, Public Policy Pamphlet 17, (Chicago, IL: University of Chicago Press, 1935), 24-25.

4. *Ibid.,* ii.

5. Sokolsky to Quincy Wright, 24 March 1933, Box 23, addenda 1, The Quincy Wright Collection, University of Chicago, Chicago, IL.

6. Quincy Wright, "When Does War Exist?" *American Journal of International Law* 26 (1932): 367.

7. *Ibid.*

8. Quincy Wright, "Legal Status of Economic Sanctions," *Amerasia* 2 (February 1939): 570.

9. Quincy Wright, "The Transfer of Destroyers To Great Britain," *American Journal of International Law* 34 (October 1940): 680-681.

10. Quincy Wright, "Political Conditions of the Period of Transition," *International Conciliation* 379 (April 1942): 265.

11. George F. Kennan, *American Diplomacy* (Chicago, IL: University of Chicago Press, 1984), 64.

12. *Ibid.,* 75-77.

13. Hans Morgenthau, *In Defense of the National Interest: A Critical Examination of American Foreign Policy* (New York: A.A. Knopf, 1951), 25; 30.

14. Quincy Wright, "The Munich Settlement and International Law," *American Journal of International Law* 33 (1939): 30.

15. *Ibid.,* 31.

16. Morgenthau, *In Defense of the National Interest,* 137.

17. *Ibid.,* 137-138. Morgenthau cites Churchill's 14 December 1950 speech to the House of Commons.

18. Kennan, *American Diplomacy,* 80.

19. *Ibid.,* 82.

20. Frederick L. Schuman, *The Nazi Dictatorship: A Study in Social Pathology and the Politics of Fascism* (New York: A.A. Knopf, 1934, 1935).

21. *Ibid.,* vi.

22. *Ibid.,* 127-128; 357.

23. William E. Leuchtenburg, *Franklin D. Roosevelt and the New Deal, 1932-1940* (New York: Harper and Row, 1963), 216.

24. Denna Fleming, *While America Slept: A Contemporary Analysis of World Events From The Fall of France To Pearl Harbor* (New York: Abingdon-Cokesbury Press, Inc., 1944), 20.

25. Frederick L. Schuman, "Nazi Dreams of World Power," *Current History* 39 (February 1934): 535-541; Schuman, "Germany Prepares Fear," *The New Republic* 77 (7 February 1934): 353-355; Schuman, "The Political Theory of German Fascism," *Ameri-*

can Political Science Review 28 (April 1934): 210-232; Schuman, "The Third Reich's Road to War," *Annals of the American Academy of Political and Social Science* 175 (September 1934): 33-43; Schuman, "The Conduct of German Foreign Affairs" *Annals of the American Academy of Political and Social Science* 176 (November 1934): 187-221.

26. Denna Fleming to J. Pardue (editor of *The Nashville Tennessean*), 25 February 1937, The Denna Fleming Collection, Vanderbilt University, Nashville, TN. In a letter to Manley O. Hudson from Fleming dated 7 September 1935 written from Geneva, Fleming noted that "more Americans than any other nationality come to Geneva to visit the seat of the League of Nations."

27. Edith Osburn to Denna Fleming, 11 March 1936.

28. Fleming to Edith Osburn, 16 March 1936.

29. Fleming to R. B. C. Howell, 14 October 1937; Doris Fleming attributes the problem to an antagonistic Senator McKellar who was upset with Fleming's beliefs. Notes from Doris Fleming, 7.

30. Document entitled "Data Concerning D. F. Fleming," Fleming Collection; Mrs. Fleming described the relationship as lasting from 1939-1947. WSM was a station with a powerful transmitter: Mrs. Fleming noted that she heard Fleming's programs in London, Ontario where she had gone for her father's funeral. Notes from Doris Fleming to Steven J. Bucklin, 8.

31. Fleming to Senator Elbert D. Thomas, 1 February 1935.

32. See notes from Doris Fleming to Steven J. Bucklin, 8; Fleming, *While America Slept*, 31.

33. Kennan, *American Diplomacy,* 83.212; 269.

34. By 1942 Schuman received $150 per engagement, sometimes plus expenses; by 1946 it was double that amount. Schuman to Charlotte Sander, 19 May 1942; Schuman to Charlotte Sander, 1 January 1947.

35. See Frank N. Trager, "Frederick L. Schuman: A Case History" *Partisan Review* 7 (1940): 143-151; Frank Warren *Liberals and Communism: The "Red Decade" Revisited,* (Bloomington, IN: Indiana University Press, 1966), 4; William O'Neill, *A Better World--The Great Schism: Stalinism and the American Intellectuals* (New York: Simon and Schuster, 1982), 27-29. O'Neill dislikes Schuman's power politics (27-28), yet O'Neill asserts that "diatribes against power politics make no sense (95)." See also David Caute *The Fellow -Travellers: Intellectual Friends of Communism* (New Haven, CT: Yale University Press, 1973, 1988), 146; 290.

36. Mrs. Albert W. Dilling, *The Red Network* (privately published in Chicago, 1934).

37. Frederick L. Schuman Collection, Memorandum to the Illinois Senate Committee Investigating Subversive Activities in Colleges and Universities, 13 May 1935, 1; Quincy Wright Collection, Paul Douglas to Wright, 1935, Box 18, folder 8, 1-2.

38. "Culture and Crisis," memo to the Illinois Senate Committee, 2-3.

39. Quincy Wright to Paul Douglas, 14 June 1935, Box 18, folder 13.

40. Editorial, Chicago *Herald-Examiner*, 16 March 1935, as quoted in Schuman's letter to the editor "Public Enemy Number One" *The Nation* 140 (24 April 1935): 480-481.

41. *Ibid.*

42. Schuman to Robert Hutchins, 12 April 1935, 1. This confirms Mrs. Fleming's assessment of his carelessness.

43. *Ibid.* The fact that he did not belong to the party or any affiliated organizations did not indicate that he was not sympathetic; nonetheless, Schuman was cleared of subversive activities on two occasions during which he gave testimony under oath.

44. *Ibid.*

45. These charges influenced Quincy Wright's recommendations of Schuman. Wright's original recommendation read: "I have seldom had a student of such marked ability and believe that he has an enviable career ahead of him as a research worker. His teaching has also been of the highest quality and I am happy to recommend him without qualification." Undated letter of Recommendation, Wright Collection, Box 9, addenda 2, folder 8. In Wright to Dean Fred C. Woodward of the University of Chicago, 9 March 1927, Box 9, addenda 2, Wright referred to Schuman as the best student I have had for some time . . . " Prior to the events of 1932-1935, Wright recommended Schuman as "one of the very best of our younger men," "[he] has an enviable career ahead of him as a re-search worker," and recommended him "without qualification." Wright to Don Young, 28 October 1932, Box 23, addenda 1; Letter of Recommendation, Box 9, addenda 2, folder 8. Yet in a 6 July 1937 letter to Charles Merriam, Wright did not support Schu-man's request to be appointed Wallgreen Professor at the University of Chicago. By 1946 his recommendations of Schuman included very negative assessments. See Wright to Leonard White, 5 March 1946.

46. Frederick L. Schuman, *American Policy Toward Russia Since 1917* (New York: International Publishers, 1928).

47. Frederick L. Schuman, "Neutrality or Sanctions," *New Republic* 85 (25 December 1935): 200.

48. *Ibid.*

49. Frederick L. Schuman, "Liberalism and Communism Reconsidered," *Southern Review* 2 (1936): 326-338.

50. *Ibid.,* 327.

51. *Ibid.,* 328.

52. *Ibid.*

53. He concluded that authority in the Soviet Union flowed from the people to the leaders and that the "Dictatorship of the Proletariat" was not a dictatorship because "the communists act not for themselves, but for the whole body of organized workers and collective peasants"; that there was a wide degree of freedom of discussion, criticism, and responsibility to the electorate within the party; that there were "genuinely representative elections"; and that the Soviet economic system had "increased production at a phenome-nal rate, abolished unemployment, eliminated slumps and booms, and expanded con-sumer demand more rapidly than productive capacity." *Ibid.,* 332-333.

54. *Ibid.,* 335.

55. Frederick L. Schuman, *International Politics: An Introduction to the Western State System* (New York: McGraw-Hill, 1933), 848.

56. Schuman, "Liberalism and Communism Reconsidered," 336.

57. Frederick L. Schuman, "Addenda to 'Who Owns the Future'," *The Nation* 152 (11 January 1941): 111.

58. *Ibid.*

59. *Ibid.*

60. Morgenthau, *In Defense of the National Interest,* 59.

61. Quincy Wright, *The Causes of War and Conditions of Peace* (London: Long-mans, Green & Co., 1935), 48. Original emphasis.

62. *Ibid.,* 2.

63. *Ibid.,* 2-4.

64. *Ibid.,* 4.

65. *Ibid.,* 99. Wright develops this concept in *A Study of War* (Chicago, IL: University of Chicago Press, 1964).

66. For moral disarmament see Wright, *The Causes of War and Conditions of Peace,* 63; for qualitative and quantitative disarmament see *A Study of War,* 71.

67. *Ibid.*, 65.

68. *Ibid.*, 53; 57-58.

69. *Ibid.*, 64-65.

70. *Ibid.*, 54-55.

71. *Ibid.*, 95-96.

72. *Ibid.*, 96-97.

73. *Ibid.*, 98.

74. *Ibid.*, 99.

75. *Ibid.*, 100. His reliance on air power is revealed in detail in his work with the CSOP.

76. *Ibid.*, 103.

77. *Ibid.*, 101-103.

78. Wright to Edith Ware, 11 April 1940, Box 5, folder 11, (2pp).

79. Wright to Edith Ware, 11 April 1940, Box 5, folder 11, (2pp).

80. Denna Fleming to Newton D. Baker, 19 May 1937.

81. Denna Fleming, "Neutrality Controversy," *Congressional Digest* 15 (January 1936): 30.

82. Fleming to Sydnor Walker, 15 January 1938. Fleming did not mention the Nye Committee's findings specifically in this letter, but it seems apparent that he was referring to them. In a letter of 26 February 1938 to the Dean of the Graduate School of the University of Pennsylvania, though, Fleming refers specifically to the revisionist works of C. Harley Grattan and Walter Mills.

83. Fleming to Dr. William C. Binkley, 4 April 1938.

84. Denna Fleming, *The Origins and Legacy of World War I* (Garden City, NY: Doubleday, 1968).

85. Fleming, *While America Slept*, 21.

86. Denna Fleming, "America's Stake in the Far East," *The China Weekly Review* 88 (20 May 1939): 373; see also, Fleming's "Roosevelt and Churchill Confer," 119, for a reference to the "correspondingly large trade" China was developing with the United States.

87. Fleming, "America's Stake in the Far East," 373.

88. *Ibid.*

89. *Ibid.*, 374.

90. *Ibid.*, 375.

91. *Ibid.*

92. Quincy Wright, "The Mandates In 1938," *American Journal of International Law* 33 (April 1939): 341-342.

93. See Wright document entitled "Meeting of Sub-Committee on Political International Organization," 27 December 1939, 2, which concludes that the new world organization should emphasize "the need of the United States for raw materials, markets and cultural inspiration from abroad, and the even greater need of other countries to have access to raw materials, markets and cultural institutions in the United States."

94. Wright, *Mandates Under The League Of Nations,* 34, 260.

95. See Chester Lloyd Jones' *Guatemala: Past and Present* (Minneapolis, MN: University of Minnesota Press, 1940) for a demonstration of the impact of the U.S. presence in a traditional society.

96. Wright, *Mandates Under The League of Nations,* 579.

97. *Ibid.*, 586.

98. *Ibid.*, 585-586.

99. Morgenthau, *In Defense of the National Interest*, 6-7.

100. Kennan, *American Diplomacy,* 40.

101. *Ibid.,* 45.

102. Fleming's papers for the period 1939-1945 are sparse. One of the librarians at the Vanderbilt archives characterized the Fleming collection as having been "sanitized," but she did not elaborate.

103. The "last vestiges of aristocracy" is a reference to the U.S. Senate and is attributed to Fleming in a *Newsweek* review of his book *The United States and the World Court* (New York: Doubleday, 1945), *Newsweek* (12 February 1945), 101; Fleming, "War Without Shooting," 35; and Fleming, "Roosevelt and Churchill Confer," 113-120.

104. Fleming, "Roosevelt and Churchill Confer," 117; Fleming, "The Coming World Order, Closed Or Free," 251.

105. Fleming, "War Without Shooting," 35.

106. *Ibid.,* 38. Fleming did not provide a citation for the Knox quotation.

107. *Ibid.,* 35.

108. Fleming, "Roosevelt and Churchill Confer," 120.

109. Wright to Tyler Dennett, 8 July 1926, Box 7, addenda 2, folder 2.

110. Among those who disagreed with his position on the Soviet Union he was known as "Red Fred." See Frank N. Trager, "Frederick L. Schuman: A Case History," *Partisan Review* 7 (1940): 143-151.

111. Frederick L. Schuman, *Design for Power: The Struggle for the World* (New York: A.A. Knopf, 1942).

112. *Ibid.,* 488; see also Frederick L. Schuman, "The Great Conspiracy," *New Republic* 96 (26 October 1938): 325-326; "The Tory Dialectic: I," *New Republic* 97 (28 December 1938), 219-222; "The Tory Dialectic: II," *New Republic* 97 (4 January 1939): 253-255; and "Toward the New Munich," *New Republic* 99 (31 May 1939): 91-93.

113. Schuman, *Design For Power*, 166-171.

114. Schuman, *Nazi Dictatorship*, 504.

115. Wright to Edith Ware, 11 April 1940, Box 5, folder 11, (2pp).

116. Wright to Father, 14 July 1917, 2.

117. Quincy Wright, "The Outlawry of War," *American Journal of International Law* 29 (January 1925): 77.

4

The New World Order

At the outbreak of World War II, Fleming, Schuman, and Wright worked diligently in support of the Allied cause. Not only that, but these three men began to consider the needs the world and the nation would have to maintain international order and peace in the years following the war. They had spent years developing their theoretical approach. Now, in the dangerous and complex context of the war, they began a consuming effort to put theory to practice.

To do so, all three served on the Committee to Study the Organization of Peace. The CSOP, the brainchild of Nicholas Murray Butler, director of the Carnegie Endowment for International Peace, was founded in 1939 under the auspices of the Endowment. The CSOP membership included a variety of luminaries from the academic, public service, and business communities. Their recommendations inspired attacks from Harry Elmer Barnes, C. Harley Grattan, and Oswald Garrison Villard that the CSOP was "interventionist."[1]

The CSOP assigned areas of special concern to experts in a given field. Quincy Wright led the investigation into regional areas and union and federal systems. John Foster Dulles was charged with examining the means for peaceful change. His brother, Allen Dulles, would assess the potential to reduce and limit armaments. Clyde Eagleton would research peace enforcement. Philip C. Jessup was to tackle the framework of court and arbitral arrangements under an international legal authority. Sarah Wambaugh would be assigned minority issues, and Raymond Buell to the needs of colonial areas.[2]

Several themes emerged from initial discussions of the CSOP that were based on a series of nine questions Wright sent to the prospective discussants.[3] Among them was a commitment to the "Open Door," to regional associations, and to recognition of the individual within the new world order. The membership reiterated "Open Door" themes throughout the meeting and they concluded that "unless reasonable commercial opportunities were assured for the states most dependent upon external markets and sources of raw materials" it would be very difficult to prevent future territorial aggressions.[4]

Their belief in the need for regional associations, such as a federation of Europe and a federation of Danubian powers, was their first specific prescription.[5] Their commitment to peaceful change led a "substantial minority" to advocate that individuals be granted international standing through a specific remedial procedure to be made available "after local remedies had been exhausted."[6] Although only a "substantial minority" solidly supported this extension of standing to the individual, the majority recognized that "the problem of peaceful change is a legislative problem, and that no international court of Equity or arbitral tribunal could solve the problem. Law can be changed only by a body so representative of public opinion that its enactments will conform to the prevailing sentiment of justice."[7] This recognition required extension of individual rights in a representative system.

Wright's report on regional areas, union and federation was completed and distributed on 25 March 1940. An underlying theme remained his commitment to the Open Door, which was evident in his insistence that "freer trade assuring more opportunity and more wealth for all through division of labor" would help prevent war. He also insisted that a functional organization concerned with "problems of commerce, raw materials and markets . . . should be developed with such competence as to assure a moderate freedom of trade and access to raw materials for all nations" was essential to a world committed to peaceful change.[8]

Wright further asserted that a new order would not necessarily perpetuate the status quo, nor would it eliminate controversy, nor would it even eliminate the use of force. If order did create the above conditions, Wright warned that there would be no progress and no variety to international affairs, and that self-defense and application of sanctions would be eliminated as well. What order would provide would be procedures for individuals, nations, and international institutions to settle disputes, to administer services, to create and enforce law, and to change even the procedures for dispute settlement when "justice requires and knowledge permits."[9]

Wright concluded that in addition to national and local governments, which he believed "should continue to have primary legal authority within the territory of the respective states," an effective world organization would require universal principles, universal institutions, regional organizations, and functional organizations.[10] The CSOP adopted this assertion, in fact the entire document, virtually unchanged, and it appeared in an article entitled "Peace and Political Organization."[11]

Wright alleged that four problems endangered peace more so than any others did. First of the four were state attempts to augment power at the expense of other states. This was so, he wrote, because many believed that the state existed first for itself. The only remedy he offered for this condition was the admonition that policy makers and people alike accept the theory that "the State exists for the benefit of its people and of humanity."[12] But what if the state and its people subscribe to a messianic ideology? Aggression could then be justified as benefiting humanity.

The second problem he recognized was that the search for self-sufficient national wealth was often the precursor to war. To remedy this he prescribed free trade to assure both "opportunity and wealth for all through division of labor."[13] This was rather nebulous as he made no mention of who or what would decide the division of labor, the share of resources, the share of profits, the share of costs, or other variables.

Third, he suggested that national and international welfare policies be adopted in order to avert depression and unemployment, both of which he believed led to "revolution and violence." George Kennan's plan for European Recovery after the war shared that assumption. Fourth, Wright argued that only properly developed legal procedures could address perceptions of or actual injustice, thus eliminating some of the fuel that fired "political and economic rivalries and social misery." But as any member of an underclass can attest, law and procedure can just as well perpetuate injustice.[14]

Wright continued his analysis with an assessment of the impact the growing interdependence of states had on the need for world organization. Because states were increasingly interdependent, domestic legislation frequently affected individuals and groups within other states. This external impact of domestic legislation required further international cooperation in order to prevent violence. From this observation he concluded that peaceful change and collective security were irreducibly connected, and that a dynamic world order would "provide for both by varying the ease of altering the elements of its structure and procedure, according as they are essential to security or obstacles to necessary change."[15]

He asserted that the institutions that developed in the new world order would do so most effectively if they served essential interests and avoided radical breaches with tradition; these, he wrote, would last longer than revolutionary changes. To facilitate this objective, he insisted that institutions designed to improve world organization "be natural developments from those that already exist."[16] Far from being radical futurists, the CSOP advocated a quintessentially conservative approach. The problem, though, was who or what would determine whether developments are "natural"? And what about the "natural" inertia of the bureaucracy necessary to such a world organization? Such questions would plague the CSOP and the new international organization.

Wright broke with his dictum on tradition, though, in his discussion of the application of sanctions. He was aware that if a state possessed sufficient force to defend itself, that same force could be used to flaunt the law. And there were no guarantees against lawlessness in an unorganized international system governed by balance of power. Therefore, in order to provide such guarantees, the new system of international sanctions had to have power greater than that of any single nation or any combination of nations that might attempt to break the law. The new international organization would have to attain such power immediately upon its creation—"all at once"—or its sanctions could be "worse than useless."[17] To make sanctions "sufficiently powerful all at once" would be revolutionary change and, in his own words, likely not to last, but it was the only way to compel the great powers to follow the rules.

Wright called for all nations to be invited to sign a pact that would be incorporated in each national constitution (presuming they had a constitution) to ensure that certain obligations under the new world order would be met. Foremost was protection of basic human rights and limits on the use of armed force. He called for measures to ensure economic fairness. In the event a problem could not be settled diplomatically, the Permanent Court of International Justice would decide the case. Wright also demanded standardized treatment of aggressors. Each nation would also support the establishment of a World Assembly representative of every considerable opinion group, a World Council composed of great powers and important political regions, and a World Secretariat to study world problems and to provide those institutions with regulatory and substantive powers.[18] The obvious problem was what to do if a nation or nations refused to sign? Unless the world organization was willing to force them to join, Wright admitted any such organization would likely fail as he declared universal membership and power "all at once" essential to its survival.

The CSOP continued to refine its objectives and its plans for accomplishing them during the war years. Dissent plagued the group as several members quit, presumably over policy disputes.[19] Wright was as well very concerned that the CSOP be careful to avoid association with "questionable" individuals or groups. Two cases in point are his attempt to distance the CSOP from Clark Eichelberger's League of Nations Association and Wright's questioning of an International Student Service (ISS) letter that referred to the CSOP in a way that indicated the two were mutually supportive.

Wright, who had a long relationship with Eichelberger, implored him not to misunderstand his interpretation of the relationship between the Association and the CSOP. He assured Eichelberger that in no way did the CSOP "wish to minimize the importance of the work of the Association in connection with the Committee, nor to decrease that relationship." Wright's concern was to make the CSOP as "efficient as possible" in its effort to develop in a public traditionally antagonistic to the concept of the League support for the principles of international organization. He noted that the CSOP was financed independently of the Association, and that the "result of its efforts are not in any way predetermined by the past program of the Association." It was evident that Wright thought the Association was tainted with a lost cause in the public mind, therefore he thought it desirable that the CSOP's independence from the Association "should be emphasized to the public as much as possible."[20] Eichelberger responded that "We are in no way going to make the effort appear to the public as a sole League of Nations Association effort."[21]

As for the ISS, Wright believed that its actions regarding the Hoover Finnish Relief Fund Drive would lead many people to believe that the ISS, like so many other student organizations, was sympathetic to communism. Wright thought every effort should be made to avoid such an impression of the CSOP.[22]

Clearly, internecine strife plagued the CSOP and groups that were, or wished to be, associated with it, but that strife did not deter the Committee from its work. The agenda remained to establish a working organization of the world's states that addressed the problems of the League and the problems of a changing world. Important in this phase of the Committee's work was emphasis on the need for a world organization committed to basic human rights, to free trade, and to collective security.

By 7 June 1941 the nucleus of the CSOP approach to world organization was outlined in a confidential document entitled "Outline of Program."[23] The document contains a proviso that indicates it was not prepared as an official statement of the CSOP program, but rather as a potential guide. Nonetheless, its contents, which declared that "civil order and normal economic processes [were] an indispensable prerequisite to the establishment of a general peace" as was establishment "of an effective system of international security," became the basis of the CSOP program. Further, the authors envisioned "a world order designed to promote stable economic progress, social justice, and cultural freedom for all national groups, races, and classes willing to accept their proper responsibilities as members of a world community."[24] The proposal also called for effective military cooperation between the United States and the British Commonwealth, apparently justifying in the minds of their opponents charges that the CSOP membership was interventionist in outlook and would ally the United States with British interests.[25]

After the United States entered the war, the CSOP called for a statement of war aims in order to avoid the public and private dissent that developed following U.S. entry into World War I. To that effect the CSOP issued seven detailed and revealing aims. First they asserted that the government of the United States was established to advance the welfare of its citizens and at the same time maintain "due regard for the welfare of citizens everywhere." Second, they declared that democratic liberalism had provided "political liberty" and must now provide "economic security" for the masses. Material and intellectual resources were, they insisted, sufficient to the task of equitable distribution. Third, they declared that industrialization had made it "impossible for any nation adequately to care for the welfare of its members by its own unaided efforts." Therefore, they reasoned that "commercial and intellectual intercourse between nations" would be best carried out "under proper rules of law, and with the protection of the community of nations."

Fourth, they observed that the nature of war had now become total, and the "necessity for continuous totalitarian preparation against war, even in peace-time," jeopardized the "very existence of democracy." In order to ensure stability and democracy, and make possible the "essential intercourse between nations," they declared that the use of force must be "brought under control." Fifth, they called upon the United States to announce its guarantee of the creation and enforcement of an international system to "prevent the use of force between nations, to provide justice between them and to give opportunity for the further improvement of the welfare of individuals everywhere." Sixth, they assured all peoples the right to the form of government they desired as long as it conformed to the "rules of the community of nations." Finally, the United States was to announce its intent to join with other states in a "union of economic and military forces" to realize the first six goals, and for the "joint study and establishment of a permanent system of law and order between the nations of the world."[26]

The relationship of the war aims to the traditional U.S. peace/internationalist movement is self-evident. They are also consistent with Wilsonian internationalism and the Atlantic Charter. And they continue to underscore commitment to economic principles consistent with the free enterprise system.[27]

In the meantime, Wright completed his book *A Study of War* in 1941. He directed the Conference of Teachers of International Law in 1942, was elected to the American Philosophical Society in 1943, and served as a consultant to the State Department from 1943-1944. Wright was president of the American Association of University Professors (AAUP) from 1943-1945, chaired the International Relations Committee and was executive secretary of the Norman Wait Harris Memorial Foundation at the University of Chicago, and was secretary of the World Citizen's Association. Despite such a demanding schedule, he was able to concentrate his energies during the war on the mission of the CSOP.[28]

By 1943 the CSOP had issued its third report and innumerable memoranda.[29] Wright attempted to reach a much broader audience than that which the Committee's journal of record, *International Conciliation*, afforded. In a flyer sent to labor unions entitled "Prepare for Victory," Wright observed that the failure of world opinion to unite behind the enforcement of peace had brought the world to war once again. The lesson could not be misunderstood: the world must not wait for victory before examining its responsibilities. He asked U.S. labor unions to increase their interest and their role in solving post-war problems, and to help create a "constructive public opinion."[30] He requested that the unions discuss the organization of the postwar world. He even offered through the Midwest office of the CSOP to provide programs for discussion, but there is no indication of a response in his papers.

As well, Wright participated in twenty-four radio broadcasts from 1939-1945, all of which were published, and whose participants included Eduard Benes, Bernard Pares, James Reston, Norman Thomas, and many others.[31] His speaking schedule included foreign policy associations, the World Citizens Association, the American Association of University Professors, the American Political Science Association, and many other professional organizations to which he addressed the need to adopt the recommendations of the CSOP.

By 31 August 1944, after many debates, many memoranda, and five years of work, the CSOP recommended to the Dumbarton Oaks Conference several proposals to maintain the peace and to prevent aggression. The most basic recommendation was that nations should pool their forces to prevent aggression. An Executive Council should be created and given control of a new international air force. As well, there should be an international general staff to serve the Executive Council in the deployment of the military contingents each nation would contribute to the security force. The CSOP believed that the international organization should use its forces to occupy strategic bases around the globe.

To accomplish these first recommendations, the CSOP declared that the general international organization must be superior to any regional security systems and that the general international organization must conduct arms inspections. In the event a nation violated its obligations, there must be agreements to break off communications and trade in order to quarantine aggressor states and supplement military measures to enforce peace.[32] With the exception of the recommendations regarding a permanent military force, the CSOP's program was an essential part of the plan the Dumbarton Oaks Conference adopted.

The need of the world organization to possess not just military forces, but a monopoly of force in certain areas, became central to Wright's and the CSOP's vision of an effective new world order. Their subscription to the limited view that technology was shrinking the world and to the belief in the potential of military offense over defense led them to conclude that the airplane was the ultimate weapon of destruction.[33] If, they reasoned, that weapon could be monopolized, its power would become deterrent. Wright pushed for the world organization to receive such a monopoly in every forum available to him.[34]

Wright anticipated the San Francisco Conference on the United Nations Organization Charter with hope. In response to Fred Schuman's article "The Dilemma of the Peace-Seekers," which was highly critical of the possibilities of Dumbarton Oaks, Wright declared that his former student had not sufficiently examined the possibilities for evolutionary change within political institutions.[35] Wright insisted that although the international organization proposed at Dumbarton Oaks was superficially "a league of equals and in substance an alliance of great powers," the organization contained the promise of federalism. It was too early to tell what might develop from it.

Ever the optimist, Wright reminded Schuman that although it took a civil war "to decide whether the United States was a league or a federation," John Marshall and Daniel Webster had made great progress in the decades prior to that war in the interpretation of the constitution that assured victory for federation. Wright thought that if great power solidarity could be maintained for a generation, and at the same time those powers could be continually subjected to pressure, influence, and the power of the lesser states, federalism might be the result.[36]

Wright saw as significant the fact that the Dumbarton Oaks provisions for coercion were "not against states which commit aggression but against acts of aggression."[37] This would allow governments or individuals to be tried for acts of aggression and perhaps free a subject people from the burden of collective guilt. He then recalled to Schuman a passage from Wright's *A Study of War* that addressed the possibility of moving from a league to a federation.[38] As well, he noted that there was greater potential for the creation of a meaningful international police force in Dumbarton Oaks than in the League Covenant.

Finally, he reminded Schuman that the basic requirement for a direct relationship between individuals and the world organization was a sense of world citizenship. He envisioned a world public opinion that adhered to universal concepts of human rights and of crimes, individual or national, against international law as the basis for such a direct relationship. Education (or indoctrination) was the fundamental element in cultivating "a sense of world citizenship along with national citizenship in individual minds. Without the germs of such sentiments," Wright concluded, "any legal arrangement however federalistic would not work."[39] It would not be too long until he wrote a text book devoted to just such an education.

It seemed to Wright in the spring of 1945 that the opportunity was at last at hand for Wilsonian principles to be established as the guidepost for world organization. He had witnessed and participated in a quarter century of debate over international theory and practice, The results had been mixed. His years of study had led him to revise certain of his beliefs, most notably those surrounding the issue of neutrality, and to temper the youthful enthusiasm of his letter to his father of 14 July 1917. His approach to the problems of international relations was now more sophisticated, more attuned to the nuances of psychology and sociology, more aware of the multiplicity of problems that faced a world organization.

Fleming's general endorsement of Franklin D. Roosevelt's wartime foreign policy, a strong independent policy that Fleming believed most Americans favored, never wavered. But the war absorbed the President's mental and physical energies to such an extent that even his most ardent followers must have wondered who would lead the executive branch once the president left office. Late in 1941, Fleming began referring to Vice-President Henry A. Wallace as "one of the best informed men on economic matters in Washington." Fleming's admiration for Wallace's economic abilities soon grew to adoration of Wallace as "one of the wisest men of our time." Fleming's identification with the man who would in 1948 become the presidential candidate of the Progressive Party and a leading advocate of peaceful competition with the Soviet Union underscores Fleming's continued emphasis on "the people" rather than the political establishment as the basis of U.S. foreign policy. By the time of the 1948 campaign, though, Fleming became disillusioned with Wallace and his movement, perhaps because "the people's" influence in Wallace's campaign was less evident than that of the elite factions within it.

In May of 1942 Fleming wrote that the world was on the path toward political unification—the only doubt that remained for him was what method would be used to bring about the unification.[40] He believed that the only hope for stable world government rested with a coalition led by the United States and the Soviet Union as "the key members of a world union." But if the terms of peace divided the superpowers, Fleming saw a world headed for another cycle of balance of power politics culminating in a Third World War.[41]

He recognized two possible courses of action, neither necessarily exclusive of the other, which might cause a split between Washington and Moscow. First, a Soviet policy of "excessive, as contrasted with extensive" expansion of Soviet territory might well alienate the United States, and, second, that U.S. "attempts to preserve semi-Fascist regimes in Europe as a counterpoise to Sovietism" would undoubtedly destroy the hope of a stable and competent United Nations.[42]

Fleming used the two emergent superpowers and their vulnerability as examples to underscore the need for strong, federated world government, but also asserted that it would be given "just as little power as will keep the peace."[43] This was obviously an effort to diffuse critics who would oppose any loss of national sovereignty to such a world organization.

In a radio address broadcast over WSM on 21 September 1943, Fleming questioned whether any state maintained sovereignty in an absolute sense under current conditions. When nations as powerful as the Soviet Union and the United States could be forced to expend so great an amount of natural and human resources at the whims of aggressor states, absolute sovereignty was to Fleming a fiction.

He questioned whether in an anarchical world, a world in which little was sacred, where even the worth of a nation's sovereignty was questionable, it was reasonable to oppose limits on sovereignty. He stated that he had accepted the idea that all international institutions must be reconciled with the dogma of national sovereignty for twenty years, but after this second collapse of civilization he could no longer accept that need. The completely sovereign nation, he declared, had died before him.[44]

Although this sounds like a lament, it was actually a celebration, for Fleming had long hoped for limits to be placed on national sovereignty. In a "rapidly shrinking world" there could be only one true sovereign, a world government, although he allowed that a federation of the type he envisioned would likely preserve the essentials of self-government for the many existing national societies.[45]

Fleming continued to battle against isolationists. His respect for the Russian war machine turned to antipathy because of the impact Red Army successes had on American isolationists and their renewed efforts to dissuade the American public from supporting their country's proper role in the war. "The sense of urgency," he observed, "was relaxed."[46] There was also the issue of clearly defined peace goals, something close to a Wilsonian's heart given the general dismay when the secret treaties were published during the last World War. Yet Fleming temporized on behalf of Roosevelt and Churchill who were, Fleming wrote, "[t]oo busy coping with the results of Hitler-Mussolini meetings. They did not have, either, sufficient assurance of final victory to justify a peace program."[47] It was not until Russia's "magnificent" resistance to the Nazi invasion during the summer and fall of 1941 that the Allies could propose a peace plan, a plan that pleased Fleming.

The Eight Point Peace Plan that Roosevelt and Churchill issued from their meeting in the North Atlantic in 1941 was a tribute to Wilson, according to Fleming. All eight points were drawn from his Fourteen Point Speech of 19 January 1918. And although the British and American leaders did not state so explicitly, Fleming argued that a "league of nations . . . is implicit in every point, for without a great international authority to administer and defend the new settlement it would be written in sand--bloody sand."[48]

This he considered a triumph for Wilsonian internationalism, but as the war continued and the United States entered as a belligerent, Fleming was ever wary of the threat of an isolationist cabal forming in the Senate. This possibility, especially imminent as the Allied victory became more certain, led Fleming to fear a repetition of the Paris Peace Conference of 1919. He sought to avoid "another grand peace conference with a monumental peace treaty issuing from it" so as to reduce the opportunities a recalcitrant Senate might have to tinker with the treaty.

Fleming supported as well the concept of unconditional surrender as announced at the Casablanca Conference of January 1943. The policy was especially attractive to him in that it advocated the annihilation of fascism, allowed for little direct Senate interference, and provided for the recognition and wholehearted support of "governments springing directly from the people."[49] George Kennan also endorsed the policy of unconditional surrender. Hitler, he declared, was not a man with whom one could obtain a compromise peace. Even though Kennan wrote that unconditional surrender "was probably not a wise thing to talk a lot about and make into a wartime slogan," he concluded that there was "no promising alternative" to it.[50] Hans Morgenthau, though, opposed total victory through unconditional surrender. For him, such a policy negated traditional diplomacy and eliminated the possibility of compromise and a peaceful settlement.[51] As a "realist," he was willing to compromise, apparently even with Hitler.

For Fred Schuman, World War II brought a new set of old problems. Although Schuman was rejected for military service in 1942 because of kidney stones, he remained qualified for alternate government service. In 1942 Dr. Goodwin Watson, head of the Analysis Division of the Foreign Broadcast Intelligence Service (FBIS), recommended Schuman for a position as Principal Political Analyst of the German Section of the Analysis Division. He began his duties on 21 October 1942.[52]

Schuman worked in the section that produced the "Weekly Review of Official Foreign Broadcasts" and published analyses of enemy radio propaganda and cable material. The section's clientele included the Departments of State, War, and Navy; the Lend-Lease Office; the Board of Economic Warfare; and the Office of Strategic Services. In addition, the German section published a second weekly, the "Central European Radio Analysis," intended for parties interested in Nazi propaganda.

These analyses were for in-house official use and their production required access to classified material.[53] Presumably, any person appointed to such a sensitive position would have been subjected to a rigorous security check and would have received confirmation only after receiving clearance. If this sort of method was in practice, Schuman must have passed an initial inspection prior to taking his position with the FBIS. At least one governmental agency, after close scrutiny, must have found Schuman fit for his post, but this was not enough to ensure his tenure as a federal employee.

Schuman's relationship with many "radical" causes, and the "Dilling Accusations" in particular, were well known to at least two government agencies. Schuman was a subject in the Department of Treasury and Bureau of Internal Revenue investigation of his former colleague and student, Brita Hyde.

Ms. Hyde, who worked in the Office of Civilian Defense, came under suspicion in 1941 when federal agents learned that she had studied sociology and anthropology at the University of Chicago, two disciplines and an institution that aroused fear among radical conservatives. She underwent interrogations about the "suspicious" circumstances that surrounded her engagement and marriage to an Army major (neither event was announced and she was not a native-born American, hence their suspicious character), the nature of sociology and anthropology, and the names of people with whom she lunched.

Hyde, referring to the agents as "the Gestapo," wrote Schuman that he was under investigation. His name had appeared for years on her employment record, and the agents had "evidently just received a report . . . that you are or were a very bad man," and they wanted to know what affect he had had on her. Had he encouraged her to become a Communist? Had she collaborated with Schuman in writing the *Nazi Dictatorship?* In a conniving and leering manner, the "Gestapo" agent then asked her if her relationship with Schuman could be described as having been "his PRIVATE secretary? Did Prof. Schuman receive considerable newspaper publicity . . . was he a Communist? etc etc etc."[54]

Schuman's life did not hang on the appointment and while he awaited his confirmation he continued to be an active speaker. By this time he had two agents: one for his Midwestern speaking engagements and another for his east coast lectures.[55] Schuman spoke frequently on such topics as "war aims, peace plans, and programs for a Free World Order" in an attempt to address the failures of the Versailles system. He believed that in order to win the war, the Allies must first win the peace. And like his fellow Wilsonians, he believed it was necessary to define the war goals in explicit terms in order to ensure that public rhetoric coincided with foreign policy, for in order to secure victory the United States had to be in a position to "tell ourselves and the world what we propose to do with our victory."[56]

Schuman's initial solution was to create a world federation modeled after the U.S. federal system. It would limit national sovereignty, legislate individual as well as state laws, and allow appeals from both.[57] Without federalism as its basis, Schuman believed any new international organization that allowed for free and willing participation would simply be another League. But Schuman had little hope for his program, for he believed that another League would most likely result from postwar attempts at international organization and would prove to be as ineffective as the first.

True to the Wilsonian idea of self-determination, Schuman championed the cause of colonial independence. He sent a telegram to President Roosevelt asking that the United States, the Soviet Union, and the Republic of China use their good offices as arbitrators in the dispute between the Indian Congress Party and the British government over Indian independence. He wrote that to "fail on the question of India is to fail on one of the crucial fronts of the war. It is also to fail on an issue that tests the capacity of the United Nations to work out post-war settlements."[58]

Schuman wanted the arbitrators to recommend a United Nations tribunal as the instrument to establish "within the next three months, a provisional government of an independent India, linked in war and peace alike to the British Commonwealth and the United Nations as a free and equal partner."[59] This was central to the way he interpreted the Atlantic Charter and its pledge to provide self-determination for all peoples. He was as fervent about the Indian situation as he was about anything else, perhaps because it represented a chance to establish peace through a system of international cooperation; perhaps because he saw the war as one of liberation for the colonies whose peoples had for so long labored under the yoke of European imperialism.[60]

Schuman managed to retain his sense of humor and perspective through it all. He told his mother that "Uncle Sam prefers to win (or lose) the war without my help."[61] Still, he continued his search for government work, and explored possibilities with Nelson Rockefeller at the Office of Inter-American Affairs, which included a meeting with both Rockefeller and Henry Wallace, and opportunities with the New York office of the Office of War Information.[62] Neither agency retained him, so when he learned that he had been confirmed for the position with the FBIS he was elated. Unfortunately for him, his excitement was short-lived.

On 30 March 1943, just five months into his work, Schuman was called before a hearing of the Special Subcommittee of the Special Committee to Investigate Un-American Activities. The Dies Committee already had a reputation among politicos for crediting the incredible and for pandering to unfounded public fears. William E. Leuchtenburg wrote in *Franklin Roosevelt and the New Deal, 1932-1940* that Texas Democrat Martin Dies "permitted witnesses to make unsupported charges of the most fantastic character, and rarely accorded the accused the right to reply."[63] Leuchtenburg concluded "The antics of witnesses before the Dies Committee, and the yahooism of some of its members, influenced a whole generation of Americans to dismiss any alarum about a communist conspiracy as ludicrous."[64]

Unfortunately for Schuman, the generation to which Leuchtenburg referred was a generation away: The Kerr Subcommittee equaled the reputation of its progenitor and employed the same tactics. The Committee had been active only five years when Schuman testified before it and the Communist threat continued to haunt many Americans.

Schuman came to the Committee's attention when, on 1 February 1943 on the House floor, Dies charged him and thirty-eight other federal employees with being "irresponsible, unrepresentative, radical, and crackpot."[65] Dies demanded that the House refuse to appropriate money for these employees' salaries. Schuman's past problems with the Illinois Senate and the Hearst press resurfaced, and given the Committee's reputation, it seemed almost certain that he would be reprimanded or discharged.

The Committee used innuendo, association, and intimidation as well as past and present behavior to establish guilt. Joe Starnes chaired the Committee and other members in attendance included Herman Eberharter, Noah Mason, and Karl Mundt. Robert Stripling advised the Committee and Dr. J. B. Matthews was its research director. Charles Denny, General Counsel for the Federal Communications Commission was present as an observer.[66]

Schuman had foreseen the possibility of a public confrontation well before it occurred. He had written Dr. Watson that he was aware that other liberals who had vigorously opposed fascism and nazism and advocated close cooperation with the Soviet Union against the common enemy who had gone to Washington to serve the war effort had been persecuted. Schuman indicated that he was "no less open to attack than these men" and concluded that it would be fruitless to accept a position from which he was likely to be discharged.[67] Apparently Watson believed that the charges of subversion against Schuman were groundless, for he approved Schuman's appointment, as did Harold Graves, Jr. and Dr. Robert Leigh, Administrative Chief of the FBIS and the head of the FBIS respectively.[68] But the fact that the Committee had targeted Watson, too, tempered his approval.[69]

Dr. Matthews conducted much of the questioning. He was a self-professed "fellow traveler" during the thirties, now an apostate. A zealous convert, Matthews pursued his targets and those who questioned his professionalism, his ethics, and his integrity, with relish. The charges against Schuman were no different than those of the Dilling Affair: that International Publishers was a Communist front, that he endorsed a "Communist" candidate for Chicago alderman, the Ford banquet, the pamphlet "Culture and Crisis," all were resurrected in order to vilify Schuman once again. And once again he refuted the charges with a combination of documentation and sworn testimony.

Schuman declared that as an unpublished author in 1928 he had no reason to question the political background of what was on the surface a reputable publishing house.[70] Quincy Wright told John Kerr that Schuman had offered the dissertation to Macmillan, to Scribner's and Harper's and that the University of Chicago Press had agreed to publish the dissertation but only with a heavy subsidy. International Publishers, Wright implied, was the publisher of last resort.[71] Schuman noted that he had endorsed Vladimir Janowicz as a former graduate student, not a budding Communist. As for the Ford banquet, Schuman claimed a professional interest in a Communist and a black candidacy. Said Schuman, "The banquet I sponsored, not Mr. Ford."[72] He explained the circumstances surrounding his endorsement of the pamphlet "Culture and Crisis" exactly as he had reported it to Robert Hutchins: that he had agreed to lend his name to the pamphlet carelessly after its publishers misrepresented it to him.[73]

These were reasonable explanations, ones that would have satisfied any court of law, but Schuman was not on trial and as such he did not have the full benefit of the law. The evidence presented against him was circumstantial and laden with innuendo, and the 105 pages of testimony and exhibits clearly indicated that he deserved to be exonerated. Regardless, Dr. Matthews ended the hearing with the statement that Schuman's "orientation is decidedly pro-Communist," implying that Schuman was unfit for federal service, and, of course, attaching a spectre to his continued employment in the private sector as well.

Nonetheless, in what was a most unexpected decision, the Committee ruled that there was "not sufficient evidence to support a recommendation of unfitness" regarding Schuman.[74]   Schuman certainly did not expect this outcome, for when he heard that a hearing was scheduled he turned in his resignation.[75] Goodwin Watson refused it. Schuman, now more confident in his tenure, requested several leaves through October so that he could lecture. The request went unanswered, for the Committee had declared Watson unfit for government service on 21 April and Schuman's duties with the FBIS ended that same month when the new director accepted his resignation.[76]

Even though Schuman was not unprepared for this event, certainly he felt betrayed, frustrated, and rejected as a result of it. Although his leave of absence from Williams College had been extended to accommodate his government service, he now returned to his academic duties, and he did so vigorously. The following summer he was a visiting professor at Cornell University and was by that time very much reacclimated to the academic environment. He continued his lectures and writings for an ever-widening public audience and published many articles in several journals and magazines during the war, including *The American Political Science Review, Current History, Antioch Review, The Nation,* and *The New Republic.* He also prepared the manuscript for a new book, *Soviet Politics: At Home and Abroad* (New York, 1946).[77] His lectures were more and more frequent, scheduled in such diverse places as Des Moines and Long Island, and at each stop he promoted the United Nations and prepared the public for his vision of the new international order.

For Schuman, association with leftist groups and the fact that anyone who was not anticommunist was *ipso facto* labeled a communist sympathizer put him doubly at jeopardy when World War II ended. Denna Fleming would also find his views quickly subject to the intrusive examination of McCarthyites. All three men would find their hopes for a powerful international organization sacrificed to traditional balance of power politics. Such an outcome, though, was one they had anticipated and for which they were not unprepared, for all three men recognized the importance of balance of power in an anarchical international system.

NOTES

1. The founding date is inferred from a letter of 20 November 1944, Box 5, folder 16, from Clark Eichelberger to Quincy Wright. The lineage of the CSOP is found in a document in the Quincy Wright Collection papers dated 24 February 1940, Box 5, folder 12, entitled "Tin Cans and Peace," #21. Harry Elmer Barnes, C. Harley Grattan, and Oswald Garrison Villard were among the document's editorial sponsors.

2. Wright document "Meeting Of Sub-Committee On Political International Organization," 27 December 1939, Box 5, folder 11, 11. Clyde Eagleton, Clark Eichelberger, Sarah Wambaugh, Quincy Wright, Samuel Guy Inman, Philip Jessup, James Shotwell, Allen Dulles, and Frederick Dunn attended this meeting.

3. Wright document, "Political International Organization," circa December 1939, Box 5, folder 11, 1-3.

4. *Ibid.,* 5.

5. *Ibid.,* 1.

6. *Ibid.,* 2.

7. *Ibid.,* 8.

8. Wright document "Proposals Respecting Political International Organization," 25 March 1940, Box 5, folder 11, 2; 15.

9. *Ibid.*, 1.

10. *Ibid.*, 11.

11. Quincy Wright, "Peace and Political Organization," Preliminary Report and Monographs, CSOP, *International Conciliation* 369 (April 1941): 454-467. This journal was the primary forum for the CSOP.

12. *Ibid.*, 454.

13. *Ibid.*, 455

14. *Ibid.*

15. *Ibid.*, 456.

16. *Ibid.*, 457.

17. *Ibid.*

18. *Ibid.*, 463-464.

19. Wright document, Box 5, folder 13 (c.1940?), indicates that CSOP membership no longer includes Allen Dulles, Thomas W. Lamont, Frederick Schuman, or Edith Ware.

20. Wright to Clark Eichelberger, 5 December 1939, Box 5, folder 11.

21. Wright to Clark Eichelberger, 7 December 1939, Box 5, folder 11.

22. Wright to Clyde Eagleton, 11 March 1940, Box 5, folder 12.

23. Wright , "Outline of Program," 7 June 1941, Box 5, folder 12.

24. *Ibid.*, 1-2, original emphasis.

25. *Ibid.*

26. Wright, "Statement of United States Aims called for by Commission to Study the Organization of Peace," undated, Box 5, folder 13.

27. More evidence of Wright's commitment to free enterprise is to be found in his later article "The War and the Peace," *Ethics* 53 (October 1942): 64-68, in which he refers to E. H. Carr's treatment of laissez-faire capitalism in *Condition of Peace* (New York: Macmillan, 1942) as "unduly critical."

28. Introduction to the Quincy Wright Collection, 1-3.

29. Quincy Wright "Human Rights and the World Order" *International Conciliation* 389 (April 1943): 238-262. Third Report of the CSOP.

30. Wright document "Prepare for Victory," 10 June 1942, Box 5, folder 14.

31. See Louise Wright, *A Bibliography of Quincy Wright: 1890-1970* (Pittsburgh, PA: The Clifford E. Barbour Library, 1974), 76-77, for broadcast titles and a complete list of participants.

32. Wright "CSOP Statement," 31 August 1944, Box 5, folder 16.

33. For their emphasis on the role of the offense in modern warfare, see Wright, *A Study of War,* 326; for their emphasis on the airplane's impact on the offensive, see *A Study of War,* 302, 809.

34. See Quincy Wright " National Security and International Police," *American Journal of International Law* 37 (July 1943): 499-505; Wright, "Responsibilities of the United States in the Post-War World," *Free World* 5 (January 1943): 35-41; Wright, "Peace Problems of Today and Yesterday," *American Political Science Review* 38 (June 1944): 512-521; Wright, "Security and World Organization," *International Conciliation* (June 1944): 30-65, 396; Wright Statement on CSOP, 31 August 1944, Box 5, folder 16; Wright, "An International Police Force," *New Europe* 4 (March 1944): 3, 16-17; and Wright, "The International Regulation of the Air," *American Economic Review* 35 (May 1945): 2, 243-248.

35. Frederick L. Schuman, "The Dilemma of the Peace-Seekers," *American Political Science Review* 36 (February 1945): 12-30.

36. Quincy Wright to Frederick L. Schuman, April 1945, Box 23, addenda 1, The Frederick L. Schuman Collection, University of Wyoming.

37. The provisions are to be found in Chapter VIII of the Dumbarton Oaks proposals.

38. The passage is to be found on 912 and 1063-76.

39. Wright to Schuman, April 1945, Box 23, addenda 1.

40. Denna Fleming, "The Coming World Order, Closed Or Free," *The Journal of Politics* 4 (1942): 253

41. Denna Fleming, "Planning For The Post-War World," *Current History* 4 (March 1943): 118.

42. *Ibid.*

43. *Ibid.*

44. Denna Fleming, "America and the World Crisis," *Vital Speeches* 10 (15 October 1943): 7-8.

45. Fleming, "The Coming World Order, Closed Or Free," 253.

46. *Ibid.*

47. Denna Fleming, "Roosevelt and Churchill Confer," *Current History* 1 (October 1941): 114.

48. *Ibid.,* 115.

49. Fleming, "Planning For The Post-War World," 8.

50. George F. Kennan, *American Diplomacy* (Chicago, IL: University of Chicago Press, 1984), 87-88.

51. Hans Morgenthau, *In Defense of the National Interest: A Critical Examination of American Foreign Policy* (New York: A.A. Knopf, 1951), 132-133.

52. Frederick L. Schuman, HUAC Testimony, 3089-3091.

53. *Ibid.,* 3089-3090.

54. Brita Hyde to Schuman, 17 July 1941, 1-2.

55. Schuman to Charlotte Sander, 19 May 1942, 1-2; Schuman to Roxanna Wells, 22 June 1945.

56. Schuman to Jack Shand, 17 July 1942, 1.

57. Frederick L. Schuman, "Might and Right at San Francisco," *The Nation* 160 (28 April 1945): 480.

58. Schuman to Franklin D. Roosevelt, 11 August 1942. Schuman's co-author was Max Lerner.

59. Schuman to Editor, *The Boston Herald* (12 August 1942), 2.

60. He even tried to enlist the aid of Henry and Clare Booth Luce, with whom he had had previous correspondence, in order to publicize his views. Schuman to Mr. and Mrs. Henry Luce, 12 August 1942.

61. Schuman to "Dearest Mom," 16 July 1942, 2.

62. Schuman to "Dearest Mom," 16 July 1942.

63. William E. Leuchtenburg, *Franklin D. Roosevelt and the New Deal, 1932-1940* (New York: Harper and Row, 1963), 280

64. *Ibid.,* 280-281.

65. Frederick L. Schuman, "'Bill of Attainder' In the Seventy-eighth Congress," *American Political Science Review* 37 (October 1943): 819.

66. Schuman, HUAC Testimony, 3087.

67. *Ibid.,* 3092.

68. *Ibid.,* 3091.

69. Schuman, "Bill of Attainder," 823.

70. Schuman, HUAC Testimony, 3095-3096.

71. Wright to John H. Kerr, 16 April 1943, Box 23, addenda 1.

72. Schuman, HUAC Testimony, 3115-3118.

73. *Ibid.,* 3104-3105; Schuman to Robert Hutchins, 12 April 1935, 1.

74. Schuman, "Bill of Attainder," 823.

75. Schuman to Goodwin Watson, 1 February 1943.

76. Schuman, "Bill of Attainder," 823.

77. Frederick L. Schuman, *Soviet Politics: At Home and Abroad* (New York: A.A. Knopf, 1946).

5

Wilsonians and the Cold War

April 1945 signaled victory not just for the Allies in the European theatre, but also a growing sense of victory for many internationalists. The San Francisco Conference established the Charter of the United Nations, although many of the details had been decided at the Dumbarton Oaks Conference. The United States was firmly encamped in the promised land of international organization, and it seemed only a matter of smoothing the transitional phase in order to replace a system of anarchical international relations with one governed by the rule of law, one that would impose limits on national sovereignty. Some of the goals the internationalists had previously sought for the post-war world were now more subdued; some of the principles they had held dear were now subject to compromise; but over all, it was an atmosphere of reverie for many.

What the United Nations Charter provided was a system committed to respect the sovereign equality of all nations; one state, one vote (somewhat modified in the cases of Byelorussia and the Ukraine); and to maintain the balance of power through the cooperation of the permanent members of the Security Council. These were essential elements of the peace that the new organization sought to obtain. Hope, though, lay in the protean character of the UN. Fleming, Wright, and Schuman believed that it could become an effective organization, perhaps even the nucleus of a world government, through the proper manipulation of world opinion, and through the evolution and enforcement of international law.

For the Wilsonians, the UN also represented an opportunity for the United States to follow the Wilson Doctrine. Given that outbreaks of unrest did not always disturb the national interest of the United States, the UN would aid the United States in judging when developments elsewhere required commitment of U.S. military forces, the weight of U.S. opinion, or no U.S. response. Although this could have been done outside any international organization, public opinion expected the United States to be involved in the UN. The good will that American participation in the new world organization generated was not only in the national interest, U.S. participation alone was worth the price of membership.

Still, in 1946 Wright considered the United Nations to be a "transitional organization."[1] From his perspective, the UN then was a hybrid of many different political systems. It was in some respects like an empire, with the five great powers exercising control via the Security Council. It resembled a world federation with the General Assembly and the Economic and Social Council at the center. And it contained the qualities of "an ethical system depending upon the self restraint of states in respecting the principles of sovereign equality, territorial integrity, political independence, nonintervention in domestic matters, abstention from aggression, and pacific settlement set forth in the first chapter of the Charter."[2] He believed the democracies should strive toward a UN that comprised a federal world order that exercised jurisdiction over individuals as well as states.[3]

To this end, Wright believed that the Nuremberg Trials had established beyond doubt that the lack of individual accountability that had crippled the old order would not hamstring the UN. One of the principle reasons previous international law had been ineffectual in the political sphere was because its rules had been directed exclusively at states and not at individual persons. Wright, who served as technical adviser to U.S. Counsel Francis Biddle at the trials, observed that the process of building precedent upon precedent in international criminal proceedings should "give greater weight to the very important principle that individuals have a direct relationship to the world community."[4]

Wright believed that a regularly enforced world criminal law that applied to individuals would limit national sovereignty and "change the foundation of the international community from a balance of power among sovereign states to a universal federation." Wright focused only on criminal law, making no reference to the potential of a world civil law to strengthen the individual in the world community. The federation would directly control individuals the world over on matters within the jurisdiction of international law.[5] Key to this observation, though, was, in Wright's own words, that "some national states . . . appear in fact more independent, powerful, and dangerous than ever."[6]

Morgenthau in particular was critical of the claim that the Nuremberg Trials had altered the international legal system. Those trials, he asserted, could not be taken out of their immediate context. Besides, he claimed, no one in the international legal community could demonstrate whether the Nuremberg Trials had applied the already existing law of the Paris Pact or whether they had created international law that had not previously existed. This, of course, was the *ex post facto* argument the lawyers for the Nazis made at the trials. To Morgenthau, Nuremberg was yet another example of a "statement of moral principle without legal effect."[7]

Denna Fleming paid little attention to the issue of individual standing in international legal venues. Instead, he focused his attention on other issues. Among those was the Wilsonian maxim of self-determination. In a review article published near the war's conclusion, Fleming refused to support extension of that principle to the people of defeated Germany. He joined other commentators in assuming that most Germans were "Pan Germans under the skin," and that they accepted the basic goals of Hitler's Reich, if not also its methods. In order to prevent a third German war, an "antidote for the lazy sentimentalism which may soon urge us to bring the boys home and let nature take its course in Germany" must be administered. Germany must be decentralized and Prussian power permanently broken.[8] Like his realist counterparts, Fleming believed the United States must maintain a strong military in the post-war environment.

In addition, Fleming reexamined sovereignty, and he paid it much less deference than did his colleague Quincy Wright. Indeed, Fleming showed a remarkable evolution during the war years in his thought about the sovereignty of nations. He transformed his concept of limited national sovereignty in order to allow for an effective League of Nations to the complete abrogation of national sovereignty.[9] In a review of Emery Reves' *Anatomy of Peace,* Fleming observed that "So long as nations remain, wars will come." He feared not only the international repercussions of unabated sovereignty, but the domestic ramifications as well. He believed that "fear of other sovereignties ha[d] driven Russian socialism to develop into a totalitarian state with an all powerful police force suppressing civil liberties" and agreed with Reves that all existing governments were bound to evolve toward fascism.[10]

For Fleming, the solution was a world state. Progress demanded it. The world was shrinking. The implications of airplanes and the atomic bomb weighed heavily in his mind. The time had come for a world government.[11]

Fear of fascism also drove him to this conclusion, although emotion rather than objective analysis guided his understanding of that system. Of the three systems into which he divided the world—capitalist democracy, totalitarian socialism, and fascist "gangsterism"—only fascism posed an intrinsic threat to both the other systems. In turn, Fleming saw no reason why capitalist democracies and socialist states could not coexist until the world state could be created.[12]

For Fred Schuman the central truth of the post-war world was that political power persisted in the form of "disparate national sovereignties."[13] There would be, he predicted, no world state following World War II, no world federation, and no world order based on a universal association of sovereign equals, for such an association could "neither succeed nor endure."[14] What would continue to dictate international relations would be "power politics," but with a new twist, for World War II had altered considerably the distribution of power. Schuman saw a world of three super-powers in 1946: the Soviet Union, the United Kingdom, and the United States. And they held the potential to rule the world in concert or to make the world a "vast arena of rivalry and conflict."[15] His only error here was in extending super-power status to the United Kingdom.

Because this distribution of power was reality, any plans for effective world organization must reflect that reality. This was precisely, in Schuman's estimation, what the proposed Charter of the United Nations failed to do. He condemned the idea that the majority of the members of the Security Council were to be lesser powers (the voting procedure was still under consideration at the time Schuman wrote this, so he could not assess the Big Five veto). Only the Big Three acting in concert could maintain peace, for if they acted separately there would be no effective action. Schuman feared that given the zealous devotion to the principle of sovereign equality, the super-powers would be unable to develop a directorate within the new organization and hence would lose interest in it.[16] And, in order for the United States to be a reliable and effective partner in such an alliance, Schuman clung to the Wilsonian demand that executive powers be strong and unfettered in foreign policy matters, because congressional debate had proven costly in the past.

Schuman's criticism was succinct. His call for a concert of powers—a Grand Alliance—recognized the distribution of power in the world. He realized that, despite the most compelling rhetoric and theory of sovereign equality, those who wielded great power were unlikely to accept limitations upon it unless such limitations served immediate interests. And he knew that peace could be procured only if the super-powers could accept the requirements each deemed necessary to its security as the *sine qua non* of future collaboration. Without such an alliance, little of durable value could come from the Dumbarton Oaks proposals or the United Nations.[17] What would result would be little more than a new League of Nations.

Schuman's vision was a reaffirmation of Wilsonian internationalism. Wilson, too, had seen the need for a concert of powers in 1919. His work in Europe, his emphasis on the Big Five in the Security Council of the League, his commitment to free trade and the open door, all required the cooperative effort of the great powers. Both Wilson and Schuman recognized that the potential of any world organization would be limited by the degree to which the great powers cooperated.

Although Schuman's analysis was in concert with Wilson's, this was not the case between Schuman and Wright. Their interpretations of the potential of the UN placed them at odds with one another. To Schuman, Wright's gradualism was a source of misapplied trust of the elites, of an inability to go beyond traditional approaches to world organization. Schuman condemned as well the inability of James T. Shotwell and Clark Eichelberger to see beyond a league, which was a thinly veiled attack on Wright, who had worked so closely with those men in the CSOP.

On the other hand, Wright saw in Schuman's position a close adherence to power politics, something Wright abhorred and sought to eliminate from international relations.[18] Surprisingly, so did Schuman, but he was willing to accept and work within the structural framework of *realpolitik.* Wright categorized Schuman as a *machtpolitker* and, although he labeled Schuman's and Morgenthau's work as among the best in the *genre,* it was evident that he fundamentally disagreed with his former student's emphasis.[19]

Perhaps most notable, though, was the key area of agreement in this exchange: the emphasis on the need for individuals to have standing under international law. The implication of this need was not lost on either man, and it was central to their understanding of what was necessary to create an effective world organization. Both saw in the U.S. constitution a model for federalism predicated on the power of the federal government to act on the individual, not just upon the member states. They agreed as well on the need for a strong executive.

Schuman continued his effort to reach the largest possible audience to encourage support for the UN. He maintained an aggressive speaking schedule
and published articles in a variety of journals. Included in this array of articles
was one entitled "Toward The World State" in the *Scientific Monthly*. Schuman
cautioned that science offered two prospects: a "golden age of plenty" or the
immolation of modern civilization.[20] Here, as was the case with so many of his
peers, Schuman's perception of how nuclear weapons would be used was
blighted: it was all or nothing and few considered the possibility of limited use
of nuclear weapons.[21]

In order to reduce the possibility of nuclear immolation, Schuman declared,
the Western state system would have to abandon anarchy for meaningful world
organization. When the separate parts of a community claim prerogatives that
only international law can limit, they will be limited "only insofar as habit, expediency, good faith, or force may dictate obedience," for international law was
comprised of only those customs and contracts that sovereigns found acceptable
to observe. In extreme situations any such restraints would "yield to the im-
peratives of survival."[22]

Schuman provided a syllogism to explain what must be done: unrestrained
national sovereignty was the basis of international anarchy; international anarchy bred power politics; power politics bred war. Therefore, abolishing power
politics would eliminate war, and power politics could be abolished only when
effective world government replaced unlimited national sovereignty and the
anarchy that accompanied it.[23]

But what defined effective world government? Schuman first identified
what would not work. International government could not be achieved through
contracted obligation between nations that clung to the concept of sovereign
equality. Nor could covenants among sovereignties to keep the peace through
collective coercion produce world government. What might work was "an organized authority . . . superior . . . to any other authority in the community."
Such organized authority would have to maintain a "decisive preponderance" or
monopoly of armed power. And that government would have authority over
individuals as well as the component nations or states. "Legislation, administration, and adjudication," wrote Schuman, "are prerequisites of all government
capable of governing. To talk of government in terms of arrangements falling
short of these essentials is to indulge . . . in an exercise in humor, hypocrisy, or
cynicism."[24]

How to achieve such a world government? Peace by conquest was, said
Schuman, impossible in the atomic age. That left peace by choice, and the only
effective choice would be to create a world federation empowered to act on individuals as well as on member states. At the time there were many advocates
(Clarence Streit of the World Federalists was perhaps the most vocal) who
wanted a union of democracies to provide the seed for a wider federal organization. But Schuman opposed an exclusive union of democracies, because the
Bolsheviks were likely to construe it as anti-Soviet, not pro world government.[25]
Stalin's response to Winston Churchill's call for an Anglo-American union in
1946 confirmed Schuman's opinion.

Instead, Schuman looked to the UN to step beyond the limitations of its Charter. Although as a league of sovereignties it did not fit Schuman's definition of a government, he argued that it had the tools to maintain the peace and provide the nurturing environment that might lead to voluntary federalization. The veto in the Security Council was a means of assuring peace, because peace could only be maintained as long as the great powers were in basic agreement.[26] This was a much different assessment of the veto than Quincy Wright had offered.

The Security Council, Schuman continued, must be granted "legislative power in the field of atomic energy" because such power was essential to building a federated world. He opposed conferring control over atomic energy upon the General Assembly because that body clung so tenaciously to the concept of sovereign equality, to an idea of participatory democracy falsely transposed to the relations of states. Democracy, Schuman observed, assumed the equality of individual persons, not states. It was because of the continued obeisance to the concept of sovereign equality that he also opposed the Truman-King-Attlee Plan, for he saw no way to ensure the peaceful use of atomic energy in a world of fully sovereign states left to their own devices. Instead, he accepted the proposal of the Report on the International Control of Atomic Energy of 16 March 1946 that called for an Atomic Development Authority, under direction of the Security Council. The ADA would own and operate all uranium mines and monopolize the technology to make it fissionable.[27]

Schuman was not optimistic about the chances of meaningful cooperation between the superpowers. The rift between United States and the Soviet Union seemed to be widening. Long an element missing in Wright's assessment of world organization, the growing tension between the former allies had for some time been something that Schuman saw as having major implications for an effective world organization. And, as a long-time apologist for the Soviets, he was anxious to combat reflexive anti-communism in the United States, for he had been its victim more than once. He believed that the future would lead to either a convergence of the two competing systems or the ultimate confrontation between them, and he sought vigorously to promote the former.

In his article "Designs For Democracy," Schuman asserted that civilization could survive the atomic age only through Anglo-American-Soviet cooperation. To achieve such cooperation, Schuman believed it was essential to develop mutual tolerance and a "synthesis of opposites" that would ultimately lead to a "global pattern for community life," recognized universally as conducive of democratic values. Such tolerance and synthesis could only be achieved through a trenchant reconsideration of ideological and institutional differences between the two world systems.[28]

Of course, a signal problem in the development of mutual trust between the two competing systems in order to ensure a peaceful world was the perception each had of the other's intent. Both governments pandered to one-dimensional interpretations of complex issues. Schuman believed this was particularly true of those in the West who labeled legitimate Soviet security interests as indicators of aggressive Soviet expansionism. The Soviet people had suffered horribly in the two world wars, not to mention the costs of a convulsive civil war and the subsequent Allied intervention. This, when coupled with Stalin's program of forced collectivization and industrialization, made the Soviet people desperate for peace and security and their foreign policy, wrote Schuman, should be understood as a reflection of those desires. Their fear of further bloodshed and of foreign invasion led to diplomatic intractability but did not represent a desire to rule the world.[29]

Contributing further to Soviet fears was the trend Schuman saw in developing regional systems of security. Schuman believed regional defense programs as they had evolved after the war created dissension between the superpowers and weakened the UN. They also contained the potential to encourage escalated tensions and action-reaction responses to critical situations rather than reasoned solutions.[30] Schuman called for a renewal of the "spirit of Yalta" to restore trust between the two systems and observed that the Soviets had enforced their Yalta agreements until the United States and the United Kingdom had begun to back out of theirs.[31]

The Yalta agreements have, since the ink dried, been the source of heated controversy, and Kennan and Morgenthau provided somewhat different assessments of them. Both "realists" condemned them as overly legalistic, yet both found value in them.

Kennan wrote that from a "practical standpoint" the wartime conferences "were somewhat redundant and led to a certain number of false hopes here and elsewhere." But he insisted that they also "had a distinct value as practical demonstrations of our readiness and eagerness to establish better relations with the Soviet regime . . . ." They were, he concluded, "important for the record."[32]

Morgenthau blamed the Soviets exclusively for violating the agreements and condemned Cordell Hull and Roosevelt for engaging in idealism and legalism when they negotiated with the Soviets. But, like Kennan, Morgenthau saw value in the Yalta Agreements, although it was of a negative sort. Soviet violations led to our rearmament, and for that Morgenthau was grateful. "With the legalistic insistence upon the violations of the Yalta agreement," he wrote, "we could build a bridge between our utopian ideals and the bitter realities of power politics, without giving up the one or disregarding the other."[33]

Schuman's understanding of the "spirit of Yalta" was essential to a peaceful system of international politics. Western rhetoric of the sovereign equality of weak states with powerful ones rang false to Soviet perceptions of their own, as well as Western, security needs. And it was incumbent upon the United States to lead the way to an empowered United Nations.[34] Schuman advocated the adoption of the Baruch Plan (and blasted Gromyko's plan to outlaw atomic weapons) as a starting point to an effective UN, for it would contribute to a limited world government that could exercise global sovereignty in the field of atomic energy.[35]

Morgenthau again led the attack on the concept of a world state. That he did so on the building blocks of Wright, Fleming, and Schuman is a tribute to their understanding of the problems that encompassed organizing world opinion. Morgenthau recognized that the call to a "world state" like the one Wendell

Wilkie issued in 1940 had reached a broad audience. Having faced the terrors of two world wars and the seemingly imminent prospect of a Cold War with great potential to turn hot, people wanted the assurance of peace that world staters said would be theirs if such a system were created. Quincy Wright had reached this conclusion in July of 1917.

The analogy world state advocates used most frequently was to a national society, usually the United States and its adoption of the federal system. That analogy, insisted Morgenthau, was false. "The community of the American people," wrote Morgenthau, "antedated the American state, as a world community must antedate a world state."[36]

Of course, organizing public opinion was at the heart of Wilsonianism, and Fleming, Schuman, and Wright knew very well what it would take to get a world state. They knew, too, that developments in Soviet-American relations were rapidly diminishing the possibilities. Although many people suspected a Cold War was brewing in 1946, events of 1947 dispelled any doubt they might have entertained. The British note of February announcing the end of the empire, the Truman Doctrine of March, the National Security Act of June, all augured a renewed confrontation with the Soviet Union. "Uncle Joe" disappeared almost as quickly as he had been created.

The announcement of the Truman Doctrine in the spring of 1947 led Schuman to conclude that the concept of a bipolar world was now institutional dogma in both the rhetoric and in the actions of the Truman administration. Schuman believed that the doctrine had little to do with the Soviet Union or with the preservation of democracy; instead, he saw it as a means to achieve partisan political goals. It was, he said, a "perfect formula for reelecting Truman . . . and for preventing or curing the next depression by a domestic and foreign policy program painfully reminiscent" of the fascist regimes of the 1930s.[37]

Schuman understood the fundamental difference between the Truman Doctrine and the Wilson Doctrine: whereas Truman's was inflexible and demanded commitment, Wilson's allowed flexible response and did not require commitment. Truman's doctrinal rigidity was the child of Kennan. The language of the doctrine parallels much of the language of the "X" article. When Truman declared that the United States must support free peoples, it was a statement of universalism not unlike Kennan's statement that the nation must meet Soviet force with counter-force. Truman's description of the two ideological camps is consonant with Kennan's. Kennan's detailed account of the life of the "X" article indicates that Secretary of the Navy James Forrestal and Secretary of State George C. Marshall had read and approved it well before Truman's Doctrine was announced on 12 March 1947.[38]

The flexibility in the Wilson Doctrine should have appealed to Kennan and Morgenthau. That it did not is a mystery. They sought to avoid reflexive commitments, and the doctrine allowed for different responses to different situations. Equally mystifying are the policies Morgenthau and Kennan advocated that the U.S. employ toward the Soviet Union. Given their critique of the moralism and legalism of foreign policy analysts with whom they disagreed, it is ironic that their policies during the early period of the Cold War relied on both those characteristics. By comparison, the suggestions of Schuman and Fleming were especially reasonable.

Kennan's Long Telegram of 1946 was the draft, if you will, of his famous "X Article" that appeared in *Foreign Affairs* in June 1947. Both documents present a formula for dealing with the Soviets that would bind diplomats to certain unalterable rules. Deviation from them meant certain failure and negative consequences. This is the hallmark of a legal system.

Kennan's later claim that he was misunderstood when it came to the application of his containment theory does not account for his statement in the Long Telegram that the Soviets were "highly sensitive to logic of force. For this reason it can easily withdraw—and usually does—when strong resistance is encountered at any point."[39] The adversary of the Soviets, then, must possess force and be perceived as ready to use it. In doing so, that adversary will likely meet with success. Morgenthau's dictum that "consistency is the moralist's supreme virtue" is as easily applied to Kennan as it was to Wilson.[40]

From the premise that the Soviets respond to force, Kennan built five cardinal rules for conducting negotiations with and for setting policies toward the Soviets. First is to "apprehend . . . the nature of the movement with which we are dealing." Second, the public must be "educated to the realities of the Russian situation" and to the fact that we have little by way of material investment to protect. Third, U.S. policy must ensure the "health and vigor of our own society." Kennan argued under this rule that "every courageous and incisive measure to solve internal problems of our society, to improve self-confidence, discipline, morale, and community spirit of our own people, is a diplomatic victory over Moscow." Fourth, Americans must formulate a positive image of the world they sought to create so that other countries can easily discern the value of American ways over those of the Soviets. Finally, U.S. citizens must be forever wary about the potential for adopting means that turn us into what we most despise about the enemy.[41]

Kennan prescribed even more direct rules for engagement in an unfinished document entitled *The United States and Russia* that he produced in the winter of 1946 in response to a request from Secretary of State James Byrnes. Kennan insisted, among other rules, that we not "act chummy with them," that we not make "fatuous gestures of goodwill," that we "take up matters on a normal level and insist that Russians take full responsibility for their actions on that level," and that we not "encourage high-level exchanges of views with the Russians unless the initiative comes at least 50 percent from their side."[42] These rules reek of moral judgments and of paternalism and proscribe meaningful negotiations.[43]

Hans Morgenthau had his own rules, nine to be precise. He established four fundamental rules for diplomacy with five corollary rules to the fourth. Morgenthau believed that to be effective, diplomacy "must be divested of the crusading spirit." National interest must govern the objectives of a foreign policy, and it must have adequate power to enforce it. Third, a foreign policy must take into account the perspectives of other nations. His fourth rule was an admonition that nations be willing to compromise on issues that were not vital to them.[44]

The corollaries were designed to facilitate compromise. He argued that a nation should reject "worthless rights for the substance of real advantage." Yet quoting Edmund Burke, Morgenthau also argued that "humanity, reason, and justice"—not legal interpretations—should govern a nation's foreign policy. This is a candid appeal to moralism as the final arbiter of compromise. Given that Woodrow Wilson argued from precisely this basis—that humanity, reason, and justice required the United States to support the League of Nations—it is odd indeed that Morgenthau would be so critical of the "Warrior Priest."

His fifth corollary—the other three are not controversial—is equally obtuse when viewed in the perspective of his criticism of Wilson.[45] "The government," Morgenthau insisted, "is the leader of public opinion, not its slave." No one did more than Wilson to buck popular opinion and lead foreign policy not by polls, but by what he perceived to be reasonable and just policies designed to secure the national interest as well as the greater interest of humanity.[46] One of the most frustrating elements of the "realist" critique is that it allows the "realists" to criticize even those who follow their rules.

Regardless of his flights of fancy concerning sovereignty and a world state, Denna Fleming remained grounded in a realistic approach to U.S.-Soviet relations. This thinking was especially evident in memoranda he wrote to Bernard Baruch.[47] Fleming explained his relationship with Baruch, long-time Wall Street financier and advisor to every president since Wilson, as one in which two men shared a common respect for Wilson, and that Baruch had read Fleming's books on the Wilson years. This led Baruch to contact Fleming during World War II and solicit his opinions on how to organize the world for peace.

Fleming visited Baruch's home in New York on several occasions and wrote position papers for the advisor to President Roosevelt. It was Baruch's intention, according to Fleming, to recommend the Vanderbilt professor as a presidential advisor, but Franklin Roosevelt's death intervened. Instead, Baruch asked Fleming "to join his group as an advisor to the Atomic Energy Section of the State Department" in 1946. At this time, Fleming observed that Baruch shared his fears that U.S. policy was moving the world in the direction of another war, but that he changed his mind in later years, perhaps due to the "wearing effects of the Cold War."[48]

His relationship with Baruch led Fleming to pursue what would be the most important study of his career, a study that would change his professional status in many ways. He began a detailed, exhaustive examination of the state of U.S.-Soviet relations that culminated in the two-volume book *The Cold War and Its Origins,* published in 1961.[49] The book heralded the New Left's revision of cold war historiography and Fleming became one of its gurus.[50] Like Schuman earlier, Fleming would suffer the attention of McCarthyites for his interpretation of the Cold War and U.S. foreign policy.

His memos to Baruch spearheaded Fleming's revisionist interpretation of the Cold War. In a document written soon after victory in Europe, Fleming assessed the prospects for U.S.-Soviet relations. First, he assured Baruch that the

United States needed Soviet aid in concluding the war with Japan. Fleming was certain that the Russians would be willing partners, for they hated "the Japs cordially and we have no reason to believe that they will not do their share, if anything like the working relations of the Roosevelt period can be preserved."[51]

As to the ultimate disposition of the Axis, Fleming urged that they be "crushed" completely. He expressed this desire not out of a sense of revenge, but from the perspective of national interest. Germany and Japan as fascist states were "incompatible with any civilized concept of living." He wrote in terms of the inevitability of battles to the death between democracy and fascism but observed that "no such final struggle between democratic capitalism and communist state socialism is necessary, for both systems maintain that they seek the largest good of society as a whole."[52] There would be, he stated, "sharp competition between the two surviving systems for the favor of mankind, but that emphatically need not mean war."[53] And, in what was his most telling observation, he declared that this world provided room enough for both systems and that the democratic west "need not fear that our way of life cannot prove its validity."

These are conclusions that Kennan arrived at, too, although somewhat later. In the spring of 1948, Kennan lay in Bethesda Hospital. Although being treated for ulcers, his mind was on a series of articles Walter Lippmann wrote attacking Kennan's "X Article." Kennan wrote a "long letter" to Lippmann, never sent, in which the author of containment declared "The Russians don't want to invade anyone. . . . They don't want war of any kind."[54] And, of course, in his famous "Long Telegram" of February 1946, Kennan observed that "we must have courage and self-confidence to cling to our own methods and conceptions of human society" or face the possibility that we become like our enemy.[55]

His memo to Baruch reveals several features of Fleming's design for international organization. As opposed to Quincy Wright and Hans Morgenthau, Fleming did not calculate the reduction of the variables within the world balance of power system as inherently destabilizing. Instead, he foresaw the possibilities for what would later be called "peaceful coexistence." He also believed that neither side was so ideologically rigid that it could not change. Although he stated that the two would not merge, he noted that both were evolving; and he declared that an irreconcilable clash between them was not inevitable.[56]

Fleming professed a faith in his system and its ability to survive and thrive in a world of peaceful competition that many of his contemporaries lacked. Struck by an almost paranoid fear of communism, the policy makers of the day came to accept means that were anathema to the values of the West—covert operations, assassinations, blackmail, and unwarranted military intervention—in order to achieve their ends.

Fleming continued his memo with an assessment of how to approach relations with the Soviet Union. There was no possibility of successful cooperation with the Soviets unless the United States remembered "the long effort of the Western Democracies to isolate and ostracize Red Russia." He would require that we deal with Russia "firmly" and that Russia "trust us as an equal." With what was probably unintended understatement, Fleming then observed that the two policies would be "hard to combine."[57] The Russians could look back on only a few years of hazardous cooperation with the West, but they recalled over twenty years when many Western leaders called for the total destruction of the Bolshevik experiment. Here Fleming anticipated what would become the heart of the revisionist interpretation of the Cold War.

Putting this into the context of national security interests, Fleming explained why the Soviets were so determined to extend and exercise complete control over their sphere of influence. He observed that the League of Nations' early policy of isolating the Soviet Union had generated Soviet mistrust for the West, and Fleming feared that impact was being recreated over the admission of Argentina to the UN.[58] Fleming believed that a few more successful efforts to impose U.S. will in the UN would give those Russians who believed cooperation was impossible the "upper hand."[59] Presumably, they would be inclined to seek the realization of their perceived national interests at almost any cost and scuttle the potential of the UN for achieving compromise.

By way of illustration, Fleming pointed to the experience of Poland. He stated that the West could not insist upon the inclusion of any "real anti-Russian elements" in the new Polish government, because the Russians would never accept them. Poland's powerful neighbor was determined to prevent any future German military adventures through Poland, and the means to that end was to establish and maintain a Polish government friendly to the Soviet Union. And, if this alone proved ineffective in containing the threat of future German expansionism, the Soviets would have the option of "taking over Eastern Germany," and would be doubly assured of doing so if the West engaged the Soviets in a balance of power competition. Rumania and Hungary were subject to the same considerations.[60]

Most of the policies Fleming advocated toward the Soviet Union were constructed in the language of appeasement—a form of negotiation both Morgenthau and Kennan said had been criticized too harshly—and from his recognition of the distribution of power. The West had treated the Soviets harshly: they deserved their rightful place among the powers, and if such status were not recognized, they would seize it anyway.

Underlying it all was the fact that the territory they were to occupy or that was to be contained within their sphere in Eastern Europe was overwhelmingly Slavic. Even though Fleming did not explicitly refer to race or ethnocentrism as a definitive element in the organization of the post-war world, it is clearly implicit in his plans. Just as racial concepts are often the unspoken assumptions of social and political values within a core ideology, so it was with the policy Fleming advocated. That he and other Wilsonians were willing to manipulate the generally held meaning of self-determination or sacrifice it altogether indicates a continued willingness to engage in power politics.

Fleming insisted, though, that the United States continually remind the Soviets at all stages of post-war organization that a coalition had gained victory in the war and that, to be successful, there must be a coalition peace. He did not expect that the Soviets would be able to impose their economic system upon all the countries within their sphere, nor that they would be able to communize

China, but, to ensure that, the West would have to provide appropriate alternatives. What the West must never do, though, would be to "start playing with the remnants of fascism as a counterpoint to communism." Fleming could envision no "more deadly game."[61]

For Fleming, the path to post-war peace was "firm, tenacious cooperation with Soviet Russia."[62] This seemed a reasonable approach from the U.S. perspective, at least unless the Soviets gave cause to believe they were acting in bad faith. Like Kennan, though, nowhere in Fleming's blueprint is consideration of what to do if the Soviets crossed the line of "reasonable" behavior. Nowhere is there a definition of what constitutes "firm dealing" with the Soviets, nor is there any discussion of the means for making the Soviets "trust us as an equal." In this failure of definition, Fleming made common ground with the so-called "realists."

In another memo to Baruch entitled "Whither Russia?" and dated 8 May 1945—V-E Day—Fleming posed the question of whether Russia was determined to conquer "much of Europe and Asia." His answer was that it depended upon the policy of the West. After a lengthy description of the many resources the Soviets possessed—political, ideological, demographic, material, and strategic—Fleming concluded that "[m]ost of what happens in Russia is beyond our control."[63]

Because of that, Fleming argued it would be in the best interest of the West to treat the Russians as partners in the United Nations and other international organizations. He believed such treatment would bring the Russians to see "tangible benefits flow to them from working with us through the United Nations, through the Bretton Woods agreements and many others; they will see the advantages of cooperation and, it is to be hoped, lose some of their brashness."[64] And, presumably, if the Soviets acted irresponsibly in the forums of the UN, world public opinion could be brought to bear against them.

The possibility of co-opting a reluctant partner was not to be discounted until tried, for the alternative as Fleming saw it would be a "most calamitous balance of power arms race . . . which would vitiate most of our own hopes . . . to meet the needs of our people."[65] Much to his disappointment, the effort to cooperate with or co-opt the Soviet Union was never attempted, and he would spend the rest of his career decrying the horrors of the Cold War.

While Fleming cautioned firm yet good faith negotiations with the Soviets, Harry Truman was not inclined to follow such a path. Deciding that he was "tired of babying the Russians" after the December 1945 Moscow meeting of the Council of Foreign Ministers, Truman embarked on a "get tough" policy. That policy would take shape in the form of the Truman Doctrine, the National Security Act of 1947, and a generally confrontational attitude toward the Soviets. Truman's beliefs turned on the assumptions of a bipolar world and monolithic communism.

Among those who had Truman's ear, although filtered by George Marshall and later Dean Acheson, was George Kennan. Far from treating the Soviets as equals, and less confident in his own system than Fleming, Kennan discounted the potential of negotiations. In the "X Article," Kennan called for the "long-term, patient but firm and vigilant containment of Russian expansive tendencies [and] the adroit and vigilant application of counterforce at a series of constantly shifting geographical and political points."

Coupled with his declaration in the Long Telegram that Soviets generally withdraw when faced with counterforce at any point, it is difficult to accept Kennan's claim that he really did not mean what he wrote. The retired diplomat wrote in his memoirs that the "X article" was seriously deficient in that he failed to make clear that he meant "political containment of a political threat."[66] In fact, Kennan found it necessary to apologize for the language of the "Long Telegram" as well. It was unfortunate, he wrote, that it sounded like something the Daughters of the American Revolution would write "designed to arouse the citizenry to the dangers of the Communist conspiracy."[67]

Taken on face value, Kennan and Truman's doctrine was more Wilsonian than Wilson's Doctrine. Wilson declared in 1916 that the United States had an interest in any war anywhere in the world. The word "interest" is critical. Wilson did not imply a vested interest, but an interest that would require investigation. Wilson did not apply force to every point in the world where war was being waged after announcing his doctrine. Instead, he weighed the national interest before committing American force. Kennan's language, which occurs in multiple places, would have the United States respond symmetrically to any Soviet push anywhere. Such a policy requires no examination to place it outside the traditional approach of a realist.

Fred Schuman, like Denna Fleming, counseled a different approach to the Soviets than did the "realists." His arguments in the thirties sought to convince the reader that the only viable solution to the problem of international organization was a social revolution in the West or a political agent that could enforce its will upon the globe. By 1941, Schuman had refined this theme. Although he professed to believe that peace was the only medium in which the common liberal and communist values could survive, and that only a liberal/communist collaboration against fascism could obtain lasting peace, he also believed that he had seen the future and that a "militant social-mindedness" characterized it. The West, he believed, would have to adopt totalitarian means to achieve freedom. He believed that collaboration between Moscow and the West could result in "a further liberalization of communism and a resurgence of liberalism as a living faith, revived and enriched, paradoxically, by Moscow's example."[68] This was the message of the convergency theory that gained credence in certain circles during the 1950s. But, if the West refused to accept Moscow as a partner, Schuman insisted, it would "perish in bloody chaos."[69]

Schuman believed that World War II validated his prediction, but his fears were resurrected with the onset of the Cold War and the Truman Doctrine. His views remained influential within a segment of the community who wrote about and made U.S. policy during the war, not least of whom was Hans Morgenthau.

Morgenthau edited a collection of essays that were published in October 1945 under the title *Peace, Security, and the United Nations*. Schuman's essay, "Regionalism and Spheres of Influence," provided a glimpse into the place that balance of power concepts held in his analysis of international relations as they would be conducted under the Charter of the United Nations.

Schuman insisted that the Charter did not alter "in any fundamental way the traditional concepts of international law and diplomacy," but instead forwarded the high moral principles that had "long been ignored by all realistic governments pursuing national interests."[70] What the Charter did accomplish, according to Schuman, was a tripartite rule of the United States, Great Britain, and the Soviet Union. The principle of unanimity in the Security Council, sustained by the veto, meant "insofar as it functions effectively, the Security Council will be indistinguishable from the superpowers."[71]

It seems that Schuman could not resist the opportunity to tweak Quincy Wright in this paper. Referring to the seemingly endless permutations of cross-references in the Charter regarding regional blocs and spheres, Schuman noted that it "was all quite necessary and quite simple to international lawyers. If you do not understand the cross-references, my old teacher, Quincy Wright, will be able to explain them to you at the drop of a hat without batting an eyelash."[72] But despite the legalism, Schuman approved of the effort at post-war international organization. There would be little hope of peace for his or future generations if the Soviets, the Americans, and the British did not work together.[73]

The postwar era provided Schuman with the opportunity to direct foreign policy issues for a political party. Schuman believed that Henry A. Wallace represented the best hope for the policies essential to world peace. It was with great misgiving that he heard of Truman's dismissal of Wallace in September 1946. It was "*very* bad news," he wrote, "for you, for me, for America, and for the world."[74] Wallace's sacking was confirmation of Schuman's worst fears on two levels: if it was the beginning of a "red bashing" reaction, then his ability to reach a large audience on the lecture circuit might be reduced; and, the possibility of an effective UN was greatly reduced, too. Both fears were realized.

But Schuman, like Fleming, had called for a more moderate approach to U.S.-Soviet relations in the early period of the Cold War, and he had come to the attention of Wallace. Schuman had immediate access to him during the 1948 presidential campaign, and Wallace frequently sought his opinions and advice. The best record of Schuman's activities on behalf of the Progressive Party campaign is Curtis MacDougall's three-volume work *Gideon's Army*. MacDougall refers to Schuman's reputation as a prophet of world events as they transpired in the thirties, and to a diary Schuman kept along with 2,500 words of notes and comments about the events in Philadelphia during the Progressive Party convention.[75]

Schuman's was a voice of reason, coupled with biting wit, among the many chants of extremism at Philadelphia. In a moment of reflection on Truman and Thomas Dewey, the major party candidates, Schuman declared that Wallace was the only businessman and capitalist currently running for president of the United States. To buttress this, he noted that neither Truman nor Dewey had ever met a payroll, run a successful business, or accrued any capital through their business efforts. The irony was that Wallace, who had accomplished all those things, was lampooned as Utopian, impractical, and a Communist stooge. It was this latter image that took hold of the imaginations of many Americans.

The Communists had "infiltrated" the Progressive Party and, along with non-communist socialists, had contributed to what some considered the radicalization of its platform.[76] Among these radical planks was the nationalization of most industry, a policy which Schuman "strongly opposed" from his position on the drafting subcommittee.[77] Schuman gave speeches in which he recommended a gradualist approach toward nationalization, which, he argued, should be accomplished on an individual industry-wide basis according to the merits. Much to Schuman's dismay, the radical proponents of nationalization carried the day.[78]

Schuman was most influential in the creation of the foreign policy plank of the Progressive campaign, which he wrote and defended at the convention. That plank contained the nucleus of Schuman's prescriptions for world order and an endorsement of world government. The opening line declared that enduring world peace could be had only through world law, because anarchy in international relations during the atomic age threatened to destroy not only Western civilization, but also humanity. There was, wrote Schuman, one alternative to the then current system of sovereign states and the wars that it brought: the establishment of a world federal legislature that could create and enforce law upon individuals as well as nation states.

The powers of that legislature would be "limited but adequate" to defend the "general welfare of all mankind."[79] Schuman continued by suggesting that the United Nations could be the basis of "peace through government" if the unity of purpose of the Great Powers was restored. "Since the death of Franklin Roosevelt," he observed, "this principle has been betrayed to a degree which not only paralyzes the United Nations but threatens the world with another war in which there can be no victors and few survivors."[80]

There was little debate over these passages of the platform, but what followed caused Wallace some uneasiness. Schuman blamed the USSR and the United States equally for the current state of affairs between them and the growing tensions in the world. He declared that U.S. bipartisan policy makers had sacrificed the nation's interests to "monopolistic profits" and military power, and that the Soviet leaders had sacrificed peace to national aggrandizement and power politics. Vice-presidential candidate Glen Taylor vigorously opposed the inclusion of such a statement in that he believed responsibility for the Cold War was exclusively the result of U.S. policies. The wording was changed to read "Responsibility for ending the tragic prospect of war is a joint responsibility of the Soviet Union and the United States," and the amendment was adopted.[81]

In a series of letters between Brigadier General T. H. Landon, Deputy Commandant, U.S. Army War College, and Schuman, the foreign policy analyst provided further insight to his perspective. In response to an invitation in 1947 to speak to the students at the War College, Schuman felt obliged to warn the commandant about his opinions before he committed himself to appear. Schuman noted that he tended to "share the views of Henry A. Wallace," that he opposed the Truman Doctrine, was "extremely skeptical" of the Marshall Plan, and had "little sympathy with U.S. diplomatic pressure on behalf of 'democracy' in

Eastern Europe."[82] In order to spare the War College any possible embarrassment, Schuman suggested a "safe" alternate speaker, but noted he would be more than willing to accept the invitation if the general thought it best.

The general thanked Schuman for his "candid" remarks, then proceeded to explain the purpose of the War College in inviting him. The college, he wrote, made an "honest effort" to present varying points of view to its students. Schuman's views were known to the college administration and served as one of the key elements in their extension of an invitation to participate. As well, the administration believed Schuman had established a reputation of being able to defend his views. The general concluded with the observation that Schuman was invited *because* of his views, *because* of his knowledge of Soviet-American relations, and *because* of his ability to express himself in "understandable" terms.[83]

Hans Morgenthau agreed with most of Schuman's criticisms. He, too, deplored the Truman Doctrine for its sentimentalism and crusading nature.[84] He was also a critic of the Marshall Plan. Although not opposed to a wealthy power helping those weaker powers whose support it needed, Morgenthau objected to the trappings of moral principle that draped the European Recovery Program. Aid to Europe was not, insisted Morgenthau, humanitarian in nature. It was "a means to a political end" that should be evaluated solely on the basis of whether it served the national interest.[85]

Schuman continued to be a sought-after participant among the various service related colleges and to enjoy invitations to the War College, even after he had gone on record in opposition to the Truman policies of peace-time conscription, universal military training, and increased appropriations for the military.[86] Schuman believed that, contrary to the proclamations of Truman and Acheson, U.S. policy would do little to contain Communism; instead, he thought U.S. policy would serve the purposes of the enemy, disintegrate the democratic traditions of the United States, and transform the free enterprise system into a "militarist economy."[87] It is to the military's credit that it sought such diverse opinions.

But when Schuman offered his ideas anew after the war, he did so as a branded man. The hearings before the various state and federal committees, the continued uncritical apologies he made for Soviet policies, his fence-riding on Western values and principles, and his unswerving embrace of *machtpolitik,* had taken from him the respect of certain of his professional colleagues.

Even his mentor, Quincy Wright, moved to distance himself from the maverick professor. Writing to Leonard White, Wright praised Schuman as "a teacher and popular writer [who] made introductory courses . . . more interesting to students than anyone ever to have taught them, and who had a capacity to absorb great quantities of material and [write] clearly, even brilliantly, about them." Yet he was not the type Wright favored for permanent faculty. Wright doubted whether Schuman could "ever be outstanding as a research man." "Perhaps," Wright mused, "his research capacity has been interfered with by his tremendous ease in popular writing." But despite the reason, Wright's "prime interest" was to recruit scholars "who can press forward the frontiers of research," qualities he thought absent in "people whose prime ability is teaching and popular writing."[88] He wrote this on the same day that he sent Schuman congratulations on the publication of *Soviet Politics: At Home and Abroad,* which he claimed was "exciting both as to content . . . and presentation."[89]

Schuman's new book ushered in the Cold War and its severe threat to Wright's grand design. Wright had not anticipated this turn of events that so inhibited the cooperation necessary for his planned expansion of international organization. A paradox developed in that the two superpowers were "more independent, powerful, and dangerous than ever" and were the states most capable of thwarting international law and organization. Yet they were also the states whose cooperation was essential to make international law and organization effective. The conflicting coalitions of power that eventually comprised the North Atlantic Treaty Organization (NATO) and the Warsaw Pact so divided the communist and capitalist worlds that they adopted the creed that other states were either for or against their coalition, with no middle ground possible. World order of the type Wright sought was not in sight.

Wright claimed as well that under new conditions of warfare, especially with the advent of airpower, there would be incentives for ambitious rulers to unleash military aggression in the expectation of rapid benefits. Because of this, the role of "balancer in a balance of power world would be extremely expensive and the opportunities for prosperity and progress in such a world would be limited."[90] In this, he shared Morgenthau's estimate that the role of the balancer, a role Great Britain had traditionally played, had disappeared.[91] Wright also expressed fears about the potential for a "garrison state" and what it could do to the freedoms the West valued so highly.

Wright's prescription was to place at the disposal of the United Nations sufficient force to support international law, to include an international airforce and other auxiliary military components. He cited the CSOP studies to suggest that a suitable distribution of air bases under the control of an international government could prevent aggression and maintain justice and world order.[92] Wright believed that the UN should also have its own security force and a monopoly over nuclear research and production of nuclear capabilities. In the Fifth Report of the CSOP he declared that the current UN machinery was sufficient to control atomic energy, to eliminate weapons of mass destruction, and to reduce conventional weapons. Security, he concluded, was attainable within the framework of the UN.[93]

Wright's prescription for the control of nuclear energy took shape when he and the CSOP subscribed to the Baruch Plan, which sought to establish international control and verification of nuclear development. But Wright warned that, even though Baruch's plan to control atomic energy was "an excellent plan," still "it was 'made in America,' and because of that the Soviets did not accept it."[94] Due to the continued gulf between the former allies, the need for the UN to control such extraordinary weapons and technology became even more immediate, but as Wright would later note in reference to the Baruch Plan, states are "extremely reluctant to limit in any way their industrial development."[95]

There had been much debate, both during and after the San Francisco Conference, surrounding the issue of the veto power of the permanent members of
the Security Council, a power some analysts thought prevented the UN from
being effective. Wright and the CSOP subscribed to the interpretation that the
veto did restrict UN action, but they were convinced that amending the Charter
to rid it of the veto was impossible in the near future. They did not perceive this
as an insurmountable obstacle, though, because they believed that amendment of
the veto power was not necessary for the development of an effective program
of security and disarmament.[96] Still, the veto power was something Wright anx-
iously sought to eliminate.[97]

The final recommendations of the CSOP were that the UN be authorized to
form an adequate armed force of its own, to include an international airforce,
strategic bases and control of narrow waterways; and the authority to regulate
arms, including nuclear weapons, other weapons of mass destruction, and conventional weapons. The CSOP also recommended adoption of the Nuremberg
Charter as the basis of an international criminal code and elimination of the
veto.[98] The CSOP concluded that the UN was capable of meeting its task and
called for renewed U.S. commitment to the UN and for world public opinion to
support it. They closed with a challenge that every effort short of appeasement
should be made to reach an overall agreement with the Soviet Union.[99]

Of course their assumption was that either the UN be granted a monopoly
over airpower or else all nations must agree to limit their airpower to less than
the UN force. There was no precedent for such a system and certainly no means
to coerce the great powers to accept such limitation. Wright and the CSOP saw
only a strategic use for nuclear weapons when in theory, they could be used tac-
tically and in a limited capacity, a possibility Wright and the CSOP either rejected or that escaped their analysis and thus limited their vision of future war to
nuclear annihilation. Wright and the CSOP relied solely on the persuasive
power of reason to accomplish their agenda, a fact that explains in part why their
suggestions were not always implemented. Other parties could claim just as
reasonably that nuclear weapons could be used without the destruction of the
world or, even more compellingly, that their mere existence and threat of use
served to protect the peace.

Missing from all their prescriptions, procedural and structural, is any emphasis on the position of the executive within the UN. This was unusual, for
Wright was a Wilsonian who emphasized the need for a strong executive. It was
a constant in his approach to government, as demonstrated in his first book, his
opposition to the Bricker Amendment's attack on executive power, and his interpretation that the president possessed the constitutional power to deploy and use
military force.[100] This omission is evident throughout the recommendations of
the CSOP and in all of Wright's examinations of the UN. Perhaps they feared
that charismatic leadership was necessary to create a strong executive in a world
body. Or perhaps they thought the public was not prepared to accept such a
strong world executive. Or perhaps they knew the great powers would object to
it. For whatever reason, they chose to ignore this cornerstone of Wilsonianism.

It was the Cold War, though, more than any other complex of events or institutional weaknesses that seemed to limit the potential of the UN. Wright greatly feared that what he perceived as the coming bipolar distribution of power was inherently unstable and placed the world in great jeopardy of yet another war. Wright noted in 1946 that, because Britain and France were still basically independent, because China had the potential to engage in power politics, and because some of the less powerful states had resisted alliance to either superpower, the world was not yet bipolar. Nonetheless, conditions were "less favorable to a stable equilibrium" than they had been in recent history.[101]

Wright believed that to remedy this situation there would have to be either the addition of several other superpowers to offset the Soviet Union and the United States, or world organization would have to be empowered to prevent catastrophe. As he wrote in the *Yale Law Journal,* "In principle it is difficult to see how an equilibrium between only two centers of power can be stable. In general, the stability of a political equilibrium increases with the number of relatively equal states contributing to that equilibrium."[102]

Although the Security Council in theory created five nearly equal legal powers within the UN structure, in practice those powers differed greatly in their ability to influence world peace. And there was the ever present threat that the superpowers could act outside the agency of the UN, as their military and economic strength could not be contained should they choose to use either for unilateral purposes. Wright's prescriptions would have created a world organization either superior or equal in military capability to even the greatest superpower. Such an organization could either effectively address the challenge if one or another great power attempted to breach international law on its own or act as the traditional stabilizing influence when the balance of power was asynchronous. This was something both the world public and the great powers were unwilling to accept.

This emphasis on coercive power is an interesting development in Wright's thought. He was a man who fervently believed in the power of reason and who had expressed optimism in the ability of humanity to recognize the necessity of world organization without being forced to accept it through imposition. Yet the experience of the League of Nations and the unwillingness of the nation states to bind themselves to international law proved to him that for law to be effective, it must have behind it the power to coerce those who are its objects.[103]

Not only that, but his emphasis on the need to make individuals jurally competent in the international legal system demonstrates that he believed it was impossible to sustain the necessary public opinion for world organization without that organization having full power to coerce the individual as well as the state. He sensed the immediate need to create a strong world organization following the allied victory in Europe, for public opinion in favor of such a world organization would, he believed, rapidly subside after the Axis powers were vanquished. He was right.

NOTES

1. Quincy Wright, "Making the United Nations Work," *Review of Politics* 8 (October 1946): 528.

2. Quincy Wright, "Accomplishments and Expectations of World Organization," *Yale Law Journal LV* (August 1946), as found in Wright, *Problems of Stability and Progress in International Relations,* (Berkeley, CA: University of California Press, 1954), 74-75.

3. *Ibid.,* 76-77.

4. Quincy Wright, "The Nuremberg Trial," *Annals of the American Academy of Political and Social Science* 246 (July 1946): 79-80.

5. Quincy Wright, "The Law of the Nuremberg Trial," *American Journal of International Law* 41 (January 1947): 47.

6. Quincy Wright, *Contemporary International Law: A Balance Sheet* (New York: Random House, 1955, 1961), 24.

7. Hans Morgenthau, *Politics Among Nations: The Struggle for Power and Peace,* second edition (New York: A.A. Knopf, 1954), 259.

8. Denna Fleming, "After Victory What?" *Virginia Quarterly Review* (21 October 1945): 602.

9. Fleming first declared the need to "establish a new layer of government above the National States" and the death of the sovereign national state in "America and the World Crisis," *Vital Speeches* 10 (15 October 1943): 7-8.

10. Fleming, "After Victory What?" 604.

11. *Ibid.,* 603; for aircraft, see Denna Fleming, "Roosevelt and Churchill Confer," *Current History* 1 (October 1941): 116-117; "The Coming World Order, Closed or Free," *The Journal of Politics* 4 (1942): 251; and "Planning For The Post-War World," *Current History* 4 (March 1943): 8

12. Denna Fleming to Bernard Baruch, Memo dated "Sunday Evening," 2, The Denna Fleming Collection, Vanderbilt University.

13. Frederick L. Schuman, "The Dilemma of the Peace-Seekers," *American Political Science Review* 36 (February 1945): 25.

14. *Ibid.,* 24.

15. *Ibid.,* 25.

16. *Ibid.,* 27-28.

17. *Ibid.,* 29-30.

18. Wright document, "The U.N. and the Organization of Peace," 11 November 1942, Box 5, folder 14; Henry Luce to Wright, 22 September 1943, Box 19, folder 6, The Quincy Wright Collection, University of Chicago.

19. Wright to Edwin Smeeth, 13 August 1934, Box 18, folder 12; Wright to Carey B. Joynt, 15 January 1963, Box 4, addenda 1, folder J, (2).

20. Frederick L. Schuman, "Toward The World State," *Scientific Monthly* 63 (July 1946): 5.

21. *Ibid.,* 6.

22. *Ibid.,* 7.

23. *Ibid.,* 8.

24. *Ibid.*

25. *Ibid.,* 11.

26. *Ibid.,* 12.

27. *Ibid.,* 13-16.

28. Frederick L. Schuman, "Designs For Democracy," *Current History* 9 (December 1945): 497.

29. Frederick L. Schuman, "A Diagnosis of the Big Three Problem," *New York Times Magazine* (30 June 1946): 6, 43.

30. *Ibid.*, 43.

31. *Ibid.*, 44.

32. George F. Kennan, *American Diplomacy* (Chicago, IL: University of Chicago Press, 1984), 85-86.

33. Hans Morgenthau, *In Defense of the National Interest: A Critical Examination of American Foreign Policy* (New York: A.A. Knopf, 1954), 112-113.

34. Schuman, "A Diagnosis of the Big Three Problem," 44-45.

35. *Ibid.*, 45.

36. Hans Morgenthau, *Politics Among Nations: The Struggle for Power and Peace*, second edition (New York: A.A. Knopf, 1954), 485.

37. Frederick L. Schuman to Dexter Perkins, 23 April 1947, The Frederick L. Schuman Collection, University of Wyoming.

38. George F. Kennan, *Memoirs, 1925-1950* (New York: Pantheon, 1967): 354-355.

39. *Ibid.*, 557-558.

40. Morgenthau, *In Defense of the National Interest,* 26.

41. Kennan, *Memoirs,* 558-559.

42. *Ibid.*, 291.

43. *Ibid.*, 291-292.

44. Morgenthau, *Politics Among Nations,* 526-529.

45. The other three are "never put yourself in a position from which you cannot retreat without losing face and from which you cannot advance without grave risks"; "Never allow a weak ally to make decisions for you"; and "The armed forces are the instrument of foreign policy, not its master." Morgenthau, *Politics Among Nations,* 530-531.

46. *Ibid.*, 530-32.

47. "Confidential Memo for Mr. Baruch, RELATIONS BETWEEN THE BIG THREE," 13 May 1946, 1-8 and a page entitled "Footnote on the Iron Curtain"; "Memorandum for Mr. Baruch, WHITHER RUSSIA?," 1-3; and a memorandum entitled "IS COMMUNISM 'JUST AS BAD AS FASCISM'?," 1-4; unsigned letter dated simply "Sunday Evening" addressed to "Dear Mr. Baruch," 1-6.

48. Fleming to Jordan A. Schwarz, 29 January 1974.

49. Denna Fleming, *The Cold War and Its Origins, 1917-1960* (Garden City, NY: Doubleday, 1961).

50. Fleming's scholarship was the subject of intense criticism. Despite that, Barton Bernstein told me in a 1990 conversation on the way to West Branch, Iowa, that the New Left was delighted to have a member of the "old school" in their camp.

51. Fleming to Baruch, Memo dated "Sunday evening," 1. Fleming used the term "Japs" consistently, although he did not employ pejoratives for the other enemies.

52. *Ibid.*, 2.

53. *Ibid.*, 3.

54. Kennan, *Memoirs,* 361.

55. *Ibid.*, 559.

56. Fleming to Baruch, Memo dated "Sunday evening," 3.

57. *Ibid.*

58. The Soviet Union opposed Argentina's membership in the United Nations because of its late entry into World War II and because its government was fascist. The United States, on the other hand, sponsored Argentina yet opposed membership for Poland because its government was communist.

59. Fleming to Baruch, Memo dated "Sunday evening," 4.

60. *Ibid.*

61. *Ibid.,* 5.

62. *Ibid.,* 6.

63. Fleming to Baruch, 8 May 1945, 1.

64. *Ibid.,* 2-3.

65. *Ibid.,* 3.

66. Kennan, *Memoirs,* 358.

67. *Ibid.,* 294.

68. Frederuck L. Schuman, "Liberalism and Communism Reconsidered," *Southern Review* 2 (1936): 338.

69. *Ibid.*

70. Hans Morgenthau, ed., *Peace, Security, and the United Nations* (Chicago, IL: University of Chicago Press, 1946), 93-94.

71. *Ibid.,* 99.

72. *Ibid.,* 96.

73. *Ibid.,* 102.

74. Schuman to Roxanna Wells, 20 September 1946.

75. Curtis MacDougall, *Gideon's Army, Volume II: The Decision and the Organization* (New York: Marzani and Munzell, 1965), 557. These notes and the diary are not among the collected Schuman documents at the University of Wyoming.

76. See MacDougall, *Gideon's Army, Volume I,* 248; *Volume II,* 539.

77. MacDougall, *Gideon's Army, Volume II,* 539; 549. Others on the drafting committee included Martin Popper, Louis Adamic, Eslanda Robeson, and Dr. Joseph Johnson.

78. *Ibid.,* 558-559.

79. *Ibid.,* 564.

80. *Ibid.*

81. *Ibid.,* 566, 570.

82. Schuman to Brigadier General T. H. Landon, Deputy Commandant, the National War College, 21 August 1947.

83. Landon to Schuman, 25 August 1947.

84. Morgenthau, *In Defense of the National Interest,* 119.

85. *Ibid.,* 123.

86. Schuman accepted another engagement at the National War College for 13 October 1949 at the request of Rear Admiral George C. Dyer, Deputy Commandant, Schuman to Dyer, 8 September 1949; still another for 2-3 April 1950 at the Air War College at the invitation Major General O. A. Anderson, Commandant, Schuman to Anderson, 15 March 1950.

87. Schuman to Senator Henry Cabot Lodge, Jr., 19 March 1948.

88. Wright to Leonard White, 5 March 1946, Box 23, addenda 1.

89. Wright to Schuman, 5 March 1946, Wright Collection, Box 23, addenda 1.

90. Quincy Wright, "Responsibilities of the United States in the Post-War World," *Free World* 5 (January 1943): 35-41.

91. Morgenthau, *Politics Among Nations,* 328.

92. Quincy Wright, "Aviation and World Politics," *Air Affairs* 1 (September 1946), 104.

93. Quincy Wright, "Security Through the United Nations," *International Conciliation* 432 (June 1947): 426.

94. Quincy Wright, "Constitution Making As Process," *Common Cause* 1 (February 1948): 285.

95. Quincy Wright, *The Role of International Law in the Elimination of War* (New York: Oceana Publications, 1961), 65.

96. *Ibid.,* 432.

97. Wright, "Constitution Making As Process," 286.

98. Wright, *The Role of International Law in the Elimination of War,* 433-447.

99. *Ibid.,* 448.

100. See Wright, *The Control of American Foreign Relations;* on the Bricker Amendment see Wright, "The Economic and Political Conditions of World Stability," *Journal of Economic History* 13 (Fall 1953): 376 and Wright correspondence, 1953, Box 19, file 12; and on executive power see Wright, "Legal Aspects of the Viet-Nam Situation," *American Journal of International Law* 60 (October 1966): 750-769.

101. Quincy Wright, "Accomplishments and Expectations of World Organization," *Yale Law Journal,* 55 (August 1946), as found in Wright, *Problems of Stability and Progress in International Relations* (Berkeley, CA: University of California Press, 1954): 75. He later accepted the bipolar interpretation of the world's power blocs.

102. *Ibid.* For more on the inherent instability of a bipolar system, see, for instance, Wright's essay "Criteria for Judging The Relevance of Researches on the Problems of Peace," *Research for Peace* (Amsterdam: North Holland Publishing Co, 1954): 26.

103. For his belief that the observance of international law was dependent on reason, see Wright, "Criteria for Judging the Relevance of Researches on the Problems of Peace," 24; for his belief that coercion may be necessary see the same article, 33.

6

Wilsonians and the Assumptions of Containment

By 1949, growing hostilities between communist and capitalist countries threatened international peace. After the success of the Chinese Communists in defeating their Nationalist opponents in October of that year, the Truman administration could ill-afford to lose another contest with the international communist conspiracy. A regional security system was in place in Europe, but Asia was up for grabs. When North Korea invaded South Korea in June 1950, the time for timidity was past. Truman would take strong measures to repel the invaders, and he did so following the advice "realist" George Kennan had provided since 1944. The possibility of a World War III now threatened world peace.

The expectations Wright held for the UN had been threatened, too. In a letter to Clark Eichelberger, then the leader of the American Association for the United Nations, Wright lamented a growing realization that the UN was inadequate for its task. Still, he believed that the United Nations was the only nearly universal political forum within which the Soviet Union and the United States could maintain a dialogue about world problems, and as such, it was the only institution capable of providing the nucleus for a "world regime of law." This was the primary reason Wright demanded that the UN be strengthened, first through a "more active and insistent public opinion" and second, through an increase in the UN's "institutional capacity to act effectively."[1]

At the time he wrote the letter, Wright could neither recall many past victories for the UN nor foresee much prospect for UN successes in the immediate future. He saw little chance for the UN to play an effective role in the civil war raging in China. Lingering problems from the Czech coup, the Berlin Crisis, and the contemplation of Western Union, all seemed to deny a meaningful role for the organization.

It was not just the strained relations between the former wartime allies that threatened the new world order. A rapidly expanding technology and the "ever shrinking world" it created also contributed to the same end. Regardless of the centers of power, if sovereign states continued to control weapons of mass destruction like the nuclear bomb and delivery systems like the jet airplane, the threat to world society remained in a system outside the control of international law and organization. He saw the airplane as the technological equal of gunpowder or the printing press in its impact on the human condition.[2] Militarily, he dwelled on the plane's destructive potential and saw it strictly as an offensive weapon; as a civilian he was anxious about its dynamic relation to the shrinking world paradigm to which he and others subscribed.

Especially when the airplane was coupled with the destructive power of the nuclear bomb, Wright had visions of apocalypse that prevented him from seeing any but that scenario in the event of another war.[3] As he stated in his presidential address to the American Political Science Association in 1949, "The race in atomic weapons and armaments of all kinds is on and experience suggests . . . that such a race will eventuate in war. . . . Disaster seems as inevitable as in a Greek tragedy."[4] Wright then called on the association to advocate a more powerful UN.

As Wright contemplated the unfolding political developments of the post-war world, he began to perceive the historical process itself as a threat to world stability. Foreshadowing Alvin Toffler's thesis in *Future Shock*, Wright declared that the vastly augmented pace of history was equally significant to the technological shrinking of the world. To Wright, new scholarship in all fields of study was exercising greater and more rapid impact than ever. In its wake, ancient customs were breaking down, seeds of doubt were cast along with seeds of hope, new debates between radicals and conservatives developed, and new methods and goals evolved jointly with new confusion and strife.

All this and more contributed to a condition of political flux within the foundations of social institutions, and Wright feared that this flux made predictions of the future less than reliable. He feared as well that flux made the education of students more difficult, for teachers could no longer rely on time-tried traditions, nor could they prepare students for a world with which they were unacquainted and could not even discern.[5]

As for world organization, by 1950, nearly one-third of the world population was not represented in the UN, including the populations of China, Tibet, Japan, the two Germanies, and the Koreas. What would be the response of these peoples to a world organization granted the military power to impose its special interpretation of international law on the rest of the world? Given the UN's dependence on individual contributions for budget maintenance, the largest of which came from Western powers, it seemed reasonable to assume that the UN could quite likely be little more than a trumpet of Western imperialism. This fear found expression later in the Bandung Conference of twenty-nine Asian and African states in 1955 and the resultant declaration of the Five Principles of Bandung, which Wright supported. These included: mutual respect for territorial integrity and sovereignty; nonaggression; noninterference in internal affairs of nations; equality of nations and races; and peaceful coexistence.[6]

As early as 1943, Wright observed that Gallup and other polls indicated that people were increasingly sympathetic to the Wilsonian agenda of international organization as the means to secure world peace.[7] But Wright had tempered his optimism with the observation that enthusiasm would wane at war's end. It was therefore imperative for the public in America and the world to be "educated to a more fundamental appreciation" of world organization than that which occurred during and following the First World War.[8]

Of course, some central questions remained, including who would constitute "the public" and what system of world government could the public be educated to support? Who would be qualified to vote in this new world order? Who would hold positions of power and influence? Wright considered himself a democrat, but to him voting was "not the essence of democracy." It was "merely" one method by which public will could be measured. "Democracy," he wrote, "is government by public opinion."[9] And public opinion could be unscrupulously manipulated. He feared that popular voting might lead to despotism and noted that "Despots have frequently risen to power through plebiscites." As a consequence, he believed "suitable safeguards" must surround any voting process.[10]

Wright was also ambiguous about the role of women in the new world order. In a letter to Edward Bernays, father of modern propaganda, Wright stated clearly that differences between men and women dictated their social roles. Although he believed in the principle of equal opportunity in business, professions and politics for women, he also believed that the biological differences of men and women would result in a much lower proportion of women-to-men in politics, in government, in the professions and in business. In his estimation, though, "such functional differentiation should not be the result of legal discrimination; rather, it should be the result of inclination."[11] Although this likely was considered an "enlightened" view in many circles of the day, it betrays his belief that women were biologically inferior to men, at least as far as their capacity to operate in the public sphere was concerned.

These remarks provide continued substantiation of Wright's paternalistic elitism. Surely, no one who understands the nuances of foreign policy and of international relations would seriously advocate that they be conducted under the immediate scrutiny of a direct participatory democracy, but foreign policy is only one part of a united peoples' agenda. Wright demanded an organized world opinion and yet his theories would deny equal standing to its majority. Wright had created for himself something of a dilemma in that he was dependent on an organized world opinion and yet he was unconvinced of the majority's ability to function properly within that opinion.

Perhaps the public's rapid exit from the lane of internationalism, if indeed Wright was correct in believing that the public had traveled in that direction, to that of support for the Cold War policies of the United States, reinforced an underlying fear that the public could be easily misled. Wright's fear of popular democracy was of long standing, at least as far back as his remarks in a 1920 article about the "crudity of Jefferson's pell mell banquet and Jackson's Peggy O'Neill cotillion."[12] Wright noted that American opinion in support of the UN in 1946 had declined precipitously.   Americans now accepted "a bipolar world of power politics, and seemed ready to support any policy designed to give the United States and its allies a military edge over the Soviet Union and its allies," and these were opinions he did not endorse.[13]

This was especially apparent in his opposition to containment theory, but Wright also criticized the position Henry Wallace and his supporters advocated toward Russia in 1948 as borderline appeasement; so the question is what policy did Wright perceive as the best for world peace and for world organization?[14] He wrote "We must keep our powder dry, but we must avoid . . . action which would increase Soviet anxieties."[15]   Much of the reason that underlay his approach of quiet preparedness, of prudence, or of straddling fences, is to be found in his acceptance of convergency theory.

In what might be a classic, although simple, statement of the implications of convergency theory, Wright declared in 1948 that the "evils of both socialism and capitalism are so manifest that the search for . . . mixed economies has proceeded."[16]   He argued for continued adherence to UN procedures and popular education to arrive at a more complex solution than the simple "black and white" solutions that radical socialists or capitalists advocated. Wright predicted in 1956 that in the next twenty years the Soviets would make gains on the United States in military potential. Assuming political stability, he also believed that relaxation with respect to civil liberties and economic opportunities occurring in the Soviet Union might lead to an improvement in Soviet morale. Given these developments, he concluded that the Soviet bloc would decentralize and that cooperative elements should increase.[17]

The key to bringing about such convergence would be to avoid tensions that lead to war. Wright was most concerned that intense competition for resources and for ideological supremacy between the superpowers could well lead to such tensions.   The U.S. policy of containment and the Soviet response to it threatened to destroy the evolution of the UN and that of world organization. Wright was especially anxious about the development of regionalism, because he saw in its post-World War II development the creation of a bipolar system that inherently threatened to upset the peace.

Wright also criticized the growing trend of regional defense strategies in a letter to Walter Lippmann, with whom Wright had an enduring correspondence and friendship. Wright informed Lippmann that he had read his book on U.S. war aims, and agreed with much of it, but thought it "over-emphasize[d] regionalism and under-emphasize[d] universalism in the constitution of a world order which can give reasonable stability."[18] Wright and the CSOP recognized that regional security systems had great potential for disrupting international peace.   That is why they emphasized the subordination of regional security systems to the general international organization in the fifth of their seven-step recommendation to the Dumbarton Oaks Conference. It was obvious, though, that the regional security systems of the post-World War II era were designed to act independently of the UN.[19]

The North Atlantic Treaty Organization (NATO) exacerbated his fears that the UN would not, or could not, regulate regional organizations. Wright believed that the formation of NATO increased tensions in the world and had perhaps contributed to what he believed was the Soviet inspired North Korean invasion of South Korea. He feared as well that the extension of the North Atlantic Pact into a federal union might serve to increase tensions further and perhaps precipitate hostilities.[20] To Wright, the implication was clear: the Soviets perceived NATO as an organization outside the UN, beyond the impact of world opinion, and thus a threat directed at Soviet interests.

Wright feared as well that, in order to be effective, NATO would have to incorporate German forces, something he was unwilling to accept at the time. He believed that the use of German forces would provoke the Soviet Union and that Germany would not cooperate unless it received a *quid pro quo* on the eastern frontier. He observed that dependence on German forces in a defense plan would likely make NATO an instrument for German policy to reunite Germany and recover the eastern provinces from Poland. Because such a development had great potential to cause hostilities, it would be premature to consider incorporating German forces in the NATO structure until Europe and the West had achieved comparable strength with the Soviet Union.[21] After Western strength had been reestablished, he was prepared to support the creation of a neutralized German buffer state as the best solution to the problem Germany posed for the international community. Wright agreed with what he called General Eisenhower's willingness to drop the idea of using German forces for the present, but Wright also entertained the possibility that a situation could develop that required Western German participation in the North Atlantic Pact.[22]

Wright also worried that the United States could find itself in the position of financing the imperial policies of the Netherlands, France, and Great Britain in Asia through financial support to NATO. That is precisely what happened in the case of France and its prosecution of the war in Indochina. The United States found itself supplying the bulk of the funds for that war with no, or insignificant, input to the policies that governed the conduct of the war, because of the perceived need to maintain Western unity.

Wright held that such a policy would prove disastrous for the United States. Asian states might come to believe that the United States had abandoned interest in their security to maintain NATO. Because of this possibility, Wright favored a U.S. policy that retained American influence in Asia, but that was not burdened with the legacy of European imperialism. This would, he believed, be the best policy to prevent the expansion of communism in Asia as well.[23] It may seem somewhat incongruous that Wright should favor an "independent" course for U.S. policy toward Asia, but it was only if the United Nations and international law failed in their obligations.

Wright was not opposed to regionalism *per se*. He opposed regionalism that would be outside the UN umbrella. In what was almost a manifesto, Wright wrote John Foster Dulles, former member of the CSOP and now with the State Department, on the evolution of regionalism. Wright recalled Dulles's report entitled "Peaceful Change," written for the CSOP in April 1941. The future Secretary of State had noted the possibility that a postwar world organization might allow for the development of great regional associations that would be as "exclusive and resistant to change" as any nation.[24]

Wright observed that the UN had given greater scope to regional arrangements than had the League of Nations and that there had been proposals to federate some of these great regions. But he likewise recognized a trend toward the bi-polarization of the allies and wards of the United States against those of the Soviet Union. Because Wright was convinced that in a balance of power system the larger the number of great powers, the more stable the balance, he feared that a bipolar regionalization would eventually produce great instability and weaken the United Nations.[25]

Wright agreed with certain suggestions that Dulles had made in his Detroit address of November 1951, entitled "Can We Stop Russian Imperialism?," especially the proposal for the creation of a "great punishing power of the free nations." Wright observed, though, that in a bipolar world of two competing ideologies, it must be made clear that such a punishing power would be used exclusively in response to unprovoked aggression. The problem he was unable to solve, though, was how to convince the Soviet Union that this was how such a punishing power would be used. The Soviet Union, once such an overwhelming punishing power was created, might perceive it as an offensive threat to the Soviet bloc and take preemptive action.[26]

To avoid that, Wright believed that the UN should exercise sovereign control over the application of the punishing power. The UN could take effective action despite the threat of vetoes, and the diversity of its membership would serve as a brake on the urge to use such force for aggression. What remained to be seen, Wright wrote, was whether the United Nations, in view of the division between "free" countries and the Soviet countries, could be developed sufficiently so that it could control such overwhelming force solely to stop aggression and never to initiate it.[27]

Although his prescriptions demonstrated a genuine concern for Soviet apprehensions, Wright was anything but sympathetic to the Soviet cause. Wright applauded Dulles's suggestion that free nations must embark on a political counteroffensive against the Soviet bloc. Wright also believed that the West should make much ado about the example of Josip Broz Tito, who led Yugoslavia independently of the Kremlin. Tito's Yugoslavia undermined the notion of monolithic Communism and served notice to the subject nations that they might be able to retain communism or socialism or whatever domestic system they wanted after they freed themselves from the Kremlin yoke.

Wright pondered as well whether the United States should adopt as one of its primary foreign policy objectives the dissolution of the Soviet Union. Such dissolution would, he thought, allow for the creation of at least three great regional organizations from the remains of the old empire: the Soviet Union itself, the countries of Eastern Europe, and China.[28]

Wright suggested that if such a breakup occurred, the free world should then contemplate a contemporaneous breakup of the North Atlantic system into three regional arrangements: Western Europe, the Inter-American system, and the British Commonwealth. This would reduce further the danger bi-polarization presented for a world system based on balance of power politics. As a third goal, he suggested that another great regional arrangement in the Near and Middle East might be created through an expansion of the Arab League. Wright concluded that if such regions were organized for their own defense, the political equilibrium of the world might be stabilized. As an added benefit, he thought that through the regional influence in the United Nations, that organization could better assure that dominant 'punishing power' would be used only to answer unprovoked aggression.[29]

Dulles replied tersely that the UN should be relieved of "primary responsibility for the maintenance of international peace and security and looked upon primarily as the 'town meeting of the world'. . . . As things are today, the United Nations professes to be both a universal organization and a security organization and, in fact, it does not do either job adequately because it tries ineffectually to do both."[30]

This must have been a great disappointment for Wright, who likely hoped that Dulles would remain sympathetic to the internationalist cause. Wright responded that "I should be afraid that a town meeting of the world unrelated to power to give affect to opinion would become irresponsible, diffuse, and uninteresting. The world press and world interest would hardly continue paying attention to such an organization."[31]

Although Wright continued to express his views in correspondence to Dulles, the letter of 6 February 1952 was the last substantive reply from Dulles. The timbre of these letters indicates that, although Wright was critical of Dulles' tactics, he was to a degree sympathetic with the cause of the cold warriors.[32] Wright's opposition to the Soviet regime was such that, although his commitment to the UN and international law prevented his outright endorsement of U.S. policy toward the Soviet Union, he was in the camp of the cold warriors.

In the letter to Dulles, Wright continued to assert his belief that a bipolar world was inherently unstable and that regionalization as it had transpired since World War II was a deterrent to an effective UN. He feared that regional groupings outside the organization of the UN (or if within it under Articles 51 and 52, then still wielding nearly complete autonomy) might disregard international law, and Wright believed such regional organizations allowed for what was essentially unilateral intervention. He did not address the fact that it was the failure of the UN, especially the Security Council, to act effectively that had led to the creation of NATO, a regional and virtually autonomous organization.

Denna Fleming shared Wright's disillusionment over the UN's few accomplishments and found much the same causes to blame for the failures. Fleming believed that the potential for continued cooperation between the United States and the Soviets was shattered after the first use of the nuclear bomb: that act "completely transformed" their relative power relationship. A strong Anglo-American diplomatic campaign in the Balkans and the complete deadlock in the London Council of Foreign Ministers in September 1945 followed the introduction of the atomic age. The resultant antagonisms, thought Fleming, led the UN to be "a battleground between giant governments unable to make peace."[33] This was precisely what Schuman had predicted in the absence of a strong alliance between the major powers and Fleming perceived its results: stalemate in the UN.

Although Fleming blamed both the USSR and the United States for the failure of the UN to organize an effective peace, his criticisms of the United States were much harsher. He observed that the Soviets successfully led the General Assembly to condemn U.S. propaganda as too inflammatory in a resolution of 17 November 1947 that he thought validated charges that the United States had engaged in "warmongering." He also noted that U.S. policy toward the Berlin Crisis had allowed the UN to assume "a mediating personality," but that it was ineffectual. And, he asserted, when the United States feared Soviet involvement in the enforcement of UN resolutions, it blocked them.[34]

At the end of the decade, Fred Schuman also viewed the UN as largely unfulfilled, but he was more concerned with defending himself against resurrected ghosts of long ago and some of more recent creation. An article entitled "The Devil and Jimmy Byrnes," which was a long review of Byrnes' book *Speaking Frankly,* caused Schuman much difficulty. A professor from Drake University in Des Moines, Iowa complained to Schuman that a known "fellow traveller" distributed the article at a United Nations Conference held at Drake. Coupled with the fact that *Soviet Russia Today,* which the professor identified as a "communist front publication," published the article, both he and his students had been embarrassed. Wrote the irate professor: "We have used your text on *International Politics* for quite awhile . . . . We also have made liberal use of your more recent books on American-Soviet Relations . . . . but I will find it difficult to further use your materials unless you can explain or denounce the use of your material at this time by agencies which we consider dangerous to our safety."[35]

Even more difficult following the "furor" over this article was his relationship with Dr. James Phinney Baxter III, president of Williams College, and the trustees. George Sokolsky took Schuman's article to task in his column for the *New York Evening Post,* citing a few passages out of context to provoke readers. Schuman received more than one letter from Williams College alumni who opposed his interpretation of U.S. foreign policy, the most moderate of which suggested that he seek psychiatric treatment.[36] The trustees of the college seriously considered relieving Schuman of his duties.[37]

In answer to his critics, Schuman attempted to demonstrate the bankruptcy of U.S. policy. In a letter to the *New York Sun,* he provided a disclaimer for the college while insisting that its students, faculty, and administration recognized his right to express his opinions. He then attacked the Truman administration and declared that he, Schuman, had been more consistently opposed to the extension of Soviet power and communism than had Sokolsky. Schuman asserted that the actual result of Truman administration policies had been to promote communism throughout the world. And aware of that result, of what Schuman called the "failure of the Byrnes-Bevin program, the debacle of the Truman Doctrine, and the impending bankruptcy of the Marshall Plan," the men who called the shots now advocated war as the means to eliminate the "Red Menace."[38] Schuman may not have been too far off the mark.

More important to his defense, he demonstrated that nowhere in his speech did he mention his affiliation with Williams College, which had been one of Sokolsky's principle charges. This revelation prompted one alumnus who disagreed with Schuman's views to write Sokolsky and chastise him for putting Schuman "in a false light in this regard," and to apologize to both Schuman and Baxter.[39]

After another public address, Schuman found himself once again the focus of criticism on and off campus. Schuman's remarks at the Cultural and Scientific Convention for World Peace held in New York in March 1949, brought him to the attention of the press, and *Time* magazine published an article entitled "Tumult at the Waldorf" that characterized Schuman's comments as those of a fellow-traveler.[40] Once again he was at odds with the Williams trustees over whether he had absolved the college from sharing his views.

In his remarks to the conferees, Schuman repeated his earlier charge that both superpowers shared responsibility for the Cold War. *Time* characterized this as a "very tentative" suggestion. When Schuman noted that some in the United States wanted war with Russia, he insisted that they were "few in number and without influence." *Time* did not report that phrase. And when a Mr. Fedayeev declared that war was the product of capitalist conspiracies, *Time* reported that Schuman agreed completely. Schuman contended that he had said that war was the inevitable consequence of "international anarchy, power politics, and mutual fear and suspicion," not just capitalist conspiracies.[41]

The speech came to the attention of the Williams College trustees, some of whom demanded Schuman's resignation. In a letter to President Baxter, Schuman admitted his negligence in not absolving the college from responsibility for his remarks and apologized for the fact that the printed program and the press releases both identified him as a professor at Williams. But he went on to say "no one in his right mind ever supposes that I am speaking for the College."[42] Baxter must have agreed, for Schuman remained with the College. But he would be tested again, and very shortly.

As the new decade opened, the prospect of defeat in the Cold War weighed heavily on the Truman administration. The National Security Council had been preparing a policy statement to address what many analysts thought to be the bleak, even desperate, situation in which the nation found itself in 1950. NSC-68 arrived just in time for Truman to consider its recommendations in response to the North Korean invasion of South Korea on 25 June 1950. The president would use the Security Council of the UN to condemn North Korean aggression and to pass a series of resolutions authorizing a multinational UN force to repel the invaders.

The subsequent Korean Conflict would serve to focus both the internationalists and their "realist" critics. Kennan wrote that it was "clear to me from the start that we would have to react with all necessary force to repel this attack and to expel the North Korean forces from the southern half of the peninsula." But he was equally clear that the goal should be only to repel and expel, not to unite the Koreas.[43] He blamed the expansion of the war goals to include unification, "rollback" if you will, on two diametrically opposite groups: "right-wing Republican circles on the Hill" and "wide-eyed enthusiasts for the UN." He reserved special criticism for the latter, stating that they, "like so many other idealists, often promoted with the best of motives causes which ultimately only added to, instead of subtracting from, the total volume of violence taking place in the affairs of nations."[44]

Morgenthau was less direct in his support of the Korean policy as it was initially implemented, but vehement in his critique of the administration's abdication of initiative to General Douglas MacArthur and his pursuit of victory. Morgenthau declared that the record was clear that MacArthur had stayed within the limits of his instructions, but that the administration had been "timid" in executing its policy, while the general had "energetically" pursued his. The administration had backed down in the face of a popular general and an influential minority and therefore only "half-heartedly and inconsistently" pursued the policies MacArthur had made "almost inevitable."[45] For Morgenthau, though, the Korean War was an abnegation of fact. Korea had been under imperial attention for centuries and nothing we could do, short of permanent occupation, was likely to alter that fact.[46]

In a polemic that almost defied belief, Morgenthau attacked the administration for, of all things, lying to the public.[47] Expressions of moral indignation from a man who cited Machiavelli's rules as a model for the conduct of diplomacy were disingenuous at best. Even more ironic is the fact that Morgenthau declared that the "great presidents of the United States have been the leaders and educators of the American people," and included Woodrow Wilson, previously his favorite whipping boy, among those great leaders.[48]

The Wilsonians generally supported American intervention in Korea. Although Wright sought an expanded role, Fleming and Schuman did not want to go beyond the goal of repelling the invaders. In this, as in so many other matters, Fleming, Schuman, Wright, Kennan, and Morgenthau found themselves sharing much in common regarding their recommendations for U.S. policy toward Korea.

Schuman's opinions regarding Korea were expressed in his defense against charges that he was a Communist sympathizer. This test came at the hands of William Loeb, publisher of the *Manchester Union*. Loeb's reputation as a red-baiting, radical conservative is well-established. Loeb wrote an unsolicited letter to President Baxter on 16 October 1950 with a twenty-one page report purporting to detail Schuman's connections to organized Communism in the United States appended to it. The basis of the report was the Dies Committee hearings, a book by Eugene Lyon entitled *The Red Decade,* and Schuman's own work, *Soviet Politics: At Home and Abroad.* [49]

Schuman responded with a seven-page letter to Baxter, refuting the charges against him in detail. He demonstrated that he had taken strong stands against Soviet actions in the past, including a public appeal in the 10 December 1939 *New York Times* for U.S. aid to Finland in its war with the USSR. He observed that he had urged public support of the United States and the UN in Korea to check Communist aggression in the 29 June 1950 *North Adams Transcript* and the 30 June 1950 *Berkshire Evening Eagle*. He also insisted that the excerpts from his book were taken out of context and that one could find in the same book many references to the failings of the Soviet Union in domestic and foreign policies.[50]

Perhaps as the result of the continued harassment he received, Schuman exercised greater caution with regards to his membership in certain organizations. In his letter to President Baxter, Schuman observed that he had been a member of the Committee for the Protection of the Foreign Born and insisted that it was not and never had been a "communist front" organization, nor had the Communist Party USA sponsored it. The Dies Committee had labeled it a subversive organization in 1940, explained Schuman, because it had successfully opposed a series of anti-alien bills which Martin Dies, Josef Starnes, and Senator Reynolds had sponsored. Among the committee's members and sponsors were Harry Elmer Barnes, Ernest Hemingway (two names unlikely to ease congressional fears about the nature of the committee), President Roosevelt, Cordell Hull, Harold Ickes, Justice Frank Murphy, Fiorello LaGuardia, and many other popular officials.[51]

Schuman resigned from the organization on 25 June 1951 with "reluctance and regret," for he had long defended the committee from charges that it was a Communist front organization. And, Schuman insisted, he remained convinced that when he defended it, it was not a Communist front organization. But that had now changed as the result of a propaganda pamphlet he had received from Prague that contained passages of an address that the co-chairman, the Reverend John W. Darr, Jr., delivered at the 21-26 February Berlin meeting of the World Council of Peace.[52] Schuman observed that he did not agree with the committee's endorsement of the "fantastically false Communist version of the Korean War and of American Foreign Policy." Wrote Schuman, "I have never knowingly belonged to or sponsored, and I do not now choose to belong to or sponsor, any organization whose leaders or officers adopt the Communist position on public questions in any context in which that position is demonstrably at variance with established facts."[53]

Schuman characterized his general approach to world problems as "a power politics-national interest-balance-of-power approach, comparable in many respects to that of Hans J. Morgenthau and George F. Kennan."[54] In an article entitled "Cold War's End" that was published just one week before the armistice was signed in Korea on 27 June 1953, Schuman declared that the problems of power politics between sovereignties could be dealt with by fighting or bargaining—nothing else. And although, according to Schuman, a few people in the United States called for meaningful negotiations, including Denna Fleming, George F. Kennan, and Hans J. Morgenthau, U.S. skepticism about negotiating prevailed, and was paralleled by the "Byzantine obstructionism of Stalinist diplomacy." Both sides had long "regarded diplomacy as a trap." Schuman believed, though, that no one could achieve victory through fighting, a conclusion that he said everyone, "whether sober with responsibility or drunk with power," shared. Therefore, he reasoned, the United States and the USSR must eventually negotiate.[55]

Preliminary to such negotiations, Schuman called on the United States to repudiate the Wilsonian basis for diplomatic recognition and accept the People's Republic of China as a member of the international community. He urged both sides to negotiate the steps necessary for a unified, neutral Germany, and said that for now they must work to maintain the balance of power in a sovereign system of states.[56] Such negotiations, he predicted, could lead the way to an era of peace and perhaps "a reformation of a strengthened United Nations in the direction of limited world government."[57] Much of his optimism that the Cold War would end in negotiation was based on his belief World War III was unlikely in the wake of Korea because neither side could convince itself that it had the "decisive margin of superiority" necessary for victory in the nuclear age.[58]

For Wright, a defining moment in UN history came as a result of the Korean Conflict. Wright saw the Uniting for Peace Resolution, which was passed on 3 November 1950 during the Korean War after the Soviets had returned to the Security Council, as a sign that the veto-bound Security Council might indeed be by-passed in the future. The resolution provided an alternative procedure in the event of a stalemated Security Council. In that event, the General Assembly could make recommendations on any situation that threatened the peace if a majority of the Assembly decided the Security Council would be unable to function.[59] Here was a direct attack on the principle of unanimity that, in his opinion, had weakened the Security Council.

Wright claimed that the Uniting for Peace Resolution allowed for effective UN action whether the great powers were united or not. He observed that unanimity was not one of the principles of the Charter, nor was it essential to the function of other organs of the UN. Members had, after all, developed viable alternative methods to accomplish UN tasks "when the Security Council veto stood in the way of achieving the purposes and . . . principles set forth in the Charter."[60]

Wright believed that U.S. intervention in Korea was legal in that it was UN sanctioned. And because the UN sponsored the intervention, it must succeed, for if it did not, the organization could face destruction. Wright told Clark Eichelberger that to withdraw from and abandon the Koreans could destroy the UN. He looked to the failures of the League of Nations in Manchuria and Ethiopia as evidence that an international organization that fails to accomplish its goals jeopardizes its credibility. Wright emphasized that "We must insist upon carrying out United Nations resolutions concerning Korean unification, elections and rehabilitation."[61]

Wright then recommended that an impartial UN commission should implement elections and rehabilitation in Korea, and that the members of the commission could include Chinese Communists and/or Soviet representatives. A multilateral withdrawal of troops should take place with a guarantee that they would not return. UN commissioners were to be allowed to function freely. Wright believed the possibility of such guarantees was probable due to the proximity of UN air and naval forces in Japan and the surrounding area that would offset the proximity of Communist Chinese forces in Manchuria.[62] That he believed this after the Chinese "volunteers" had attacked *en masse* indicates a deep misunderstanding of Chinese fears.

The Korean intervention brought as well increased pressure on internationalists to address the situation of Chinese representation in the UN. Wright examined this issue in a December 1950 letter to Eichelberger. Wright was highly critical of the non-recognition policy of the United States, of the leadership of the Republican Party, of General MacArthur, and of Senator Joseph McCarthy, all of whom Wright believed followed a course doomed to failure.

Instead of pursuing a Wilsonian policy of non-recognition of a morally distasteful government, the United States should, in Wright's estimation, accept the Chinese Communist government in Peking as the *de facto* government and the government entitled to represent China in the UN. As a *quid pro quo* for the voluntary removal of Chinese forces from Korea, Wright was willing to admit the Communist government to the United Nations, recognize Formosa as a part of China and allow the Communist government to occupy it, and to withdraw all support from the Nationalists.[63] George Kennan agreed. There was, he wrote, "no fundamental objection from the standpoint of U.S. interest" to the seating of the People's Republic of China in the United Nations.[64]

Then, in a passage that reveals Wright's strategic grasp of the geopolitics of the day and that furthered his idea of possible friction within the "monolithic" communist region that he had referred to in his letter to Dulles, Wright emphasized again the potential for a rift in Sino-Soviet relations. He may have subscribed to the bipolar model of the world, but he knew that Moscow could not direct every policy within its "sphere." He wrote that, aside from the need to support such a position for the People's Republic of China in the United Nations, there existed a "purely political" reason: that failure to do so would serve the cause of the Kremlin policy makers.

Wright believed that, because Soviet officials were aware of the potential for discord between Communist China and the Soviet Union over Manchuria, Mongolia, Sinkiang, Tibet, and other areas of historic dispute between the two countries, the Soviets had surreptitiously fostered the U.S. led movement to prevent recognition of the PRC. He also thought it possible that the Soviets wished to "divert Western military force to a hopeless struggle in China in order to free [Soviet] hands for taking over Western Europe."[65] Soviet imperialism, in Wright's view, might provide the mechanism to divide the Communist world. In retrospect, this was a remarkably accurate foresight.[66] Again, it was a conclusion that Kennan shared. The issue of admitting the People's Republic of China to the UN revealed to Kennan a "serious difference of policy between the Soviet and Chinese communist governments."[67]

His concluding remarks to Eichelberger also revealed Wright's realistic approach to world organization. As an analogy, he offered the "bribe" paid to Franco after the Allied landing in North Africa to justify dealing with ideological enemies.[68] This was a policy many liberals had criticized because of

Franco's collusion with Hitler and Mussolini. Nonetheless, Wright observed that the policy had worked well in 1943 and declared that had we first negotiated with the People's Republic of China, which represented the most serious threat to a successful operation, before initiating the operation in Korea we might have avoided Chinese entrance into the war. Wright laid the blame for this failure on what he labeled "the unthinking opposition in this country to everything Communist" and the actions of the Senate in the winter of 1949.

Those mistakes now came to haunt the United States, and Wright believed that everything possible must be done to rectify the situation through the United Nations.[69] Wright maintained that "implementation of collective security is of the utmost importance but that in the present state of the world it implies that a legalistic position of operating against aggressors must always be accompanied by a realistic political recognition of the actual power position."[70] As much as he abhorred power politics, he remained aware of the limitations of international law within a system in which just such politics prevailed.

Fleming condemned U.S. policy as hypocritical when it could support UN membership for Franco's repressive regime in Spain but oppose membership for the People's Republic of China because it was a dictatorship. And although he believed intervention in Korea was legally justifiable, he perceived in the U.S. response to "totalitarian" aggression a growing reflexiveness. "No principle," he wrote, "is more fixed in the American mind than that appeasement of totalitarian aggression does not pay."[71] He had perceived the indelible mark of the "Munich Syndrome" upon U.S. policy makers. That concept, he argued, led to the tragic mistake of crossing the 38th parallel and of branding the People's Republic of China an aggressor, an act that prolonged the war.[72] The example of Fleming contradicts Kennan's assertion that UN advocates and "idealists" supported expanded war efforts.

As well, Fleming feared that U.S. policy in Europe might allow the Eastern world to dominate civilization. In a letter to a former student, Ching-ling Chao, Fleming declared that current U.S. policy threatened to create a "greater disaster" in Europe, one which will destroy Western civilization . . . . I have said repeatedly that if this happens the Orientals, whom we cannot destroy, are likely to inherit the earth."[73]

Together with the total lack of sensitivity for his audience, who was, after all, "Oriental," Fleming demonstrated a sort of monolithic approach to the concept of race, the assumptions of which were without substantiation. Of course, if the West could destroy itself, it could destroy the East. This escaped him. It was a visceral racial concept of the ability of Asians to breed that must have informed Fleming's opinion. As well, he assumed that Asians, and people of color in general, would act in unison to achieve shared goals.[74] Did the experience of World War II and the Japanese treatment of other Asians in their co-prosperity sphere support such a concept? Did Asians even think of one-another as members of some over-arching group?

Another of Fleming's fears was that the UN might become an organization to protect the "free" world from the "totalitarian" threat. He, like Wright, saw value in the Uniting for Peace Resolution of 3 November 1950, but he also recognized that the UN General Assembly did not possess sufficient means to enforce its resolutions. And, like Schuman, he believed that the veto power created unanimity of purpose, for the veto mechanism made the UN "an instrument of conciliation and compromise rather than one of coercion."[75] He concluded that to assume that the USSR alone had prevented the success of the UN would assure its collapse. The UN was, wrote Fleming, "our only hope of averting a permanently divided world, with the odds heavily in favor of a final struggle for world domination between the two sides." And he found little solace in having "the law always on our side" if the result was the destruction of the world.[76]

By 1951, Fleming was convinced that the real threat to U.S. security was not the Soviet Union, but those who claimed it was, a message Schuman had broadcast for several years. Fleming found particularly offensive efforts like those of the editors of *Collier's* to incite passions when a more reasoned discourse would better serve the cause of peace. *Collier's* had enlisted the talents of many influential journalists, commentators, and analysts to write an issue length scenario of "Russia's Defeat and Occupation, 1952-1960." The account came replete with details of nuclear devastation in both the U.S. and the USSR, and a cover depiction of a member of the U.S. Military Police with his bayonet thrust at a map of the USSR.

Fleming warned that the effect of one type of propaganda on the other was symbiotic, that *Collier's* "feeds the Soviet propaganda machine." And he asked his readers to consider the following syllogistic relationship: that because out of World War I the West encountered communism in Russia, out of World War II it encountered communism in China, what would be the odds that World War III would spread democratic capitalism?[77] American values, he observed, could only be preserved through the "energetic pursuit" of peace and prevention of war, both of which seemed to entail in Fleming's mind a neo-isolationism. But the methods U.S. policy makers had adopted to fight the Cold War were threatening to destroy the values that they sought to save.[78] Here, too, Fleming, Kennan, and Morgenthau agreed that the crusading nature of American Cold Warriors and their mouthpieces was inflicting untold harm upon the nation.

Fleming believed there were three likely alternative endings to the Cold War: a stable balance of power; a Soviet initiated preventive war; or a U.S. initiated war of liberation.[79] None was correct. He believed that in bipolar political systems the hegemons always confronted one another in a fight to the death. Fleming observed that "if the history of the past has any clear lessons" the world was headed toward "a war to the death between two giant powers . . . fighting with atomic missiles and gigantic V-2 rockets."[80]

Fleming continued his critique with an attack on Dean Acheson's seven-point plan for coexistence. It was a plan, noted Fleming, which could only be achieved through armed conflict, for the USSR would not, at least in the foreseeable future, abandon Eastern Europe without resort to arms, an estimation Schuman shared. Acheson's policy to negotiate only after the United States achieved a dominant and superior position was, for Fleming, disingenuous in that dominant and superior powers do not negotiate, they dictate.[81] U.S.

officials, he wrote, should stop seeing their Soviet counterparts in starkly evil terms, for it made compromise that much more difficult.[82]   And he criticized the growing trend in U.S. policy toward subversive warfare aimed at countries with which the United States was not at war.[83]

In conclusion, he voiced his fear that such "officially sanctioned" articles as the one in *Collier's* were designed solely to provoke. Fleming believed that it was representative of a flaw in the American character: the belief that compromise was unacceptable and that the world could not exist "half slave and half free."[84] He took hope in the knowledge that both sides knew neither could decisively defeat the other, knowledge that might prevent the arms race from running its natural course. But to hedge his bet he called on the Allies (whom, he asserted, believed the United States to be a greater threat to peace than the Soviets) to deny the United States use of their air bases.[85] Without such a change in course, Fleming believed that only two to three years remained before the inevitable explosion, one that would destroy democracy. Unlike his assessment in 1946 for Baruch, Fleming was no longer optimistic about the possibilities of peaceful coexistence between two hostile ideologies.

Following a visit with Fleming at Vanderbilt, Wright asked him to produce an article based on twenty-five assumptions that Fleming attributed to U.S. policy as it developed from 1945-1952.[86] In "How Can We Secure Dependable Allies?," Fleming provided a litany of how the U.S. bludgeoned countries into alliances with it following World War II and the outbreak of the Cold War. Fleming believed this was partly the reason for allied breaks with U.S. attempts to push policies in the UN regarding new members and NATO command of UN forces in 1951. He reiterated his belief that most allied states and their peoples believed that the USSR was not as great a threat as the United States portrayed it to be. In fact, he asserted that most U.S. allies believed its huge expenditures on arms and its insistence that they follow suit was unproductive and reduced their standards of living. He concluded that U.S. "rashness and impatience are driving [the Allies] rapidly toward a world war which will destroy them, whatever it does to [the U.S.] and the Soviets."[87]

His prescriptions were moderate; some even fell within the "realist" camp. The arms race should be slowed. America must negotiate settlements as we go and not wait on the policy of sufficient strength. The West should promote independent action on the part of Kremlin satellites—it was an "illusion," he wrote to believe Moscow could control the vast Chinese people. Economic aid to the allies and depressed peoples should be accelerated and delivered through the UN. The West must substitute pro-democracy for anti-communism in the ideological conflict. Finally, every effort must strive to avoid war and to provide the UN with sufficient moral authority to "alleviate and regulate the stresses and strains in an ever changing world."[88]

And what was illusory for the Soviets was equally so for the United States. Fleming, as did Schuman, Wright, Morgenthau, and Kennan, opposed the emphasis on regionalism as it evolved in the post-war world. The United States had engaged in what Fleming called "pactomania" in an effort to ally all the world's "free" nations with it, many of whose leaders were as odious as those of the Soviet Union. Fleming believed this effort was self-defeating and would strain the United States beyond its limits to lead. The United States, he warned, should accept and act upon its full share of responsibility in the world, but no more. It was Fleming's desire to live in a world that accepted many diverse creeds, systems, and cultures.[89] Although not a return to isolationism, this is an assertion that the United States should not continue Truman's style of universalism, a policy that could not tolerate undemocratic creeds.

All, though, was not doom and gloom in Fleming's scenario. He saw cause to hope in that the USSR was evolving inexorably toward, if not democracy, then a system more palatable to the United States. This theme pervades his work from approximately 1953 to the end of his life. Fleming observed that the Soviet system had evolved into a bureaucratic state capitalism not too far removed from that in the West and that the law of diversity dictated that Mao's communism would differ from Stalin's.[90]

Fleming adopted a one-dimensional interpretation of convergency theory, for although he asserted the Soviets gradually adopted parts of the Western system, rarely did he state that the reverse corollary applied to the situation.[91] Fleming claimed that as Communist societies advanced, the people demanded and received more both materially and intellectually, and that as the world progressed, competition between socialism and capitalism would result in the "modification of each."[92] Fleming also attacked the notion of monolithic communism and observed that Khrushchev had rapidly modified the Soviet system toward "freer institutions."[93] Fleming urged U.S. policy makers to bear in mind what he referred to as "the greatest law of life on earth, that every social system is in constant evolution." The implication, of course, was that the communist system would change and progress. There would be, he thought, "many communisms, all changing and adapting . . . and some of them evolving into forms distinctly more acceptable to us."[94]

The Korean War served as the vehicle for Kennan and Morgenthau to launch their "realist" critique of Truman's policies and of so-called "idealists" who sought to influence that policy. Yet Denna Fleming, Fred Schuman, and Quincy Wright, three men long associated with Wilsonian internationalism, articulated policies that were remarkably similar to those of their "realist" opponents. The difference between the two camps was minute.

NOTES

1. Quincy Wright to Clark Eichelberger, 11 January 1949, Box 6, folder 1, The Quincy Wright Collection, University of Chicago.

2. Quincy Wright, "Aviation and World Politics," *Air Affairs* 1 (September 1946): 107.

3. See Quincy Wright, "Comment," *Air Affairs 1* (December 1946): 242-245; Wright, "The Effect of the Atomic Bomb on World Politics," *Air Affairs* 1 (March 1947): 383-399; Wright to E. M. Earle, IAS Princeton, regarding Meade's *The Influence of Air Power Upon History,* 22 November 1946, Box 19, folder 19; Wright, "The United Nations Charter and the Prevention of War," *Bulletin of the Atomic Scientists* 3 (February 1947): 57-58, 61; and Wright, "Political Consequences of the Soviet Atom Bomb," *Air Affairs* 3 (Spring 1950): 414-428.

4. Quincy Wright, "Political Science and World Stabilization," *American Political Science Review* 44 (March 1950): 1-2. Presidential Address given at 45th annual meeting 28 December 1949.

5. Quincy Wright, *Contemporary International Law: A Balance Sheet* (New York: Random House, 1955, 1961), 5-6.

6. Quincy Wright, William M. Evan, and Morton Deutsch, eds., *Preventing World War III: Some Proposals* (New York: Simon and Schuster, 1962), 415.

7. Quincy Wright, "Responsibilities of the United States in the Post-War World," *Free World* 5 (January 1943): 35-36.

8. *Ibid.,* 36.

9. Quincy Wright, "Democracy and Power," *Free World* 5 (May 1943): 396.

10. *Ibid.,* 399.

11. Wright to Edward Bernays, 5 March 1946, Box 19, folder 9.

12. Quincy Wright, "The Understandings of International Law," *American Journal of International Law* 14 (October 1920): 369.

13. Quincy Wright, *The Study of International Relation* (New York: Appleton-Century-Crofts, Inc., 1955), 71.

14. Quincy Wright, "On the Application of Intelligence to World Affairs," *Bulletin of the Atomic Scientists* 4 (August 1948): 252.

15. Quincy Wright, "American Policy Toward Russia," *World Politics* 2 (Summer 1950): 480.

16. Wright, "On the Application of Intelligence to World Affairs," 250.

17. Quincy Wright, "America 1975 Series: The U.S. Position in the World," *Challenge* 5 (December 1956): 13-17.

18. Wright to Walter Lippmann, 18 July 1944, Box 18, addenda 1. Their relationship extended to their spouses and it was Wright who presented Lippmann on 11 November 1955 when the University of Chicago conferred an honorary doctorate on him. See Wright to Walter Lippmann, Box 18, addenda 1.

19. Wright statement, 31 August 1944, Box 5, folder 16.

20. Wright to Livingston Hartley (Atlantic Union Committee), 27 October 1950, Box 4, addenda 1, folder H (4).

21. Wright to Dana C. Backus, Board of Directors, American Association for the United Nations, 2 May 1951, Box 6, folder 4.

22. *Ibid;* Wright to Margaret Olson (CSOP), 30 October 1950, Box 6, folder 2.

23. Wright to Lippmann, 11 February 1949, Box 18, addenda 1, 1-2.

24. Wright to Dulles, 28 January 1952, Box 6, folder 5.

25. See Wright, *A Study of War* (Chicago, IL: University of Chicago Press, 1964) for Wright's beliefs on stability within a balance of power system; Wright to Dulles, 28 January 1952.

26. Wright to Dulles, 28 January 1952.

27. *Ibid.*

28. Wright did not foresee the impact of fundamentalist Islam and the potential for a fourth regional body comprised of the Central Asian Islamic Republics of Kazakhstan, Kyrgyzstan, Tajikistan, Turkmenistan, and Uzbekistan apparent after the actual collapse of the Soviet Union.

29. Wright to Dulles, 28 January 1952.

30. Dulles to Wright, 6 February 1952, Box 13, addenda 1.

31. Wright to Dulles, 11 February 1952, Box 13, addenda 1.

32. See Wright to Dulles, 9 February 1953, Box 13, addenda 1; Wright to Dulles, 23 February 1953, Box 13, addenda 1; Wright to Dulles, 8 January 1957, Box 2, addenda 1, folder D (2); Wright to Dulles, 16 July 1957, Box 2, addenda 1, folder D (2).

33. Denna Fleming, "The United States in the United Nations," *Annals of the American Academy of Political and Social Science* 278 (November 1951): 73.

34. *Ibid.,* 74-75.

35. Professor James B. Holtzclaw, Chairman, Department of Political Science, Drake University, to Frederick L. Schuman, 17 March 1948, The Frederick L. Schuman Collection, University of Wyoming.

36. Fred Lee to Schuman, 1 March 1948.

37. Unsigned letter to the Office of the President, Williams College, 22 March 1948.

38. Schuman to the Editor, *New York Sun,* 19 March 1948.

39. James Rich to James Phinney Baxter, 26 March 1948.

40. "Tumult at the Waldorf," *Time* (4 April 1949), 23.

41. Schuman to the Editor, *The North Adams Transcript* (29 March 1949), 2.

42. Schuman to Baxter, 10 June 1949.

43. George F. Kennan, *Memoirs,1925-1950* (New York: Pantheon, 1967), 486.

44. *Ibid.,* 489.

45. Hans Morgenthau. *In Defense of the National Interest: A Critical Examination of American Foreign Policy* (New York: A.A. Knopf, 1951), 238-239.

46. *Ibid.,* 202.

47. *Ibid.,* 239.

48. *Ibid.,* 241.

49. Dies Committee hearings; Eugene Lyon, *The Red Decade* (New Rochelle, NY: Arlington House, 1941); Frederick L. Schuman, *Soviet Politics: At Home and Abroad,* (New York: A.A. Knopf, 1946).

50. Schuman to Baxter, 20 October 1950, 1-7.

51. *Ibid.,* 3-4.

52. Schuman to John W. Darr, Jr., 25 June 1951, 1.

53. *Ibid.,* 2.

54. Schuman to Howard DeVoe, 6 February 1953, Box 15.

55. Frederick L. Schuman, "Cold War's End," *The Nation* 176 (20 June 1953): 518.

56. *Ibid,* 519.

57. *Ibid.,* 520.

58. Frederick L. Schuman, "The Paradoxes of Dr. Toynbee," *The Nation* 179 (6 November 1954), 406.

59. For Wright's assessment of the Uniting For Peace Resolution, see his testimony before the U.S. Congress, Senate Foreign Relations Committee, *Senate Congressional Resolution 44,* 90th Congress, 26, 27 October 1967.

60. Quincy Wright, *International Law and the United Nations* (Bombay, India: Asia Publishing House, 1960), 23. This volume is based on lectures he gave in 1956 at the Inter American Academy of Comparative and International Law in Havana, Cuba.

61. Wright to Eichelberger, 5 December 1950, Box 6, folder 3, 2. This indicates a changed assessment of the League's performance in the Manchurian crisis. Wright praised the League's devotion to procedure in his article "Manchurian Crisis," *American Political Science Review* 26 (1932): 45-76.

62. Wright to Eichelberger, 5 December 1950, 2.

63. *Ibid.,* 3.

64. Kennan, *Memoirs,* 493.

65. Wright to Eichelberger, 5 December 1950, 3. He was aware that such a policy would have to be pursued with caution as it was bound to be unpopular with the U.S. public due to the efforts of the friends of Nationalist China.

66. Wright addressed the issue of recognition and how it served the Soviet Union's interests as well in the following: "Some Thoughts About Recognition," *American Journal of International Law* 44 (July 1950): 548-559; "The Chinese Recognition Problem," *American Journal of International Law* 49 (July 1955): 320-338; "The Status of Communist China," *Journal of International Affairs* 11 (Summer 1957): 171-186; "Non-Recognition of China and International Tensions," *Current History* 34 (March 1958): 152-157; Wright to Walter Bingham, 22 September 1955, Box 1, addenda 1, folder B; and Wright to Stanley Hornbeck, 23 August 1956, Box 4, addenda 1, folder H (2).

67. Kennan, *Memoirs,* 491.

68. The bribe he refers to is the fact that the United States allowed Franco to purchase American oil while the United States purchased strategic materials from Spain at high prices in order to get the fascist dictator to ignore Operation TORCH.

69. Wright to Eichelberger, 5 December 1950, 3.

70. *Ibid.*

71. Denna Fleming, "The United States in the United Nations," *Annals of the American Academy of Political and Social Science* 278 (November 1951): 75.

72. *Ibid.,* 76-78.

73. Denna Fleming to Chao, 6 December 1950, 1, The Denna Fleming Collection, Vanderbilt University. Fleming counsels Chao in the letter as to how to behave now that he is in China and expresses great concern for his well-being as well as "profound respect" for his culture.

74. In his article "Our Brink-of-War Diplomacy in the Formosa Strait," *Western Political Quarterly* 9 (September 1956): 545, Fleming referred to the Bandung Declaration in response to the brinkmanship of Dulles as a meeting of "twenty-nine colored nations at Bandung in Indonesia--all have-nots, anti-colonial, and highly allergic to atomic war."

75. Fleming, "The United States in the United Nations," 80-81.

76. *Ibid.,* 82.

77. Denna Fleming, "Collier's Wins World War III," *The Nation* 173 (10 November 1951): 394.

78. *Ibid.,* 395.

79. Denna Fleming, "What Follows the Arms Race?" *Journal of Politics* 14 (May 1952): 203. Fleming was a past president of the Southern Political Science Association that published this journal.

80. *Ibid.*

81. *Ibid.,* 221.

82. *Ibid.,* 213-214.

83. *Ibid.,* 216.

84. *Ibid.,* 219.

85. *Ibid.,* 221.

86. Wright to Fleming, 21 May 1952.

87. Denna Fleming, "How Can We Secure Dependable Allies?" *Annals of the American Academy of Political and Social Science* 283 (September 1952): 15.

88. *Ibid.,* 18-21.

89. Fleming to Mr. Schreiner, 11 February 1957, 1.

90. Denna Fleming, "The Failure of Western Policies," *Annals of the American Academy of Political and Social Science* 288 (July 1953): 46. Fleming notes evolutionary progress in communist countries in "Can Pax American Succeed?" *Annals of the American Academy of Political and Social Science* 360 (July 1965): 137; and in "Is Containment Moral?" *Annals of the American Academy of Political and Social Science* 362 (November 1965): 24.

91. In the "Sunday Evening" 1945 memo to Baruch, Fleming wrote that he did not "anticipate that the two systems would merge, but that they were both evolving and that there was no reason that the two should be irreconcilable. Fleming to Baruch, 1945, 3. See also Fleming to Baruch, 13 May 1946, 6.

92. Fleming to Baruch, 8 May 1945, 2; Fleming, "Beyond the Cold War," *Annals of the American Academy of Political and Social Science* 324 (July 1959): 124-125.

93. Denna Fleming, "The Broken Dialogue on Foreign Affairs," *Annals of the American Academy of Political and Social Science* 344 (November 1962): 135-137.

94. These general ideas are first found in the Fleming papers in an undated essay entitled "Is Communism 'Just As Bad As Fascism'?" 3; and Fleming, "The Costs and Consequences of the Cold War," *Annals of the American Academy of Political and Social Science* 366 (July 1966): 136. See also Fleming to Mr. Schreiner, 11 February 1957, 1.

Conclusions: The Failure of the Realist Critique

In the years after the Korean War, Quincy Wright came to believe that the UN Charter had corrected the most glaring weaknesses of the earlier League Covenant. Speaking in 1955 to the Turkish Institute of International Law at Istanbul and at Ankara in commemoration of the tenth anniversary of the Charter's adoption, Wright observed that the old international law had undergone radical change. A system that had once "recognized the sovereign state to the exclusion of almost everything else" no longer recognized war as a legal means to ends, and no longer recognized neutrality as a legal condition in the face of aggressive behavior.[1] The world system now gave the individual standing, recognized the "public interest of the world society in many transactions," and had established the "jural personality of international organizations with rights and powers embodying that public interest."

A related development was reduced emphasis on the state in international law, while individuals and the new world organization gained prominence. Wright cautioned that although this reflected the legal situation, states that exercised efficient control over "thought, economy, and military action," could be "more independent, powerful, and dangerous than ever."[2] "Is it possible," he asked, "that the new principles of international law can be realized in practice?"[3] His invariable answer was "yes," although he recognized the need for continued development of the UN at the expense of national sovereignty.

This was especially true because of the continued tensions between the United States and the Soviet Union. Wright believed that the two big errors of post-World War II U.S. policy were to call "Kremlin imperialism" Communism, and to call the policy of preventing Kremlin expansion "containment."[4] By accepting the Kremlin thesis that it spoke for and led all Communists, Wright thought the United States had fallen into a Kremlin trap: because the United States thought the Kremlin was committed to the overthrow of capitalism, all Communists were necessarily the enemies of the capitalist world. Such a framework prevented the United States and its policy makers from exploiting future Titos. It was only as an instrument of Kremlin imperialism that the West should fear Communism, not as an indigenous manifestation of self-determination in a sovereign state. "I doubt," wrote Wright, "whether we know how much of the Communism in Asia and Africa is Kremlin inspired and how much is a local reaction against the sense of unequal treatment and conditions of low economic standards."[5]

Like Fleming, Kennan, Morgenthau, and Schuman, Wright maintained that the United States did not possess the resources to contain the Soviet Union along all its frontiers. Plausibly, the United States could "provide an adequate force so that if a war should occur, the Soviet Union would inevitably be defeated," but the best defense, he believed, was a strong UN with a genuine police force.[6] Containment doctrine was, said Wright, the product of a "Maginot mentality."[7]

As well, he feared the costs and increased potential for confrontations that attended containment. For Wright, the question was whether the West could build a power so overwhelming that the Soviets could not hope for victory in any confrontation and thus "gradually fade into their orbit," or whether the West should concentrate on the development of "a more stable equilibrium" through a strengthened UN. He believed that although the first alternative was desirable if possible, it increased greatly the risks of World War III.[8]

By 1961 Wright had concluded that the pursuit of containment had caused American military and economic power relative to the Soviet Union to decline, and undermined America's reputation in the underdeveloped world.[9] He had developed a new appreciation for the potential of underdeveloped nations to contribute to or detract from a stable world order, and of the potential for an unsophisticated U.S. foreign policy to aggravate problems in those areas. In an article entitled "America 1975 Series: The U.S. Position in the World," Wright declared that the United States was squandering its "great and deserved reputation" by maintaining racial discrimination at home and favoring colonial powers over peoples seeking self-determination.[10] Clearly, Wright now believed that support for colonial regimes was outside the interest of the United States, of the UN, and of peace. The tug-of-war between the Soviets and the West for influence in the developing world tempered his earlier position on the need to prepare people for independence.

In a letter to Walter Lippmann, Wright agreed that it was difficult to judge the real intentions of a nation. He noted that, although many believed that Russia was "guided entirely by expansionist motivations, entirely by fear of attack, or entirely by Communist ideology," the influence of these and other factors was relative to circumstances.[11] Wright had stated in a previous letter to Lippmann that it was safe to assume that the Soviet government had alternative policies, one of which was to "establish normal relations and develop mutually beneficial trade."[12]

These convictions about Soviet behavior remained substantially unchanged for the rest of his life. In the article "International Conflict and the United Nations," he alluded sympathetically to the evolving New Left interpretation of Soviet Communism. U.S. policy makers, Wright believed, would benefit from a study of Soviet policy makers that sought to answer whether they intervened around the globe from a conviction that such interventions were a defensive necessity or whether they were reacting spontaneously to acts that they interpreted as hostile. Too often, and without sufficient evidence, U.S. policy makers assumed that Soviet actions were inherent characteristics of the Soviet state and/or that the ambition to dominate and convert the world motivated its leaders.[13]

In a document entitled "Improvement of Relations With Russia," Wright declared that the universal nature of Marxist ideology gave cause to hope. The faith of Marxists that Communism would ultimately and inevitably triumph over capitalism kept the Soviets from experiencing a sense of urgency to spread their program across the world. He contrasted the confidence of the Marxists to the decline of confidence he believed was infecting Western democracy, and concluded that should the advocates of liberal democracy recapture the confidence they once held, their cause would triumph in the long run.[14]

Wright also insisted that Marxism might not have been the monolithic entity that the administrations portrayed it to be. It would be wise if the West rejected the Soviet thesis that all Communist states follow the Kremlin lead, for it might then discover "that states other than Tito's Yugoslavia have within them strong nationalist roots and resist [the] Kremlin."[15] Perhaps nonaligned states, like India, which harbored no wish to become a satellite of either the Kremlin or the United States, might "in time establish third, fourth, and fifth forces in the world," which would have the effect of stabilizing a bipolar system.[16] Wright continued to adhere to what was basically a balance of power system for maintaining stability and order.

This framework of conflict and progress led Wright to advocate the concept of peaceful coexistence. He had little doubt as to the outcome of the peaceful confrontation between the two ideologies: in his mind, democracy would always prevail over the long term. But Wright greatly feared the consequences of a prolonged ideological conflict. Ideological wars were historically insoluble, he believed, and he provided as evidence the wars from the seventh to the seventeenth centuries between Christians and Muslims, and those between Catholics and Protestants from the sixteenth through the seventeenth centuries. In neither instance was one side able to overcome the other. Wright believed that the best means of resolution would be to adopt the formula of the Treaty of Westphalia, where each country was free to adopt its own ideology. The only constraint he would impose would be adherence to the Universal Declaration of Human Rights.[17]

Wright intended, if not to replace them, to offer a counterbalance to the ideologies of capitalism and Communism with an ideology of internationalism. In his article "International Law and Ideologies," he wrote that accommodation, "a middle way" between Western capitalism and Kremlin socialism, was the best solution. Wright observed that international law recognized a state's right to deal with ideological problems without external interference but noted, too, that both technology and the development of international standards of human rights had qualified that freedom of action.[18]

Wright's sympathies in the confrontation between Marxism and democratic capitalism were clear. He believed that democracy's greatest advantages over Communism were its respect for human liberty, and that under conditions of peace, democracy can advance materially, socially, and intellectually with greater speed than any other form of society.[19] But he was equally adamant that the UN should adopt a neutral role in the contest between democracy and totalitarianism. What he sought was, as John Kennedy put it, a "world safe for diversity," because a world safe for democracy, in the phrase of Wilson, did not necessarily imply a democratic world.[20]

The United Nations must be ideologically neutral to prevent it from perpetuating the *status quo* in the face of needed change. Wright asserted that because the UN represented all ideologies, it must provide an opportunity for all ideologies to expand by legitimate means in order to maintain stability. Those means would include what Wright referred to as "genuine self-determination of peoples and legitimate transnational communication."[21] He concluded that, if an ideology expanded through legitimate methods, "this would be evidence that it deserves to expand according to Jefferson's idea of the testing of ideas in a free forum of opinion."[22] Of course the UN's advocacy of the Universal Declaration of Human Rights tempered any such neutral position, for presumably a people could, through self-determination and legitimate means, abandon the democratic principles Wright and the UN Charter held so dear.

In an address delivered at Washington and Lee University, 14 February 1956, Denna Fleming assessed ten years of collective security and arrived at similar conclusions. As usual, he praised Wilson, Franklin Roosevelt, and Cordell Hull as visionaries, but observed that in 1945, the Allies did "merely what should have been done in 1920." They had created another league that retained many of the strengths and flaws of the old one. What was needed in 1945 was a "real advance toward the organization of a world community, but by this time there was no community."[23] The UN could not discipline either the United States or the USSR and the "chance to organize the world which we lost in 1920 had not been regained."[24]

He declared the Geneva Summit of July 1955, a summit that led the United States to declare publicly its opposition to atomic war and renounce the policy of liberation, a success even though Eisenhower and Nixon retained a recalcitrant posture afterwards.[25] But he observed that U.S. support of colonial and feudal regimes propelled "most of the Asian-Arab world away from us and into neutralism." This led to the UN vote of 14 December 1955, which admitted sixteen new states over heavy U.S. opposition and was, noted Fleming, a great defeat for U.S. diplomacy and U.S. efforts to lead the UN.

The big governments, he insisted, had learned little about collective security and regarded the UN as a "tool for their own purposes," one "just as expendable as the League was." To counter this, he called for the United States to support the UN in efforts to aid underdeveloped countries or U.S. leadership would be rejected just as it had been on the vote for universality of membership. The UN, he concluded, would not have the power to enforce peace, but it would be a forum where 'the organized opinion of mankind,' a force he believed the great powers could not disregard in the atomic age, could find expression.[26]

Fleming's conclusions were based largely on his negative assessment of U.S. policies, both domestic and foreign, since 1917. U.S. policy makers had failed to maintain the balance of power, failed to suppress Bolshevism, failed to maintain isolationism, failed to appease the dictators, failed to contain Communism, failed to roll-back Communism, failed to limit the demands the military made on the U.S. economy, and failed to curb the consequent negative impact this had on personal freedom.[27] These failed policies all indicated to Fleming the need to negotiate from mutual recognition of legitimate regional defense interests.

Eastern Europe was, according to Fleming's logic, a legitimate defense zone for the USSR as was Western Europe for the United States and Eastern Asia for China. The former Axis powers of Japan and Germany, he stated, must come to terms with both East and West or they might serve as the nucleus of a future conflict. No one sphere could dictate terms to the other two, a situation that demanded that the UN be developed to assist cooperation. To facilitate that goal, the UN, Fleming insisted, should be moved from the United States, and a relief and rehabilitation type program for the underdeveloped world should be designed and funded.

Fleming declared that the nations of the world must welcome diversity and evolution and promote freedom of trade as well as civil liberties, especially in the already free world where McCarthyism had taken hold. In a telling observation, he declared that the creation of deterrent strength was "indispensable" in an international system of anarchy: "There must be," he wrote, "arms sufficient to deter our opponents from any attempt at world conquest, and vice-versa."[28] Here again is a demonstration of his commitment to balance of power politics.

Somewhat incongruously, given his calls for disengagement, Fleming also feared a resurgent isolationism in the United States. The immediate evidence for this fear was public opposition to a treaty concerning race relations and human rights in the UN. This indicated to Fleming that it would be difficult for the United States to engage a "[r]esponsible, long-sighted leadership of the noncommunist world" because only the United States feared "the comparatively feeble efforts of the United Nations to establish some common standards of human rights."[29]

Fleming continued to express this fear of neo-isolationism during the fifties. He thought that what he perceived as the failure of containment would generate pressure for a "Fortress America." The pressure of the Communist bloc against the "ring of containment"; the desire of U.S. allies to distance themselves from the Cold War and "our erratic leadership"; and the "costs of global containment" would all feed the demand for isolationism. He criticized what he labeled as the "mad U.S. rush" to join alliances after World War II, but he did not oppose alliances *per se.* He noted the irony, though, of a country that had rejected the League as an entangling alliance yet now had so many alliances it was difficult to keep track of them.[30]

He also claimed that U.S. suppression of the United Kingdom and France during the Suez Crisis "turned loose long-term impulses toward unification and neutralism in Western Europe." In that context, he wrote that the U.S. must repair relations or face imposed isolation.[31] Yet his other remedies included a call for the United States to withdraw from most of its "nearly 900 overseas bases."[32] He called for the UN to become a "permanent place for negotiation, co-operation, and for getting the world's work done" and warned "peace will be precarious until a functioning world community is organized."[33] But nowhere did he indicate how the UN was to do this.

The publication of *The Cold War and Its Origins* in 1961 provided the medium for Fleming's criticism of U.S. foreign policy. His analyses of the fifteen years that followed the end of World War II asserted that because the United States had failed to accept the lessons of the Second World War, its policies reacted to, rather than created, the dynamics of world politics. Franklin Roosevelt was a leader who really understood Soviet politics, but Harry Truman was confused and therefore botched relations with the Communist world.

Fleming urged the United States to retake the initiative for positive, not negative goals, and remember that the people of the USSR and the PRC wanted what U.S. citizens wanted—peace, a better standard of living, and more personal freedom.[34] Furthermore, the United States, he believed, must purge itself of a series of false assumptions in order to change the direction of its foreign policy. Americans needed to relinquish their belief that Communists sought to conquer the world and embrace instead the idea of peaceful coexistence. They should reject the notion that Communism, if not actually worse, differed very little from fascism, or risk an inadequate understanding of the enemy. They must divorce themselves from the domino theory and its unfounded assumptions. Equally important, Americans had to realize that rapid and constant economic growth was not essential to maintain their values.[35]

Fleming insisted that to move beyond the Cold War, the United States must account for the trend of counter-encirclement and growing Soviet arms: U.S. encirclement of the Soviet Union had "generated the very power we feared."[36] Containment was based on the faulty interpretation of a Soviet ideology of world revolution which excluded from the "defensive category any action that the Soviet Union or China could take."[37] This also contributed to the fear of appeasement, which Fleming claimed was a false analogy, for the USSR and Nazi Germany were, he observed, very different.[38]

Fleming concluded that neither the Soviets nor the Americans perceived war as in their own interest. This was based on his understanding of convergency. "The Communists," he declared, "give two hostages to fortune which must be redeemed: universal education and the promise of a higher standard of living. This was fully evident, say by 1928, and it is the reason why no war to the death with Communism was or is necessary. These two solvents change the character of the Communist societies as they advance. As people have more, materially and intellectually, they demand and receive more."[39]

In what was clearly a rejection of the global scope of U.S. military policy, Fleming called for the United States to disengage. Although he did not say so in explicit terms, this was a rejection of Truman's policy of universalism, a policy Fleming would later condemn as the "disastrous decision" for globalism.[40] In the absence of an effective world organization, the basic means to accomplish universalism was unilateral action in pursuit of a balance of power. Both Wright and Fleming believed isolationism had killed the League of Nations, global imperialism had nearly killed the UN, and few people understood that internationalism was the corrective to both.[41]

Fleming assured the reader that U.S. attempts to "surround" the USSR were provocative and could lead to war. He believed that the policy of universalism had required the United States to associate with some strange fellows, notably Franco, and had thus compromised U.S. values.[42] He also feared that because the United States had "prospered phenomenally" in the past two wars, its people and leaders might be more inclined than the Russians, or the Europeans, or the Asians, all of whom had suffered so horribly from the last two wars, to accept a third war.[43]

Schuman's response to a request in August 1952 to speak to a Friends Service Committee (FSC) on the state of the society and bipartisan foreign policy revealed his views on U.S. foreign policy and its domestic impact. He wrote to Russ Johnson of the FSC, "We are no longer living in a free society. We shall not retain such freedoms as we have left or recover any of those we have already lost until and unless the present bipartisan foreign and defense policy of our government, all but unanimously endorsed by press, pulpit, and people, is drastically revised."[44]

Carey McWilliams, editorial director for *The Nation*, continued to seek Schuman's contributions to his magazine. McWilliams referred to Schuman as "one of this country's authentic prophets," and the author used the opportunity to articulate new prophecies.[45] His correspondence with McWilliams reveals Schuman's thought and sense of humor. Paraphrasing John Hay's characterization of the Spanish-American War, Schuman wrote McWilliams that he had come to view the Cold War as "a splendid thing" and that it should "be perpetuated indefinitely." This tongue-in-cheek belief resulted from Schuman's embrace of the thesis that the Cold War was the "chief means of maintaining full employment and full production in the American economy." Schuman wrote that the Cold War had "become in large part, for the U.S.A., a kind of glorified W.P.A.—i.e., a scheme of public spending to maintain full employment and full production. Unless we are bright enough to find a substitute, our prospects are rather dismal."[46]

He also voiced his support of Arnold Toynbee's thesis that "the Cold War represented a major spiritual challenge on both sides." On a positive note, though, Schuman claimed that the Supreme Court would likely not have ruled as it did on segregation in *Brown v. the Board of Education* in the "absence of the Cold War."[47] In a domestic context, then, the Cold War served, at least in one instance, to liberate suppressed peoples.

McWilliams asked Schuman to provide a list of questions to be asked the editors of *Pravda*, a list in which Schuman defined his agenda for superpower relations. Schuman replied that he wanted to know whether the Soviet Union would accept the reunification of Germany on the basis of permanent nonalignment and permanent disarmament or severely limited arms. Would the Soviet Union accept Eisenhower's proposal for "reciprocal aerial inspection, coupled with local checkpoint control of strategic centers" if the United States would pledge not to use atomic weapons in a first strike? Would the Soviets cooperate in a joint investment venture for the underdeveloped areas of the world? His fourth question was whether further democratization in the wake of the revelations of the XXth Party Congress could be expected to include "genuine mass participation" and "multiple candidacies." In the end, Schuman requested a contemporary explanation from Soviet ideologists of the concepts for a classless society, economic Communism, and the withering away of the state.[48]

Despite the fact that he was critical of Soviet policies, yet another incarnation of the Dilling charges plagued Schuman. Arthur Schlesinger, Jr., in his book *The Politics of Upheaval,* identified Schuman as a supporter of the Foster and Ford Communist Party ticket in the 1932 presidential election.[49] Schuman wrote a letter that detailed his exculpation from such charges in both the Illinois Senate and the U.S. Senate, and requested that Schlesinger renounce his error.[50] Schlesinger responded by phone and letter to assure Schuman that the error would be corrected, sent to him two dozen errata statements, and offered further assistance if the implication that Schuman was a Communist cost him any employment.[51]

Convergency theory, as we have seen, influenced Schuman throughout his career. He had "long suspected that the end result of Soviet Communism would be an approximation to the ideal social order as defined by spokesmen of American capitalism, and that the America of days to come would somewhat resemble to the objective observer, the Marxist-Leninist vision of the 'classless society' and the 'cooperative commonwealth.'"[52] By the mid-1950s he believed that the United States and the USSR and their peoples were experiencing problems common to industrialized super-powers. Because of this, he thought it likely that the Communist-capitalist division of the world would not dictate future political divisions.[53] The important division in the future, he observed, would likely be a North-South division, industrial versus underdeveloped. This could prove to be a compelling reason for the United States and USSR to pursue a joint program designed to benefit the third world.[54]

And Schuman still believed that the UN, an association of sovereignties, could be the catalyst for such cooperation between the superpowers, although as such it could not be a world government. The UN had encouraged "détente" and survived the efforts of both sides of the Cold War to politicize it. The UN Charter, unlike the League of Nations Covenant, recognized that collective security, which Schuman read as the coercion of states by states, "was a formula not for peace but for war unless the Great Powers are unanimously in concert and disposed to cooperate for common purposes."[55]

For Fleming, Schuman, and Wright, competition between socialism and capitalism would result in the "modification of each."[56] If the UN could facilitate this, that would be all to the good. But the focus of their scholarship and prescriptions had long ago moved away from international law and internationalism. Coexistence between the super-powers and the power politics of that relationship was their only logic for the present and the near future. Coexistence was the road to progress, the road to new frontiers.

Hans Morgenthau closed his 1951 critique of American foreign policy with a blistering attack on the policy makers of the Truman administration. They had "deceived once" and now, he claimed, must do so again. They had "falsified the real issue between the United States and the Soviet Union into a holy crusade to stamp out Bolshevism everywhere on earth" in order to arouse the public. Having done so, the leaders would now have to "act as though you meant it." The same held true of U.S. policy toward China. Morgenthau criticized Truman and Acheson for presenting "the Chinese Communists as the enemies of mankind, in order to appease the China lobby: now you must act as though you meant it." The deceptions, he continued, were the result of "passion and prejudice." Government leaders were taking the nation down the road of hatred rather than reason. The policy makers had become the voices of "what is vulgar, blind, and weak" in the people.

Morgenthau's remedy was to understand the past and adhere to its lessons. He called on the nation to "remember the great and simple truths . . . of the early statesmen of the Republic." Americans should remember that the "golden age of isolated normalcy is gone forever," that "diplomacy without power is feeble, and power without diplomacy is destructive and blind." He cautioned that "no nation's power is without limits" and that consequently "its policies must respect the power and interests of others." Americans, he stated, "have shown throughout their history that they are able to face the truth and act upon it with courage and resourcefulness in war, with common sense and moral determination in peace."

Americans must forget the "sentimental notion that foreign policy is a struggle between virtue and vice, with virtue bound to win." They must forget the "utopian notion that a brave new world without power politics will follow the unconditional surrender of wicked nations." And they must forget "the crusading notion that any nation, however virtuous and powerful, can have the mission to make the world over in its own image."

Most importantly, Morgenthau urged Americans to "remember always that it is not only a political necessity, but also a moral duty for a nation to follow in its dealings with other nations but one guiding star, one standard for thought, one rule for action: The National Interest."[57]

These admonitions were out of character coming from a man so critical of what he contemptuously referred to as the moralist/legalist strain in American foreign policy. There were great rules after all, ones that Morgenthau wrote about in moral terms that evoked Mosaic law.

Equally important was what Morgenthau did not state. Although it was true that American leaders had aroused the passions of the American people, the fact of the matter was that the enemy professed a universal ideology, too. The Soviet people had been propagandized and perhaps the American people needed to be as well. Obviously, Morgenthau disagreed with the goal of the policy makers, but he never offered them a definition of what was in the national interest in the early 1950s.

As for the Chinese Communists, it would be difficult to formulate an argument that they were not the enemies of mankind. Whether in the form of the export of arms and revolution, of the mass executions and imprisonment of their own people, or their attacks on the liberties of neighboring states like Tibet, the Chinese Communists were not the friends of world civilization and Morgenthau knew it. But, like his "idealist" peers, he was correct in asserting that U.S. insistence on an ideological test for diplomatic recognition would eliminate the opportunity for dialogue.

George Kennan was at least more consistent in his critique of American foreign policy. He declared that the greatest deficiency of that policy was its "inevitable association of legalistic ideas with moralistic ones." When nations perceive of each other in terms of right and wrong, it leads, claimed Kennan, to uncompromising policies, both in times of peace and times of war. Unconditional surrender was such a policy, and it was one that Kennan disliked immensely.[58]

Kennan held that the "legalistic approach to world affairs . . . makes violence more enduring, more terrible, and more destructive to political stability than did the older motives of national interest. A war fought in the name of high moral principle finds no early end short of some form of total domination." Concepts like "total war," and "total victory" were, in his opinion, particularly ill-suited to the nuclear age.[59]

Kennan did not believe that in order to escape the problems of the moralist/legalist approach the United States would necessarily have to abandon them. In fact, he declared that there was reason to hope that international law would prove useful as a "gentle civilizer of events." Nor would we have to "go in for anything that can properly be termed 'appeasement'—if one may use a word so cheapened and deflated by the abuse to which it has been recently subjected."[60]

What the United States must do, was to develop a new attitude toward events "outside our borders that are irritating and unpleasant today." Like a doctor viewing a patient wracked with disease, we must maintain, he insisted, an "attitude of detachment and soberness and readiness to reserve judgment." Americans must "admit that our own national interest is all that we are really capable of knowing and understanding." Americans must, he concluded, realize that "if our own purposes and undertakings here at home are decent ones, unsullied by arrogance or hostility toward other people or delusions of superiority, then the pursuit of our national interest can never fail to be conducive to a better world."[61]

Again, though, a supposed "realist" failed to identify what constitutes the national interest and how one determines whether it impedes on those other nations whose power and interests Morgenthau told Americans they must respect. And the notion that "what is good for the United States is good for the world" has about as much meaning as "what is good for General Motors is good for America."

The sole reason for the label "idealist" was to cast aspersion on those who disagreed with the realist interpretation of what constituted the national interest. As the evidence demonstrates time and again, the analysts portrayed as idealists provided policies that were at least as grounded in national interest as any that Morgenthau or Kennan advocated. None of those policies were more "realist" in their approach than those based on the Wilson Doctrine.

Precisely because the "golden age of isolated normalcy," if indeed there ever had been such an era, was gone, Americans could not afford to assume that French suppression of Vietnamese Nationalists was outside our national interest. Or that cannibalism on the streets of Port-au-Prince did not affect us. Such events would require the opposite assumption: that they might influence American national interests and therefore require investigation. In this assumption, the Wilson Doctrine has dominated the twentieth-century in an even greater way than the Monroe Doctrine did the nineteenth-century.

All five men believed neutrality was an untenable policy for modern industrial nations. All believed that the negative connotation attached to appeasement had unnecessarily tarnished the art of diplomacy and compromise. They believed that the United States had bungled its relations with the Soviet Union and the People's Republic of China. They all valued the stability balance of power politics afforded the world. They agreed on the need to strengthen the executive branch; on the need to remove partisan politics from the planning and execution of foreign policy; that the nation required a long-term foreign policy; that professionalization of the foreign service was incomplete and required further reform; that the adoption of a parliamentary system would aid in accomplishing all of these goals; and that "backward" peoples required civilized ones to act *in loco parentis* for them. And as these five men aged, their opinions continued to converge. All opposed American intervention in Vietnam; all opposed the arms race; and all sought an end to the Cold War through negotiation.

Truly, the only significant divergence between Kennan and Morgenthau on the one hand and Fleming, Schuman, and Wright on the other was that the Wilsonians were not resistant to change. They were not tradition bound to the characteristics of an international system born in the Middle Ages. Contrary to Hans Morgenthau's assertion that consistency was the mark of the "idealists," their flexibility was their most identifiable characteristic. They saw the UN and international law as vehicles to accomplish the national interest. That interest was, in the opinion of a variety of administrations from both major parties, the maintenance of the "Open Door," the recognition of universal individual rights, and the preservation of peace.

NOTES

1. Wright hedged somewhat on his definition of neutrality. In a letter to Margaret Olson of the Committee to Study the Organization of Peace, he wrote that "I think we should attempt to develop . . . neutralized zones subject, of course, to the overriding principle of the Charter that aggression anywhere is to be opposed by all members of the United Nations including the states in such a zone." Wright to Olson, 30 October 1950,

The Quincy Wright Collection, University of Chicago. Of course, such a qualification eliminates the meaning of "neutral."

2. Quincy Wright, *Contemporary International Law: A Balance Sheet* (New York: Doubleday, 1955), 24.

3. *Ibid.* For further discussion of his concept of the "new" international law see Wright's prize winning essay "Criteria For Judging The Relevance Of Researches On The Problems Of Peace," in *Research For Peace* (Amsterdam: North-Holland Publishing Co., 1954): 34.

4. Wright to Dulles, 9 February 1953, Box 13, addenda 1, 1.

5. *Ibid.*

6. Wright to Eichelberger, 23 February 1949, Box 6, folder 1.

7. Quincy Wright, "American Policy Toward Russia," *World Politics* 2 (Summer 1950): 477.

8. Wright to Dana Backus, 11 December 52, Box 6, folder 5.

9. Quincy Wright, Testimony, 86th Congress, 112; Wright "Western Diplomacy Since 1945," *Annals of the American Academy of Political and Social Science* 336 (July 1961): 144.

10. Quincy Wright, "America 1975 Series: The U.S. Position in the World," *Challenge* 5 (December 1956): 13-17. This is one of Wright's first attacks on racial discrimination to appear in print.

11. Wright to Lippmann, 29 January 1948, Box 18, addenda 1. In a previous letter from Lippmann to Wright of 23 January 1948, Box 18, addenda 1, Lippmann suggested a parallel between Marxist ideology and Islamic fundamentalism with which Wright agreed.

12. Wright to Lippmann, 20 January 1948, Box 19, folder 11.

13. Quincy Wright, "International Conflict and the United Nations," *World Politics* 10 (Autumn 1957): 40.

14. Wright, Confidential Draft, "Improvement of Relations With Russia," 31 March 1950, Box 6, folder 2, 18.

15. Quincy Wright, "The Nature of Conflict," *Western Political Science Quarterly,* 4 (June 1951) 209.

16. *Ibid.*

17. Wright to Dulles, 9 February 1953, Box 13, addenda 1, 2.

18. Quincy Wright, "International Law and Ideologies," *American Journal of International Law* 48 (October 1954): 625.

19. Wright, Testimony, 86th Congress, 112.

20. Wright to George Ball, 27 May 1970, Box 1, addenda 1, 2.

21. Wright to Richard Falk, 5 April 63, Box 14, addenda 1, Falk Folder.

22. *Ibid.*

23. Denna Fleming, "Woodrow Wilson and Collective Security Today," *Journal of Politics* 18 (November 1956): 617.

24. *Ibid.,* 618.

25. *Ibid.,* 619-620.

26. *Ibid.,* 619-623.

27. Denna Fleming, "The Failure of Western Policies," *Annals of the American Academy of Political and Social Science* 288 (July 1953): 36-41.

28. *Ibid.,* 45. For more on his views of McCarthy, see Fleming, "Are We Moving Toward Fascism?" *Journal of Politics* 16 (February 1954): 39-75.

29. Denna Fleming, "The Failure of Western Policies," 46.

30. Denna Fleming, "Needed: A Purge of Obsession," *The Nation* 188 (21 February 1959): 163.

31. Denna Fleming, "Are We Moving Toward Fortress America?" *Annals of the American Academy of Political and Social Science* 312 (July 1957): 14; 19.

32. *Ibid.,* 17.

33. *Ibid.,* 20.

34. Denna Fleming, "A Diplomacy for Free Men," *The Nation* 186 (3 May 1958): 384-386.

35. Fleming, "Needed: A Purge of Obsessions," 164-165; Fleming, "Beyond the Cold War," *Annals of the American Academy of Political and Social Science* 324 (July 1959): 118.

36. Fleming, "Beyond the Cold War," 115.

37. *Ibid.,* 117.

38. *Ibid.,* 118-119.

39. *Ibid.,* 124.

40. Denna Fleming to *New York Times,* 11 January 1969.

41. Quincy Wright to Fleming, 22 November 1963 (copy). Wright observed that he had just heard of Kennedy's assassination when he finished writing the letter.

42. Denna Fleming, "What Follows the Arms Race?" *Journal of Politics* 14 (May 1952): 206. Fleming would ask rhetorically in 1971: "Also, is there a reactionary regime in the world that we have not tried to prop up or been cozy with, when the world is not moving their way?" Fleming to Edwin S. Gardner, 29 May 1971, The Denna Fleming Collection, Vanderbilt University.

43. Fleming, "What Follows the Arms Race?" 209-210.

44. Johnson to Frederick L. Schuman, 25 August 1952; Schuman to Johnson, 10 September 1952, The Frederick L. Schuman Collection, University of Wyoming.

45. For the remark on being an authentic prophet, see McWilliams to Schuman, 27 July 1955; for his requests for articles see McWilliams to Schuman 10 September 1954; Schuman to McWilliams, 20 September 1954; Schuman to McWilliams, 23 December 1955; McWilliams to Schuman, 27 July 1955.

46. Schuman to Lily, Don, and Bette, 24 January 1959, Box 16.

47. Schuman to McWilliams, 7 February 1955, Box 15.

48. Schuman to McWilliams, 23 December 1955, Box 15.

49. Schuman referred to 165 of Arthur Schlesinger's *Politics of Upheaval* in Schuman to Arthur Schlesinger, Jr., 5 October 1960, 1.

50. *Ibid.,* 2.

51. Schuman to Schlesinger, 17 October 1960; Schlesinger to Schuman, 24 October 1960. Schuman believed that he had lost a summer appointment for 1961 as a result of the book. See Schuman to Schlesinger, 17 October, 1960. Also, see a letter from Noam Chomsky to Denna Fleming in which Chomsky chastises Schlesinger for sloppy quoting practices. Chomsky to Fleming, 17 June 1969.

52. Frederick L. Schuman, "Moral Insight Into Power," *The Nation* 182 (21 January 1956): 54.

53. Frederick L. Schuman, "How Many Worlds?" *New Republic* 138 (3 February 1958): 13.

54. *Ibid.,* 14. For more on convergency, see Frederick L. Schuman, "Designs For Democracy," *Current History* 9 (December 1945): 497-502; Schuman, "The Geographic Setting," *Current History* 25 (August 1953): 76-80.

55. Frederick L. Schuman, "United Nations: The First Decade," *The Nation* 181 (30 July; 10 September 1955): 98.

56. *Ibid.,* 125.
57. Morgenthau, *In Defense of the National Interest,* 239-242.
58. Kennan, *American Diplomacy,* 100.
59. *Ibid.,* 101.
60. *Ibid.,* 102.
61. *Ibid.,* 102-103.

Bibliography

COLLECTIONS

The Denna F. Fleming Collection. The Jean and Alexander Heard Library, Vanderbilt University, Nashville, Tennessee.
The Frederick L. Schuman Collection. The American Heritage Center, University of Wyoming, Laramie, Wyoming.
The Quincy Wright Collection. The University of Chicago Library, Chicago, Illinois.

UNPUBLISHED DOCUEMENTS

Fleming, Doris A., telephone interview with author, 12 February 1989.
Fleming, Doris A., letter to Steven J. Bucklin, 23 January 1989.
Hill, Emily. "The Myth of American Idealism?: Intellectuals and International Relations in the Interwar Years." Paper presented to the Mid-America Conference on History, Topeka, Kansas, 1996.

PUBLIC DOCUMENTS

Illinois Senate. Committee Investigating Subversive Activities in Colleges and Universities. 13 May 1935.
United States Congress. House. Committee on Foreign Affairs Hearings. Seventy-fifth Congress, First Session, February 1937, 120-130.
United States Congress. House. Special Subcommittee of Special Committee to investigate UnAmerican Activities. Seventy-eighth Congress, 1943, Senate Library, volume 1035.
United States Congress. Senate. Foreign Relations Committee, *Senate Congressional Resolution 44.* 90th Congress, 26, 27 October 1967.

BOOKS

Blumenthal, Henry. *Illusion and Reality in Franco-American Relations, 1914-1945.* Baton Rouge, LA: Louisiana State University Press, 1986.

Cantor, Milton. *The Divided Left: American Radicalism, 1900-1975.* New York, NY: Hill and Wang, 1978.

Caute, David. *The Fellow-Travellers: Intellectual Friends of Communism.* New Haven, CT: Yale University Press, 1973, 1988.

Conkin, Paul. *Gone with the Ivy: A Biography of Vanderbilt University.* Knoxville, TN: University of Tennessee Press, 1985.

Cronon, E. David. *The Political Thought of Woodrow Wilson.* New York, NY: Bobbs-Merrill, 1965.

Dilling, Mrs. Albert W. *The Red Network.* Privately published in Chicago, 1934.

Fleming, Denna. *The Cold War and Its Origins, 1917-1960.* Garden City, NY: Doubleday, 1961.

_____. *The Origins and Legacy of World War I.* Garden City, NY: Doubleday, 1968.

_____. *The Treaty Veto of the American Senate.* New York, NY: G. P. Putnam's Sons, 1930.

_____. *The United States and the League of Nations, 1918-1920.* New York, NY: Putnam,1932.

_____. *The United States and the World Court.* New York, NY: Doubleday, 1945.

_____. *The United States and World Organization, 1920-1933.* New York, NY: Columbia University Press, 1938.

_____. *While America Slept: A Contemporary Analysis of World Events From The Fall of France To Pearl Harbor.* New York, NY: Abingdon-Cokesbury Press, 1944.

Hicks, John D. *Republican Ascendancy, 1921-1933.* New York, NY: Harper and Row, 1960.

Hunt, Michael. *Ideology and U.S. Foreign Policy.* New Haven, CT: Yale University Press, 1987.

Jones, Chester Lloyd. *Guatemala: Past and Present.* Minneapolis, MN: University of Minnesota Press, 1940.

Kennan, George F. *American Diplomacy.* Chicago, IL: University of Chicago Press, 1984.

_____. *Memoirs, 1925-1950.* New York, NY: Pantheon, 1967.

Keylor, William. *The Twentieth Century World: An International History.* New York, NY: Oxford, 1992.

Leuchtenburg, William E. *Franklin D. Roosevelt and the New Deal, 1932-1940.* New York, NY: Harper and Row, 1963.

Link, Arthur. *Wilson The Diplomatist.* Chicago, IL: Quadrangle Books, 1957.

Lyon, Eugene. *The Red Decade.* New Rochelle, NY: Arlington House, 1941.

MacDougall, Curtis. *Gideon's Army.* Two volumes. New York, NY: Marzani and Munzell, 1965.

Morgenthau, Hans. *In Defense of the National Interest: A Critical Examination of American Foreign Policy.* New York, NY: A. A. Knopf, 1951.

_____, ed. *Peace, Security, and the United Nations.* Chicago, IL: University of Chicago Press, 1946.

_____. *Politics Among Nations: The Struggle for Power and Peace.* Second edition. New York, NY: A. A. Knopf, 1954.

O'Neill, William. *A Better World—The Great Schism: Stalinism and the American Intellectuals.* New York, NY: Simon and Schuster, 1982.

Paterson, Thomas. *Major Problems in American Foreign Relations, Volume II: Since 1914.* Lexington, MA: Heath, 1995.

Purcell, Edward A., Jr. *The Crisis of Democratic Theory: Scientific Naturalism and the Problem of Value.* Louisville, KY: University of Kentucky Press, 1973.

Schuman, Frederick L. *American Policy Toward Russia Since 1917.* New York, NY: International Publishers, 1928.

_____. *Design for Power: The Struggle for the World.* New York, NY: A. A. Knopf, 1942.

_____. *International Politics: An Introduction to the Western State System.* New York, NY: McGraw-Hill, 1933, 1937.

_____. *The Nazi Dictatorship: A Study in Social Pathology and the Politics of Fascism.* New York, NY: A. A. Knopf, 1934, 1935.

_____. *Soviet Politics: At Home and Abroad.* New York, NY: A. A. Knopf, 1946.

_____. *War and Diplomacy in the French Republic.* New York, NY: AMS, 1931.

Warren, Frank. *Liberals and Communism: The "Red Decade" Revisited.* Bloomington, IN: Indiana University Press, 1966.

Williams, William Appleman. *American Russian Relations, 1781-1947.* New York, NY: Rinehart, 1971.

Wilson, Joan Hoff. *American Business and Foreign Policy, 1920-1933.* Boston, MA: Beacon Press, 1973.

Wilson, Woodrow. *Congressional Government: A Study in American Politics.* New York, NY: Meridian, 1956.

_____. *Constitutional Government in the United States.* New York: NY: Columbia University Press, 1908

Wright, Louise. *A Bibliography of Quincy Wright: 1890-1970.* Pittsburgh, PA: The Clifford E. Barbour Library, 1974.

Wright, Quincy. *The Causes of War and the Conditions of Peace.* London: Longmans, Green & Co., 1935.

_____. *Contemporary International Law: A Balance Sheet.* New York, NY: Random House, 1955, 1961.

_____. *The Control of American Foreign Relations.* New York, NY: Macmillan Co., 1922.

_____. *International Law and the United Nations.* Bombay, India: Asia Publishing House, 1960.

_____. *Mandates Under The League Of Nations.* Chicago, IL: University of Chicago Press, 1930.

_____. *Problems of Stability and Progress in International Relations.* Berkeley, CA: University of California Press, 1954.

_____. *The Role of International Law in the Elimination of War.* New York, NY: Oceana Publications, 1961.

_____. *The Study of International Relation.* New York, NY: Appleton-Century-Crofts, Inc., 1955.

_____. *A Study of War.* Chicago, IL: University of Chicago Press, 1964.

_____. *The United States and Neutrality.* Public Policy Pamphlet 17. Chicago, IL: University of Chicago Press, 1935.

_____., William M. Evan, and Morton Deutsch, eds. *Preventing World War III: Some Proposals.* New York, NY: Simon and Schuster, 1962.

Yergin, Daniel. *Shattered Peace: The Origins of the Cold War and the National Security State.* Boston, MA: Houghton Mifflin, 1977.

ARTICLES

Baldwin, David. "Security Studies and the End of the Cold War." *World Politics* 48 (October 1995): 117-142.

Editorial, Chicago *Herald-Examiner* (16 March 1935) as quoted in "Public Enemy Number One," *The Nation* 140, (24 April 1935): 480-481.

Fleming, Denna. "The Advice of the Senate in Treaty-Making." *Current History* 32 (April-September 1930): 1090-1094.

_____. "After Victory What?" *Virginia Quarterly Review* 21 (October 1945): 601-605

_____. "America and the World Crisis." *Vital Speeches* 10 (15 October 1943): 7-8.

_____. "America's Stake in the Far East." *The China Weekly Review* 88 (20 May 1939): 373-375.

_____. "Are We Moving Toward Fascism?" *Journal of Politics* 16 (February 1954): 39-75.

_____. "Are We Moving Toward Fortress America?" *Annals of the American Academy of Political and Social Science* 312 (July 1957): 10-21.

_____. "Beyond the Cold War." *Annals of the American Academy of Political and Social Science* 324 (July 1959): 111-126.

_____. "The Broken Dialogue on Foreign Affairs." *Annals of the American Academy of Political and Social Science* 344 (November 1962): 128-140.

_____. "Can Pax American Succeed?" *Annals of the American Academy of Political and Social Science* 360 (July 1965): 127-138.

_____. "Collier's Wins World War III." *The Nation* 173 (10 November 1951): 392-395.

_____. "The Coming World Order, Closed Or Free." *The Journal of Politics* 4 (1942): 250-263.

_____. "The Costs and Consequences of the Cold War." *Annals of the American Academy of Political and Social Science* 366 (July 1966): 127-138.

_____. "A Diplomacy for Free Men." *The Nation* 186 (3 May 1958).

_____. "The Failure of Western Policies." *Annals of the American Academy of Political and Social Science* 288 (July 1953): 36-46.

_____. "How Can We Secure Dependable Allies?" *Annals of the American Academy of Political and Social Science* 283 (September 1952): 10-12.

_____. "Is Containment Moral?" *Annals of the American Academy of Political and Social Science* 362 (November 1965): 18-27.

_____. "Is Isolation Dead?" *Vital Speeches* 11 (1 December 1944): 110-111.

_____. "Needed: A Purge of Obsession." *The Nation* 188 (21 February 1959): 162-167.

_____. " Neutrality Controversy." *Congressional Digest* 15 (January 1936): 30.

_____. "Our Brink-of-War Diplomacy in the Formosa Strait." *Western Political Quarterly* 9 (September 1956): 535-552.

_____. "Planning For The Post-War World." *Current History* 4 (March 1943): 113-120.

_____. "The Role of the Senate in Treaty-Making: A Survey of Four Decades." *American Political Science Review* 28 (August 1934): 583-598.

_____. "Roosevelt and Churchill Confer." *Current History* 1 (October 1941): 113-120.

_____. "The United States in the United Nations." *Annals of the American Academy of Political and Social Science* 278 (November 1951): 73-82.

_____. "War Without Shooting." *Current History* 1 (September 1941): 32-38.

_____. "What Follows the Arms Race?" *Journal of Politics* 14 (May 1952): 203-223.

_____. "Woodrow Wilson and Collective Security Today." *Journal of Politics* 18 (November 1956): 611-624.

Gramer, Regina. "On Poststructuralisms, Revisionisms, and Cold Wars." *Diplomatic History* 19 (Summer 1995): 515-524.

Schuman, Frederick L. "A Diagnosis of the Big Three Problem." *New York Times Magazine* (30 June 1946): 6, 43.

_____. "Addenda to 'Who Owns the Future'." *The Nation* 152 (11 January 1941): 36-39.

_____. "American Foreign Policy." *American Journal of Sociology,* 37 (May 1932): 883-888.

_____. "Benighted Diplomacy." *The Nation* 134 (18 May 1932): 563-564.

_____. "'Bill of Attainder' In the Seventy-Eighth Congress." *American Political Science Review* 37 (October 1943): 819-829.

_____. "Cold War's End." *The Nation* 176 (20 June 1953): 518-520.

_____. "The Conduct of German Foreign Affairs." *Annals of the American Academy of Political and Social Science* 176 (November 1934): 185-221.

_____. "Designs For Democracy." *Current History* 9 (December 1945): 497-502.

_____. "The Dilemma of the Peace-Seekers." *American Political Science Review* 36 (February 1945): 12-30.

_____. "The Geographic Setting." *Current History* 25 (August 1953): 76-80.

_____. "Germany Prepares Fear." *The Nation* 77 (7 February 1934): 353-355.

_____. "The Great Conspiracy." *New Republic* 96 (26 October 1938): 325-326.

_____. "How Many Worlds?" *New Republic* 138 (3 February 1958): 13-16.

_____. "Liberalism and Communism Reconsidered." *Southern Review* 2 (1936): 326-338.

_____. "Might and Right at San Francisco." *The Nation* 160 (28 April 1945): 479-481.

_____. "Moral Insight Into Power." *The Nation* 182 (21 January 1956): 53-54.

_____. "Nazi Dreams of World Power." *Current History* 39 (February 1934): 535-541.

_____. "Neutrality or Sanctions." *New Republic* 85 (25 December 1935): 200.

_____. "The Paradoxes of Dr. Toynbee." *The Nation* 179 (6 November 1954): 405-407.

_____. "The Political Theory of German Fascism." *American Political Science Review* 28 (April 1934): 210-232.

_____. Schuman to the Editor. *The Boston Herald* (12 August 1942): 2.

_____. Schuman to the Editor. *New York Sun,* 19 March 1948.

Schuman, Frederick L Schuman to the Editor. *The North Adams Transcript* (29 March 1949): 2.

_____. "The Third Reich's Road to War." *Annals of the American Academy of Political and Social Science* 175 (September 1934): 33-43.

_____. "The Tory Dialectic: I." *New Republic* 97 (28 December 1938): 219-222.

_____. "The Tory Dialectic: II." *New Republic* 97 (4 January 1939): 253-255.

_____. "Toward the New Munich." *New Republic* 99 (31 May 1939): 91-93.

_____. "Toward The World State." *Scientific Monthly* 63, sup. 3 (July 1946): 5-19.

_____. "United Nations: The First Decade." *The Nation* 181 (30 July; 10 September 1955): 98, 232.

Trager, Frank N. "Frederick L. Schuman: A Case History." *Partisan Review* 7 (1940): 143-151.

"Tumult at the Waldorf," *Time* (4 April 1949): 23.

Wright, Quincy. "Accomplishments and Expectations of World Organization." *Yale Law Journal* 55 (August 1946): 870-888.

_____. "Amending or Developing the U.N. Charter." *Common Cause* 2 (June 1949).

_____. "America 1975 Series: The U.S. Position in the World." *Challenge* 5 (December 1956): 13-18.

_____. "American Policy Toward Russia." *World Politics* 2 (Summer 1950): 463-481.

_____. "An International Police Force." *New Europe* 4 (March 1944): 16-17.

_____. "Aviation and World Politics." *Air Affairs* 1 (September 1946): 97-108.

_____. "The Chinese Recognition Problem." *American Journal of International Law* 49 (July 1955): 320-338.

_____. "Comment." *Air Affairs* 1 (December 1946): 242-245.

_____. "Conflicts of International Law with National Laws and Ordinances." *American Journal of International Law* 11 (January 1917): 1-21.

_____. "Constitution Making As Process." *Common Cause* 1 (February 1948): 284-286.

_____. "Criteria for Judging the Relevance of Researches on the Problems of Peace." *Research for Peace.* Amsterdam: North Holland Publishing Co, 1954.

_____. "Democracy and Power." *Free World* 5 (May 1943): 395-399.

_____. "The Destruction of Neutral Property on Enemy Vessels." *American Journal of International Law* 11 (January 1917): 358-379.

_____. "The Economic and Political Conditions of World Stability." *Journal of Economic History* 13 (Fall 1953): 363-377.

_____. "The Effect of the Atomic Bomb on World Politics." *Air Affairs* 1 (March 1947): 383-399.

_____. "The Enforcement of International through Municipal Law." *University of Illinois Studies in the Social Sciences.* Urbana, IL: University of Illinois Press, 1916, 1-264.

_____. "The Future of Neutrality." *International Conciliation* 242 (September 1928): 1-98.

_____. "The Government of Iraq." *American Political Science Review* 20 (1926): 743-769.

_____. "Human Rights and the World Order." *International Conciliation* 389 (April 1943): 238-262.

_____. "International Conflict and the United Nations." *World Politics* 2 (Summer 1950): 24-48.

_____. "International Law and Ideologies." *American Journal of International Law* 48 (October 1954): 616-626.

_____. "International Law in its Relation to Constitutional Law," *American Journal of International Law* 17 (April 1923): 234-244.

_____. "The International Regulation of the Air." *American Economic Review* 35 (May 1945): 143-148.

_____. "The Interpretation of Multilateral Treaties." *American Journal of International Law* 23 (1929): 93-107.

_____. "Lansing and Neutrality." *Southern Review* 2 (1936-37): 419-420.

_____. "The Law of the Nuremberg Trial." *American Journal of International Law* 41 (January 1947): 38-72.

_____. "Legal Aspects of the Viet-Nam Situation." *American Journal of International Law* 60 (October 1966): 750-769.

_____. "The Legal Liability of the Kaiser." *American Political Science Review* 13 (February 1919): 120-132.

_____. "Legal Status of Economic Sanctions." *Amerasia* 2 (February 1939): 569-570.

_____. "The Lend-Lease Bill And International Law." *American Journal of International Law* 35 (April 1941): 305-314.

_____. "Making the United Nations Work." *Review of Politics* 8 (October 1946): 528-532.

_____. "Manchurian Crisis." *American Political Science Review* 26 (1932): 45-76.

_____. "The Mandates In 1938." *American Journal of International Law* 33 (April 1939): 342-349.

_____. "Meaning of the Pact of Paris." *American Journal of International Law* 27 (1933): 39-61.

_____. "The Munich Settlement and International Law." *American Journal of International Law* 33 (1939): 12-32.

_____. "National Security and International Police." *American Journal of International Law* 37 (July 1943): 499-505.

_____. "The Nature of Conflict." *Western Political Science Quarterly* 4 (June 1951): 193-209.

_____. "Non-Recognition of China and International Tensions." *Current History* 34 (March 1958): 152-157.

_____. "The Nuremberg Trial," *Annals American Academy of Political and Social Science* 246 (July 1946): 72-80.

_____. "On the Application of Intelligence to World Affairs." *Bulletin of the Atomic Scientists* 4 (August 1948): 249-252.

_____. "The Outlawry of War." *American Journal of International Law* 29 (January 1925): 76-103.

_____. "The Palestinian Problem." *Political Science Quarterly* 41 (1926): 384-412.

_____. "Peace and Political Organization." Preliminary Report and Monographs, CSOP, *International Conciliation*, 369 (April 1941): 454-492.

_____. "Peace Problems of Today and Yesterday." *American Political Science Review* 38 (June 1944): 77-86.

_____. "Political Conditions of the Period of Transition." *International Conciliation* 379 (April 1942): 264-299.

_____. "Political Consequences of the Soviet Atom Bomb." *Air Affairs* 3 (Spring 1950): 414-428.

_____. "Political Science and World Stabilization." *American Political Science Review* 44 (March 1950): 1-13.

_____. "The Project of the American Institute of International Law on Maritime Neutrality." *American Journal of International Law* 21 (1927): 127-136.

_____. "Responsibilities of the United States in the Post-War World." *Free World* 5 (January 1943): 35-48.

_____. "Security and World Organization." *International Conciliation,* June 1944, 30-61.

_____. "Security Through the United Nations." *International Conciliation* 432 (June 1947): 423-446.

_____. "Some Thoughts About Recognition." *American Journal of International Law* 44 (July 1950): 548-559.

_____. "Sovereignty of the Mandates." *American Journal of International Law* 17 (1923): 691-703.

_____. "The Status of Communist China." *Journal of International Affairs* 11 (Summer 1957): 171-186.

_____. "The Transfer of Destroyers To Great Britain." *American Journal of International Law* 34 (October 1940): 680-689

_____. "Treaties and Constitutional Separation of Powers in the United States." *American Journal of International Law* XII (January 1918): 64-95.

_____. "The Understandings of International Law." *American Journal of International Law* 14 (October 1920): 564-580.

_____. "The United Nations Charter and the Prevention of War." *Bulletin of the Atomic Scientists* 3 (February 1947): 57-58, 61.

_____. "The War and the Peace." *Ethics* 53 (October 1942): 64-68.

_____. "The Washington Conference," *American Political Science Review* 16 (May 1992): 290-297.

_____. "Western Diplomacy Since 1945," *Annals of the American Academy of Political and Social Science* 336 (July 1961): 144.

_____. "When Does War Exist?" *American Journal of International Law* 26 (1932): 367.

Wright, Quincy and James Russell. "National Attitudes on the Far Eastern Controversy." *American Political Science Review* 27 (1933): 555-576.

Index

Nations, 2, 60, 95, 111, 117, 122-
123, 129, 130, 143; Uniting for
Peace Resolution, 128, 130-131;
Universal Declaration of Human
Rights, 141; University of Chicago,
2, 11, 40, 81, 88; University of
Illinois, 11-12; University of
Minnesota, 11; University of
Virginia, 11; veto, 98, 107, 111, 122,
128; Vietnam, 36; voting, 119;
Wallace, Henry, 120; war crimes, 17;
war power, 13; Washington
Conference, 12, 34; Williams
College, 68; Wilson, Woodrow, 4, 7,
9, 13-15, 17-18, 34, 37, 53, 96, 101,
142; women, 120; World Court, 17,
40; world federation, 12, 94; world
government, 12, 60, 62, 69, 93, 119,
128; world organization, 4, 8, 60-62,
68, 76-77, 78-79, 81, 82, 94, 96, 98,
112, 120, 121-122, 129; World War
I, 52; World War I debts, 61; World
War II, 3, 9, 59, 68, 76, 85, 89, 96,
107, 120, 123, 130, 131, 132

Yalta Agreement: Kennan, George
Frost, 99; Morgenthau, Hans, 99;
Schuman, Frederick L., 99
Yugoslavia, 68; Fleming, Denna, 27;
Tito, Josip Broz, 122

About the Author

STEVEN J. BUCKLIN is Professor of Modern American History at the University of South Dakota.